LEGENDARY LOCALS

OF

NEW ORLEANS

LOUISIANA

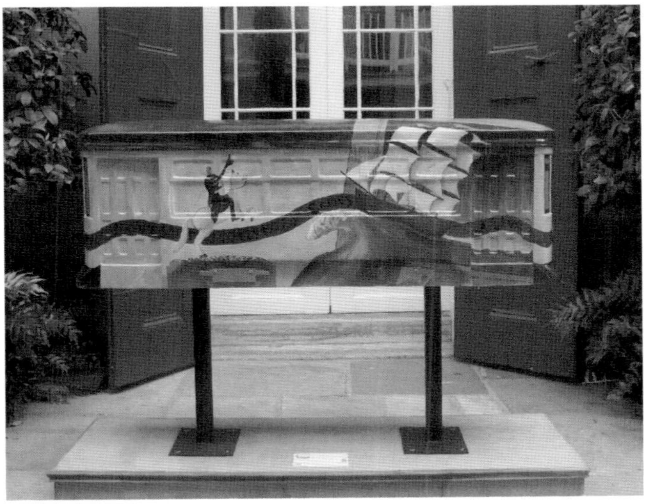

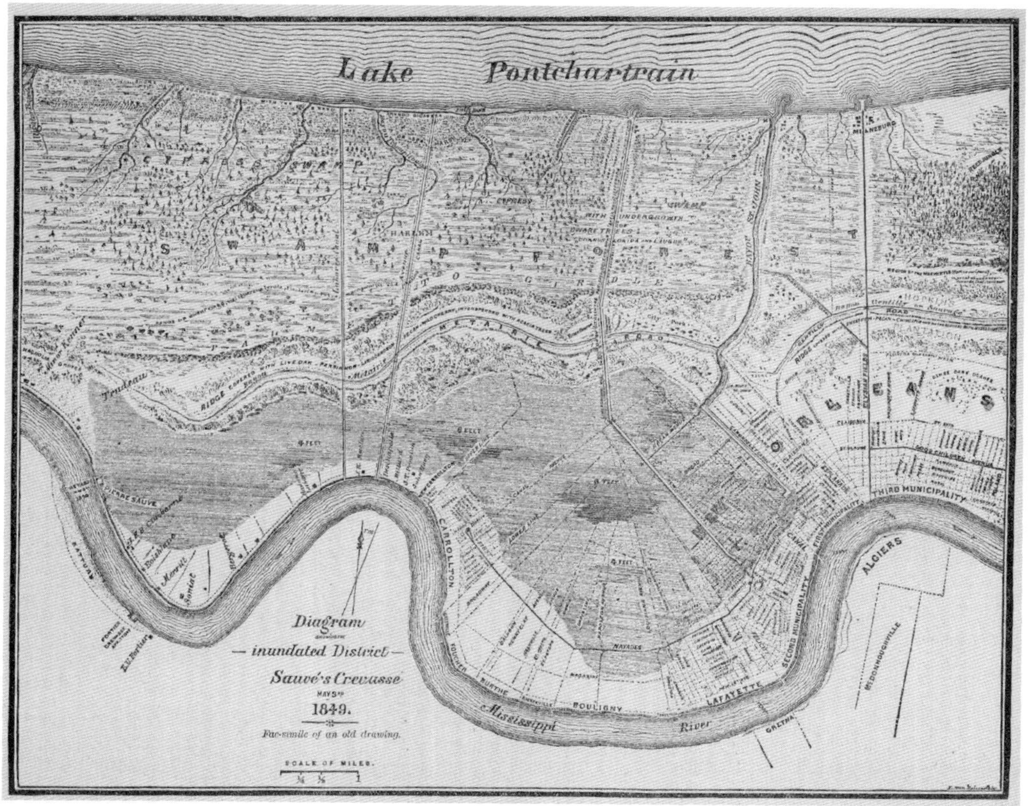

Sauve's Crevasse

This 1849 map shows most of what is now the city of New Orleans and its suburban neighbor to the west, Jefferson Parish. The map documents "Sauve's Crevasse," a levee breach along the Mississippi River in what is now River Ridge, Louisiana. The floodwaters spread from Pierre Sauve's plantation all the way to Canal Street, rising as high as six feet in some places. It took a team of engineers led by George T. Dunbar weeks to close the crevasse, and over a month passed before the water receded. It was the worst flood in the history of the city until Hurricane Katrina in 2005. Both floods demonstrate how dependent New Orleans is on its levees for protection. (Courtesy New Orleans Public Library.)

Page 1: Young Leadership Council's "Streetcar Named Inspire" 2009 Campaign

This streetcar, titled "Louisiana History Comes Alive," was painted by Anna Hilderbrandt. Sponsored by the Historic New Orleans Collection, it is on display at THNOC's gallery on Royal Street in the French Quarter. (Courtesy Stephen Faure.)

LEGENDARY LOCALS

OF

NEW ORLEANS

LOUISIANA

EDWARD J. BRANLEY

LEGENDARY LOCALS

ISBN 978-0-7385-0039-7

Legendary Locals is an imprint of Arcadia Publishing
Charleston, South Carolina

Printed in the United States of America

Library of Congress Control Number: 2012941163

For all general information, please contact Arcadia Publishing:
Telephone 843-853-2070
Fax 843-853-0044
E-mail sales@arcadiapublishing.com
For customer service and orders:
Toll-Free 1-888-313-2665

Visit us on the Internet at www.arcadiapublishing.com

Dedication:
This book is dedicated to Irene Wainwright, archivist, New Orleans Public Library; and Wayne Everard, archivist emeritus, New Orleans Public Library. Irene and Wayne, you are brilliant archivists, creative curators, and wonderful people. Thank you for being such great facilitators!

On the Cover:
(TOP ROW) Ernest N. "Dutch" Morial, judge and 57th mayor of New Orleans (Courtesy NOPL), Marie Laveau, "Voodoo Queen" (Courtesy NOPL); P.G.T. Beauregard, soldier and entrepreneur (Courtesy NOPL); Micaela Almonaster, Baroness Pontalba, businesswoman (Courtesy Louisiana State Museum); Austin Leslie, chef and restaurateur (Courtesy LSM).
(MIDDLE ROW) Joseph F. Rummel, ninth archbishop of New Orleans (Courtesy NOPL); Sidney J. Besthoff III, businessman and philanthropist (Courtesy Mr. Besthoff); Louis Armstrong, musician and bandleader (Courtesy Library of Congress); Alcee Fortier, educator (Courtesy *Popular Science Monthly*); Bob Breck, meteorologist (Courtesy Jeffrey Kent).
(BOTTOM ROW) Norman Francis, educator (Courtesy The White House); Dorothy Dix, newspaper columnist and author (Courtesy NOPL); Stanton Moore, musician (Courtesy Mike & Ali Kerr, Southern Exposure Photography); Wendell Pierce, actor and philanthropist (Courtesy Mr. Pierce); Mahalia Jackson, singer (Courtesy LOC).

CONTENTS

ACKNOWLEDGMENTS

Thanks and a big hug to my editor at Arcadia, Erin Vosgien, for following up on this idea in the first place and shepherding me through the process (which is still a challenge no matter how many books one does), and to her boss, Tiffany Frary, along with all the wonderful folks at Arcadia. My deepest appreciation to Irene Wainwright and the Special Collections staff of the New Orleans Public Library. Thanks to all the photographers and sources who contributed to making this project successful: Stephen Faure, Sheila Moragas, Sydney J. Besthoff, III, Jeffery Kent, Ali and Mike Kerr, Wendell Pierce, Alan Scott Walker, St. Augustine Catholic Church, Carlos "Froggy" May, Stephanie Schoyer, Robbie Mendelson, Masahiro Sumori, Carl Lender, Robert Avery, the Netherlands National Archives, Louisiana State Museum, Library of Congress, Klaus Hiltscher, Darlene Susco, Derek Bridges, Mark Ghstol, National Archives, US House of Representatives, Sister Helen Prejean, Brother Martin High School, People's Health Network, Tonya Armbruster, Justin Branley, and Arthur Hardy.

All my love to my wife, Helen, and my boys Kevin and Ens. Justin Branley, USN, who put up with me being distracted while working. Thanks to my friends who encouraged the project, particularly those who joined the book's Facebook page and offered suggestions. All the best to Jenifer Hill Akers, whose particular brand of humor keeps me smiling. Heartfelt thanks to the staff of P.J.'s Coffee at Clearview Mall and on Annunciation Street for giving me a comfortable place in which to work and write.

The following photograph credit abbreviations are used throughout the book: NOPL (New Orleans Public Library); LSM (Louisiana State Museum); UNO (Earl K. Long Library, University of New Orleans); LOC (Library of Congress); and Author (Edward J. Branley).

INTRODUCTION

So many clichés have been used over the decades to describe New Orleans and its people—it's a jambalaya, the locals are like a gumbo. Those trite lines do not do justice to the combinations of influences, cultures, and peoples that are drawn to any major port city. Lured by the Mississippi River, explorers assessed the value of the high ground of the city as far back as 1699. Founded by the French, developed by the Spanish, and matured under American control, New Orleans became the link that joined the sea-going vessels that made their way through the Gulf of Mexico and Caribbean Sea and the central part of the United States.

While the French may have founded New Orleans, saying the city is "French" is an oversimplification. Its role as a sheltered harbor and port guaranteed from the beginning that the city would absorb many cultures. Those first French explorers traded with the Native Americans who lived in the vicinity. Once established as a settlement/town/city, New Orleans was surrounded by Spanish colonies. Sailors and traders called on the port, often settling there. The English were not far behind, with merchants from their colonies along the Atlantic Coast turning into the Gulf, seeking new markets for their wares. Irish and German immigrants soon made their way to the New World via New Orleans, leaving some of their numbers behind. Then came the Italians in the late 19th century. This flow of new people and cultures continues to this day. Large numbers of Vietnamese were relocated to the Gulf Coast after the fall of Saigon and South Vietnam, and Mexican itinerant migration took place in large numbers in the wake of Hurricane Katrina in 2005.

The forced migration of Africans to New Orleans and south Louisiana as slaves left a permanent mark on the city's culture and makeup. Europeans of all nationalities recognized the potential of farmland along the Mississippi, establishing plantations to grow a range of crops. With slavery being legal in French and Spanish colonies, as well as the southern United States, those planters purchased and transported Africans to their newly claimed lands to develop them.

All these groups brought their culture to New Orleans, integrating it into what they found when they arrived. The wooden buildings of the French gave way to brick-based construction that was required by the Spanish in the wake of the massive fires of 1788 and 1794. French folk music melded with Spanish sea shanties, church hymns in Latin, and the African drums of Congo Square. Wealthy planters, desiring all the best Europe had to offer, brought classical music and opera to the city. Regular merchant ship runs from New York to New Orleans ensured that the locals knew of the latest trends in music from Paris, London, and Vienna. European traditions of escorting their loved ones to the grave, accompanied by music, morphed over time into the city's wonderful "second-line" parades. Black musicians took the European and African influences with which they grew up and improvised their way to a new and native musical form: jazz.

Battles and war never destroyed New Orleans like they have so many of the world's cities, but they still played a major role in the city's growth. Members of the community knew they had to defend the city from the British in 1814–1815, lest the Royal Navy and the troops they transported burn everything. They also knew that the Union army would not burn New Orleans once its coastal naval defenses were breached, so the city surrendered. The locals did not like Benjamin "Spoons" Butler and his military government, but they also knew they would absorb the Yankee soldiers and sailors into the community, just like they did for generations.

Governing New Orleans has never been a pretty thing. The mixture of so many different influences and cultures is not always smooth. French collided with Spanish until they eventually fused together. Anglo-Americans pushed the Creoles. The Creoles pushed back. Not everyone believed in the Confederacy, nor did they accept blacks among them easily. The diversity that makes the flame of New Orleans burn so brightly also threatens to snuff it out with a strong gust.

Oh, and the food! Continental attitudes and traditions won out over the Puritan mores of Britain and its American colonies. Many recognized the importance placed on food by the French and Spanish. Once deciding that "living to eat" was a better philosophy than "eating to live," others easily joined the original Creole families, adding their own twists and turns to the city's food. No group in the city embraced the New Orleans passion for good food like the city's Irish immigrants. Give people who come from a history and culture of famine and starvation the bounty of South Louisiana's plantations and farms, and you see one of the biggest reasons the "Irish Channel" grew as a sphere of influence.

New Orleans has never suffered the ravages of war that waged man against man, but it still has been at war. The city exists because of and in spite of the water that surrounds it. The Mississippi River is its lifeblood, connecting the interior of the United States with the rest of the world. Nature's bounty also flows from the river, as rich, fertile soil spreads along her banks. The more the city grew, the more people were threatened by the water. Some of the community's most talented dedicated themselves to developing and improving flood defenses and controls. Their efforts have been successful, for the most part. When they have not been a success, the city suffers greatly, as in 1849 (Sauve's Crevasse), 1965 (Hurricane Betsy), and 2005 (Hurricane Katrina). The community rises in the face of each new adversity, and new legends are born each time.

Throughout all the good times as well as the hard times, many New Orleanians have stepped forward to leave a mark on the community. This book offers a sampling of those people. Some of their stories are familiar; some are unsung heroes. Many are stories of success, but some were cut short by tragedy. These legendary locals contributed to making the sum that is New Orleans better than the parts.

Panorama

This 1909 panorama was shot by an unknown photographer from the top of the Grunewald Hotel on Canal Street. The Grunewald is now the Roosevelt Hotel (a Waldorf Astoria property). The tall building in the left foreground is the recently completed Maison Blanche building. Behind the Maison Blanche

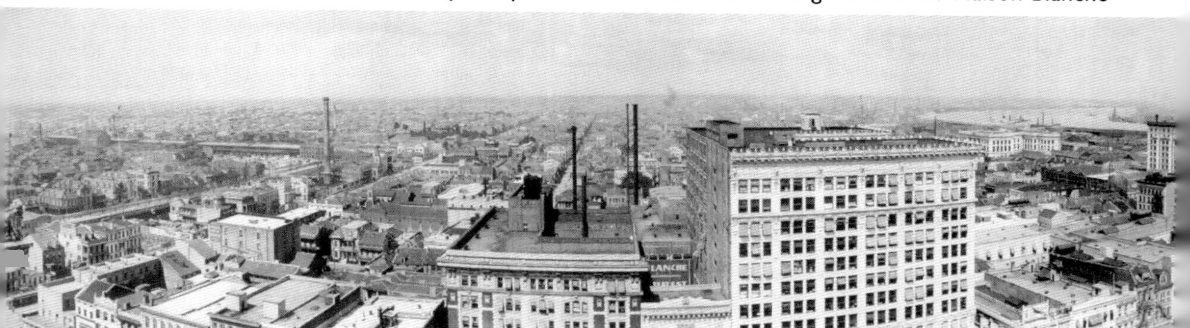

building is the French Quarter, then Faubourg Marigny in the background. To its left is Faubourg Treme. The right half of the photograph shows Canal Street, then the Central Business District (Faubourg Ste. Marie), 25 years before the "skycrapers" of Carondelet Street were constructed. (Courtesy LOC.)

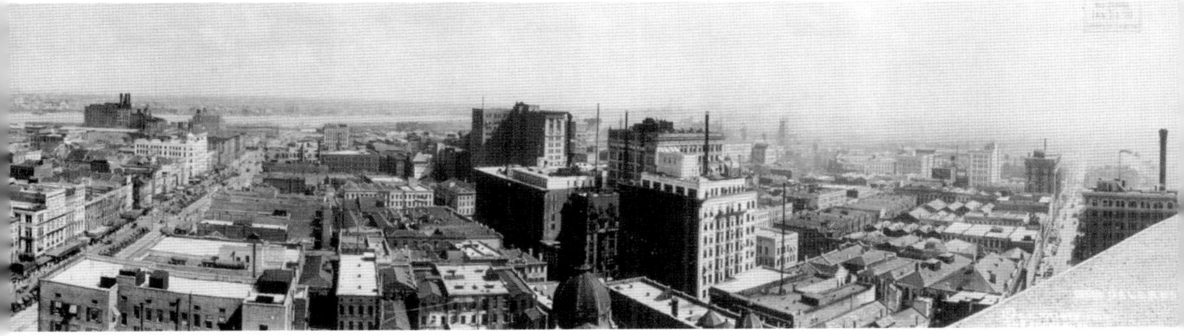

CHAPTER ONE

Early History

Native Americans in what is now the southern part of the state of Louisiana were drawn to the fertile land in between the Mississippi River and Lake Pontchartrain, at what is now New Orleans, for more than 1,000 years. The waterway known by the Native Americans as "Bayou Choupique" extended south for several miles from the lake to the river, making it an easy portage for those traveling by small boat. French explorers, starting in New France (Canada), passed along this portion of the river in the late 1600s. Men such as de La Salle and Tonti named the territory and established claims for the Mississippi and all the land that drains into it. Fur trappers and other traders followed the explorers into Louisiana, establishing an encampment on Bayou Choupique. They renamed the waterway Bayou St. Jean, and they named their encampment at the mouth of the bayou, by Lake Pontchartrain, Fort St. Jean. In 1699, Pierre LeMoyne, known as Sieur d'Iberville, retraced de La Salle's path to the river's mouth, then returned upriver to establish a more permanent settlement on the high ground of the riverbank, close to the bayou portage route.

Pierre LeMoyne left a man named Sauvolle, along with his brother Jean-Baptiste at this encampment. Sauvolle died in 1701, leaving Jean-Baptiste (who is better known by his title, Sieur d'Bienville) the temporary governor of the Louisiana colony. Bienville returned to Mobile when a replacement for Sauvolle was sent but found himself in charge again in 1717, when John Law's Company of the Indies took control of Louisiana. Bienville convinced the directors of the company that the crescent in the Mississippi by Bayou St. John would be a better site for a permanent settlement than Mobile, and he was authorized to go forward with the plan. He founded Nouvelle Orleans in 1718. By 1720, Bienville had transferred enough materials, men, and supplies from Mobile to truly start development of the city. He tasked an engineer, Adrien de Pauger, to create a plan for the city. That plan became the grid of streets now known as the Vieux Carre, the French Quarter.

From 1720 until the 1760s, New Orleans continued to grow under French control. In 1763, the French—having lost the Seven Years War to the British—secretly ceded Louisiana to Spain. The Spanish sent a governor to the colony in 1766, establishing their style of government. The devastating fires of 1788 and 1794 forced the city to rebuild more than 80 percent of the structures in Pauger's grid. The Spanish did so using their architectural style and building codes. Over the last third of the 18th century, Spaniards came from Havana and other New World colonies to New Orleans. Frenchmen, running from slave rebellions in Haiti, as well as the French Revolution, sought refuge in New Orleans. The Spanish governors accommodated these newcomers, and the city continued to grow.

A hundred years after Iberville camped near New Orleans, Napoleon Bonaparte declared himself first consul of the French Republic. Napoleon's wars and plans required cash, and that meant his government had to sell territory. Getting Louisiana back from the Spanish was no problem for Napoleon, since he installed his brother Joseph as king of Spain. Joseph transferred the colony back to Napoleon, who turned around and sold it to Thomas Jefferson and the Americans in 1804.

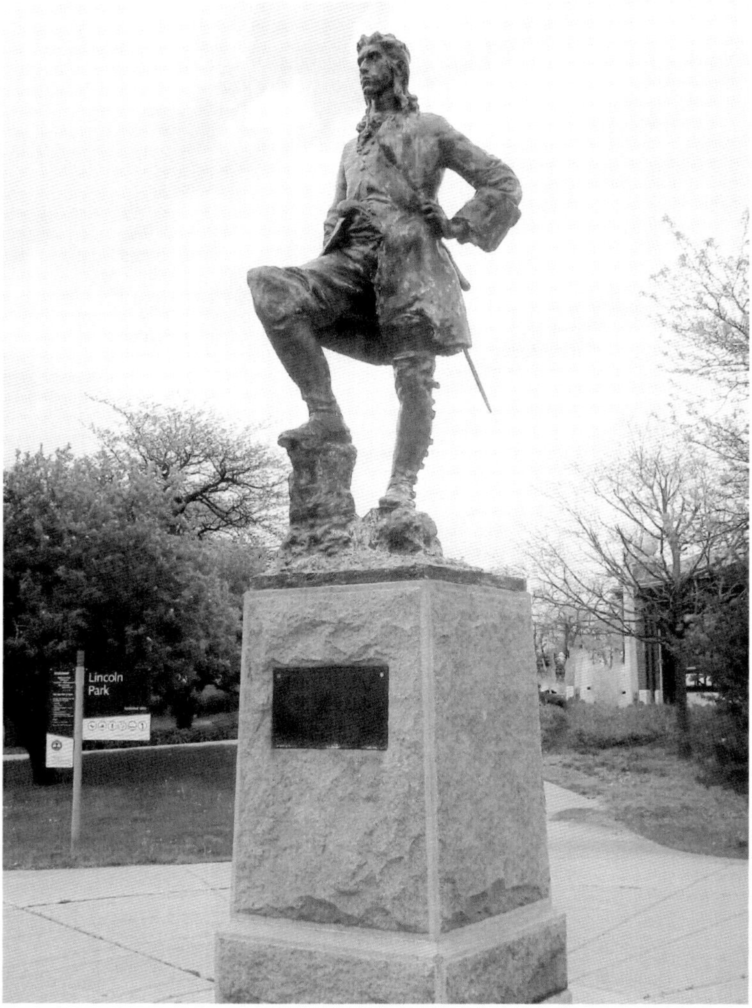

Early Explorer

René-Robert Cavelier, sieur de La Salle (1643–1687), was born in Rouen, France, and came to Montreal, Canada, in 1667. Obsessed with finding a passage across North America to China, La Salle traveled west from Montreal, exploring the Great Lakes region, making his way down Lake Michigan to present-day Chicago. He continued south over various expeditions and, in 1682, picked up the Mississippi River in what is now Illinois, traveling to the river's mouth. Upon reaching the mouth of the river, La Salle buried a plaque and a cross, claiming the river and all the territory it drains for France. La Salle returned to France in 1683, where he organized an expedition of 300 men and four ships, with the intention of starting a colony at the mouth of the Mississippi. After losing a ship to pirates in the Caribbean, La Salle overshot the Mississippi, landing in Matagorda Bay near present-day Houston, Texas. Using this as a base camp, La Salle ventured back into the Gulf of Mexico to find the Mississippi but failed on each attempt. In 1687, La Salle's crew mutinied, killed him, and returned to Montreal. In spite of this final failure, La Salle's claim to the Mississippi established France's presence in the Gulf of Mexico, setting the stage for French colonization and the founding of New Orleans. La Salle is remembered in New Orleans most notably by De La Salle High School, a coed, Catholic school founded by the Christian Brothers. (Above, courtesy Alan Scott Walker; opposite page, top, courtesy of author; opposite page, bottom, courtesy New Orleans Public Library.)

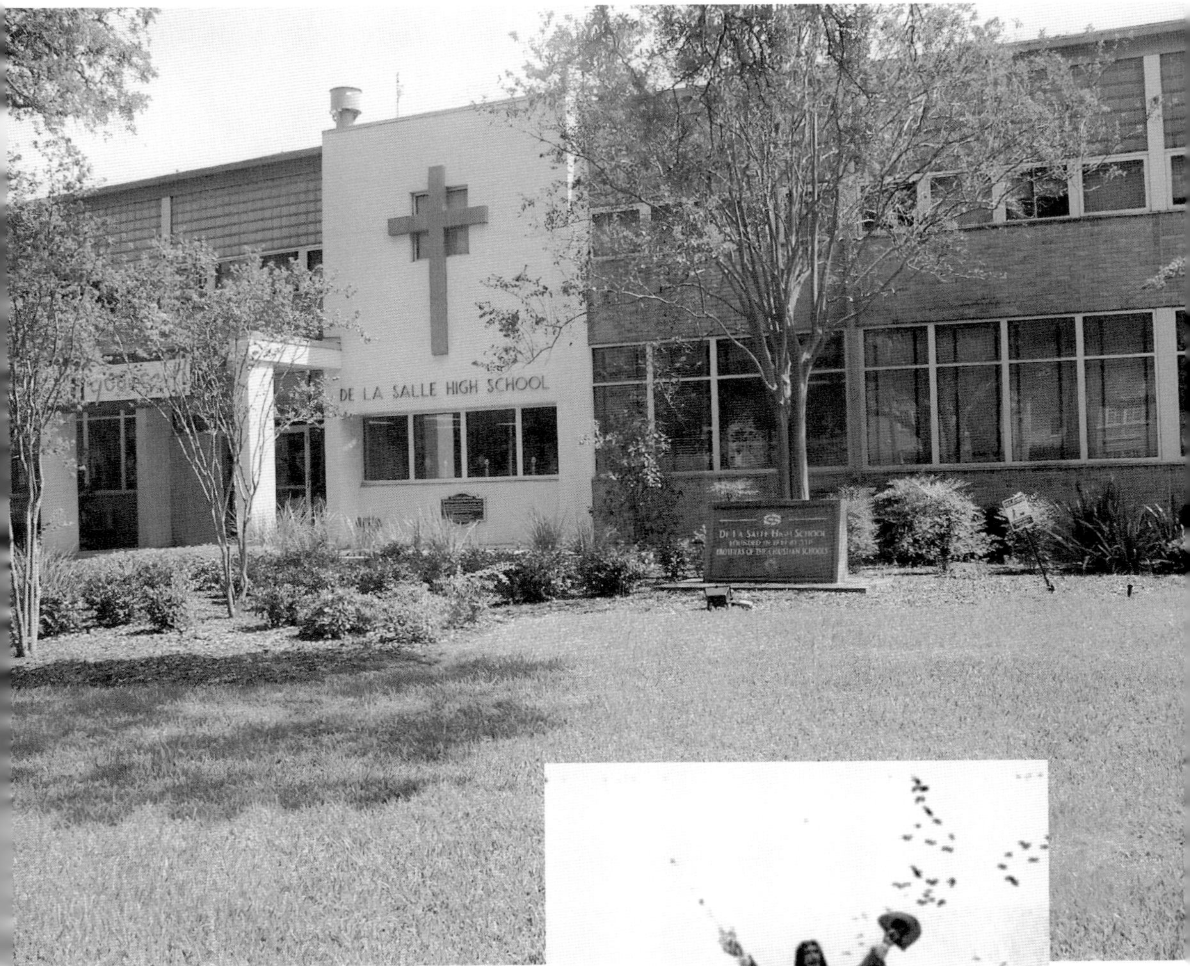
DE LA SALLE HIGH SCHOOL
BROTHERS OF THE CHRISTIAN SCHOOLS

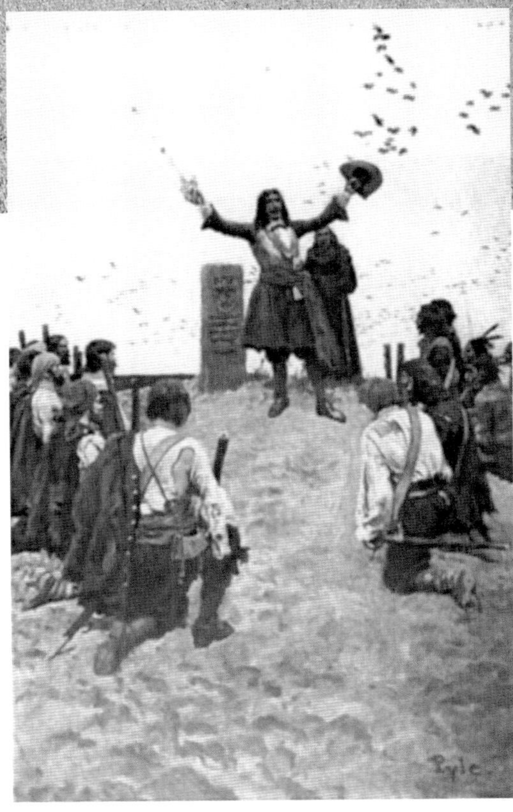
Pyle

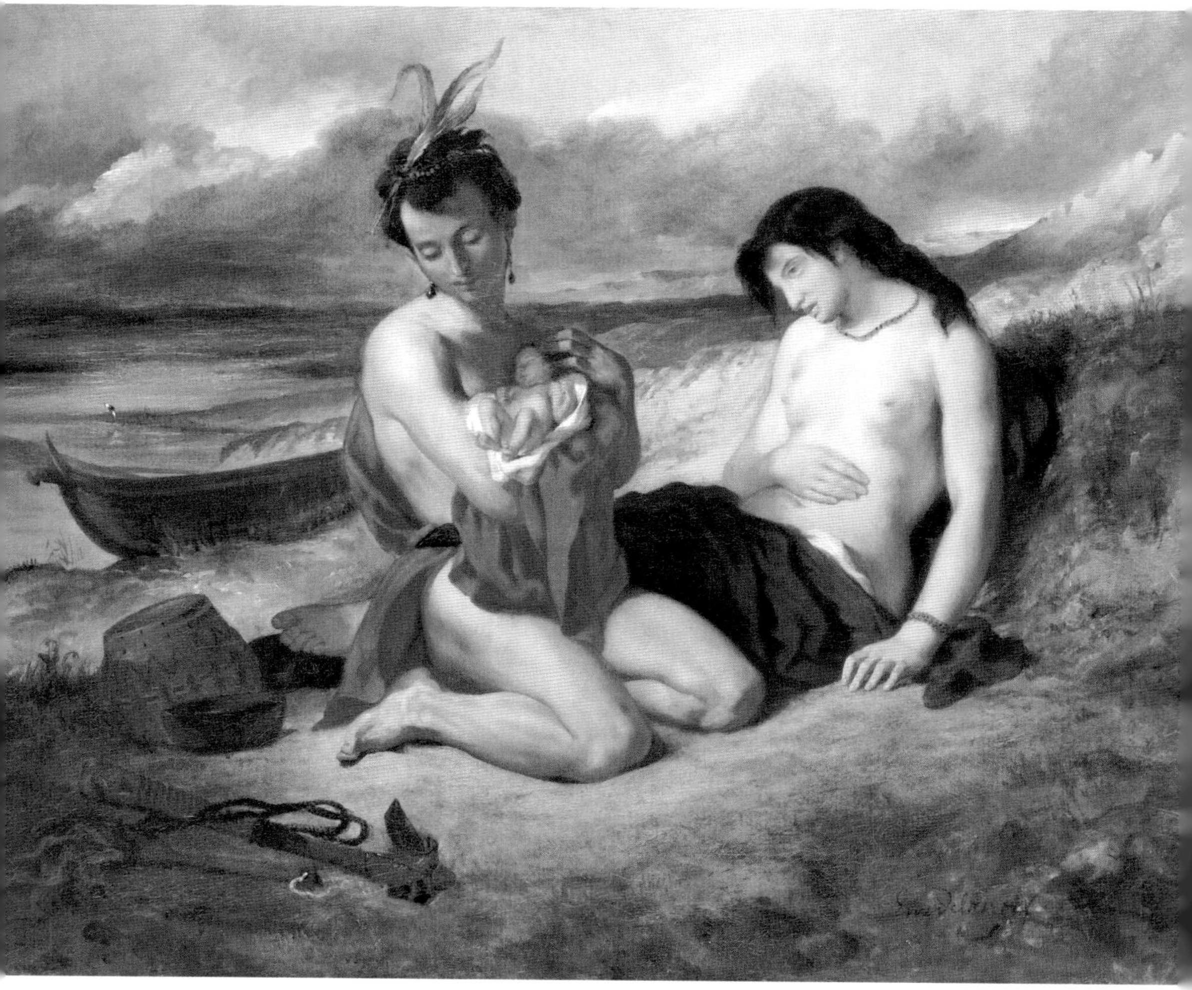

Native Americans

This 1801 painting by Eugene Delacroix was inspired by the novel *Atala* by Chateaubriand. The scene features a man and woman of the Natchez tribe with their newborn, resting on the banks of the Mississippi as they escape from a massacre upriver. (Courtesy Metropolitan Museum of Art.)

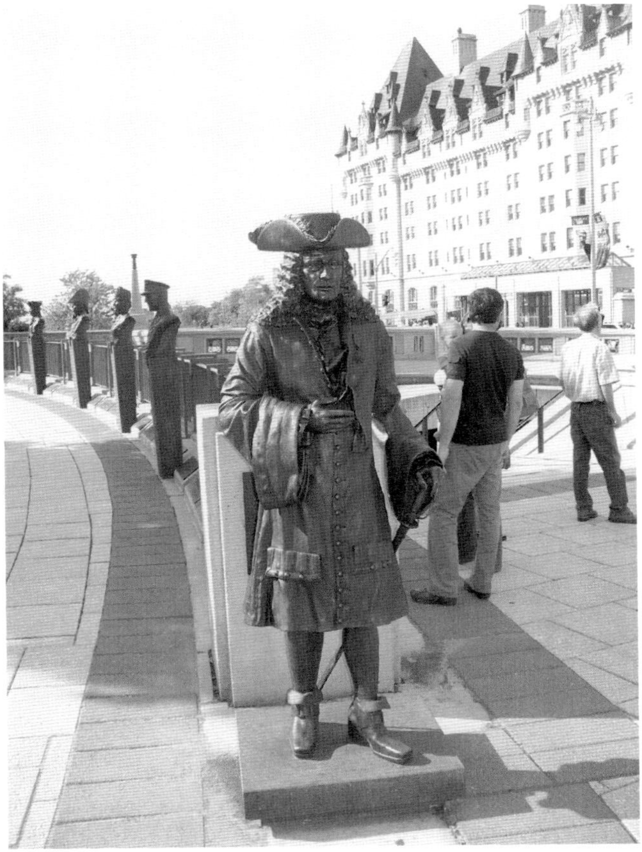

Entrepreneur
Pierre LeMoyne, sieur d'Iberville (1661–1702), was a French explorer, soldier, and 17th-century entrepreneur. Tasked in 1698 by Louis Phélypeaux, comte de Pontchartrain, France's Naval Minister, with finding the Mississippi River and reestablishing La Salle's claim, Iberville reached the river's delta in 1699. He established an outpost at Biloxi, Mississippi, in 1701, leaving his brother Jean-Baptiste there to firm up the French position. Pierre contracted malaria in 1702, and his health deteriorated. Iberville died in France in 1706 and is remembered throughout the areas he explored, like this statue in Ottawa's "Valiants Memorial." (Courtesy author.)

Founder
Jean-Baptiste Le Moyne, sieur d'Bienville (1680–1767). Born in Montreal, Jean-Baptiste accompanied his older brother on his 1698 expedition to the Gulf of Mexico. Remaining in Biloxi while Pierre returned to France to plot his next adventure, Jean-Baptiste worked through the French government and John Law's company to strengthen French colonies in Mobile and Biloxi. Seeking shelter from hurricanes, Bienville convinced his directors to move the main settlement to a section of the Mississippi about 90 miles north of the mouth, near a large lake named after the comte de Pontchartrain. Bienville established the city in 1718 and remained a major influence in the colony's politics until he grew weary of battling hurricanes and Native Americans. He returned to France in 1743 but maintained a keen interest in the affairs of New Orleans and was opposed to the transfer of Louisiana to Spain in 1763. He died in France in 1767. (Courtesy LSM.)

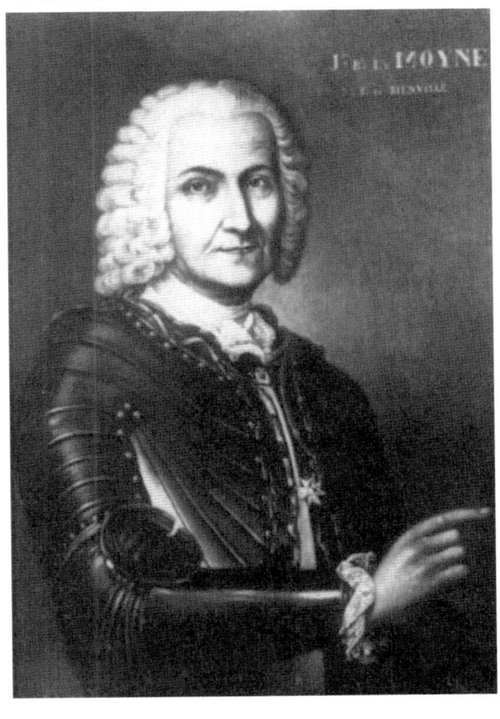

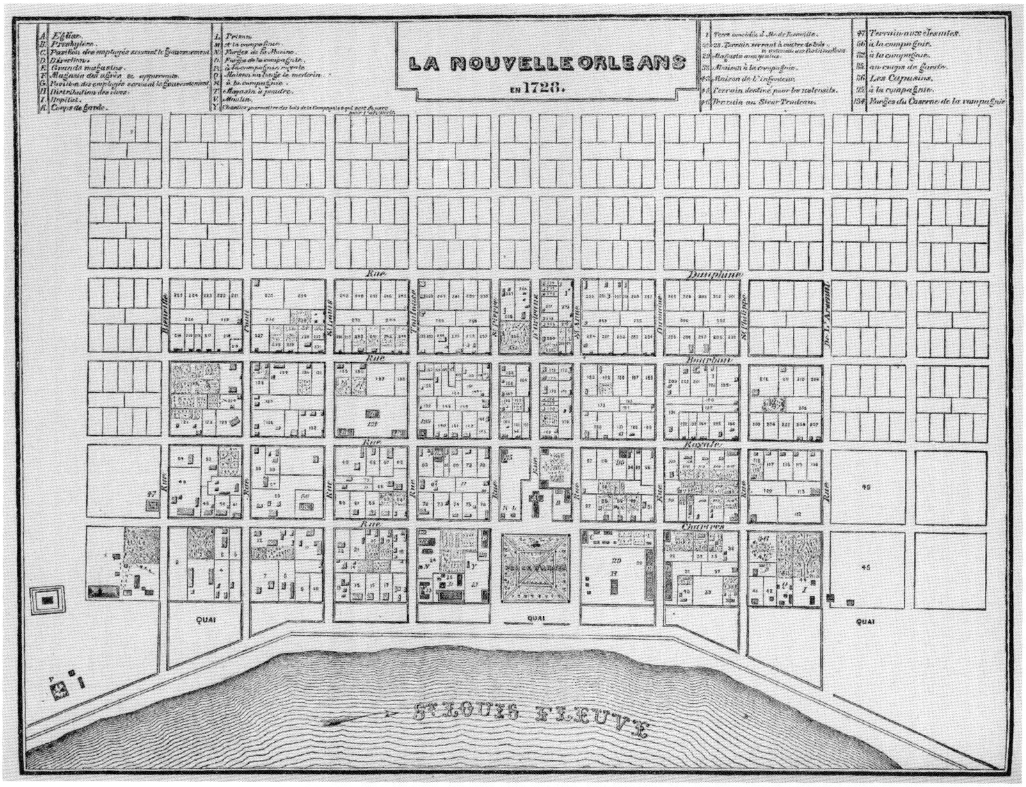

Designer

Adrien de Pauger (?–1726), engineer and cartographer, accompanied the LeMoyne brothers to Biloxi. In 1720, Bienville (see page 13) tasked de Pauger with drawing up a plan for the city of New Orleans. He arrived in New Orleans in the spring of 1721 and completed the street plan of the city later that year. In 1724, de Pauger drew plans for the Church of St. Louis, the first parish church in New Orleans. He then turned his attention to the French settlement of Mobile, developing its original street plan in 1725. (Courtesy LSM.)

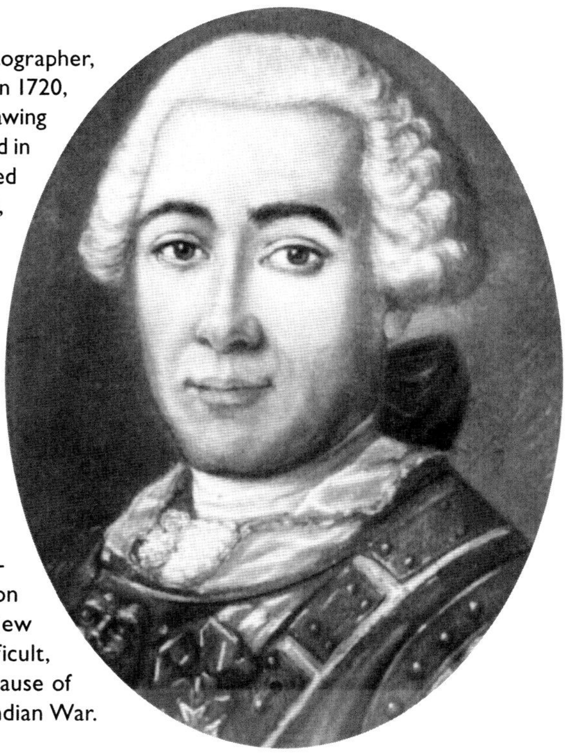

Governor

Louis Belcourt, chevalier de Kerlerec (1704–1770), succeeded the Marquis de Vaudreuil-Cavagnal as governor of Louisiana in 1753, upon the latter's appointment as governor of New France. Kerlerec's tenure in Louisiana was difficult, as he received little support from France because of the country's involvement in the French and Indian War. (Courtesy LSM.)

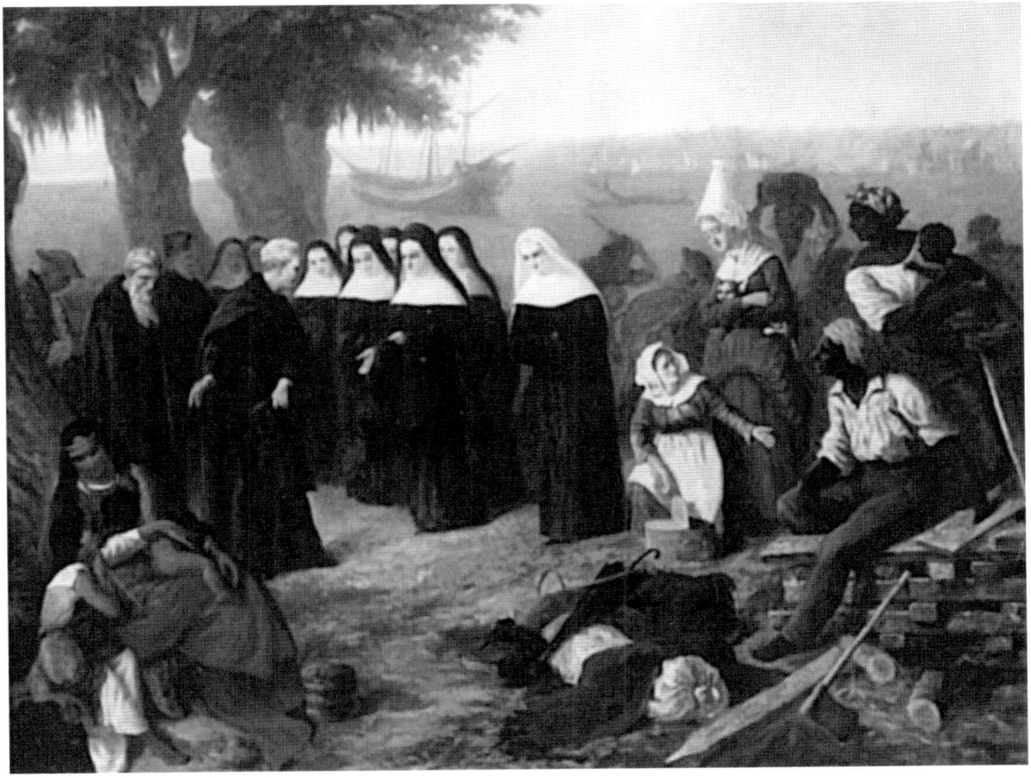

Ursulines
In 1726, under the leadership of their mother superior, Sister Saint-Augustin, 12 Ursuline nuns and two postulants left France for New Orleans. They arrived in New Orleans in 1727, establishing a presence in the city that remains to this day. The city built a convent for the Ursulines in 1734 in the French Quarter. A second convent, built adjacent to the original building and completed in 1751, survived the fires of 1788 and 1794. The "Old Ursuline Convent" is now a National Historic Landmark. (Courtesy NOPL.)

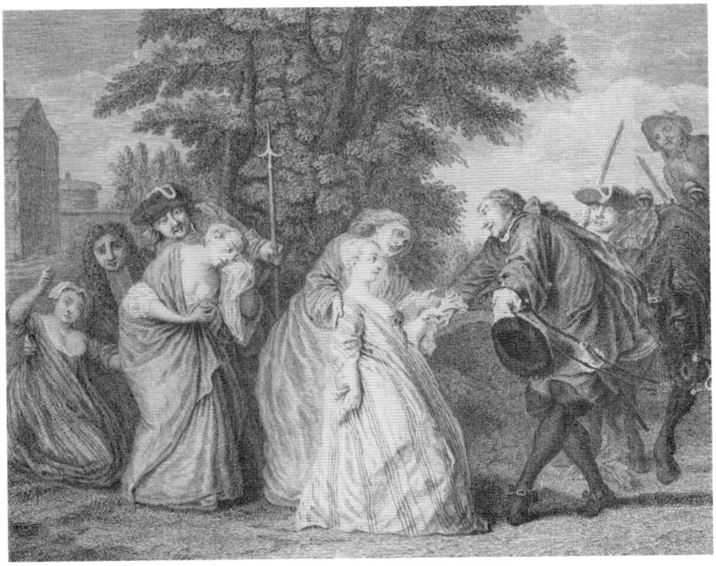

Casket Girls
Following in the tradition of the "King's Daughters" of French Canada, young French women were recruited to be brides for colonists in the French colonies of the Gulf Coast. They carried their belongings in a small trunk, or *cassette*, which was anglicized to "casket" over the years. (Courtesy LSM.)

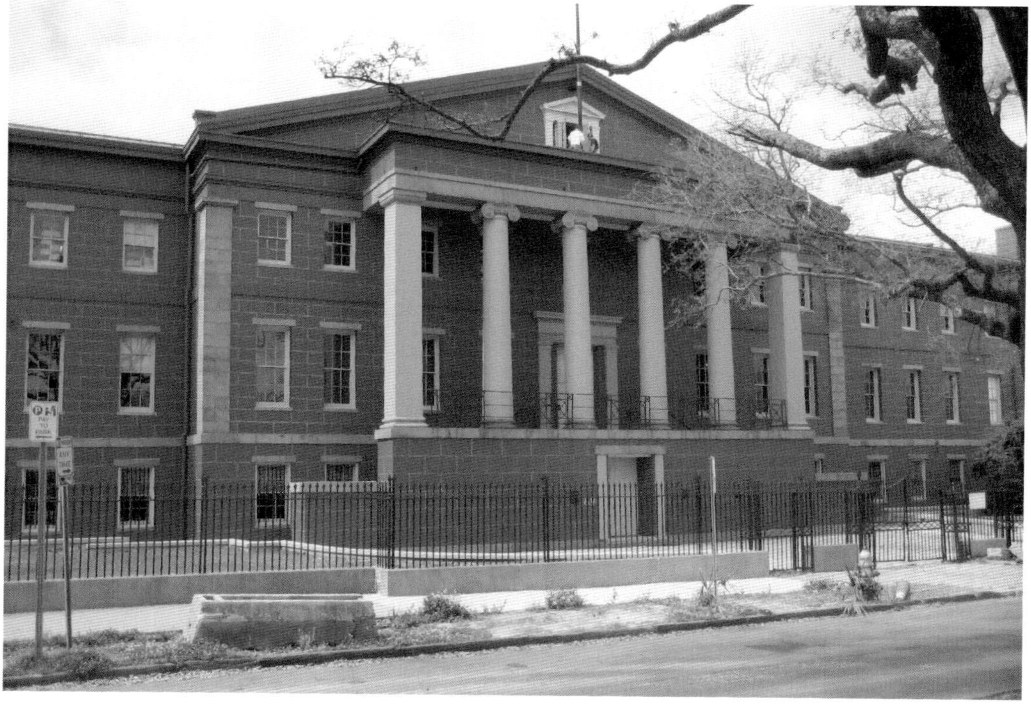

"Bloody O'Reilly"

Alejandro O'Reilly (1722–1794) was the second governor sent from Havana to Louisiana by Spain after France transferred control of the colony to that country in the wake of the French and Indian War. O'Reilly received his nickname because in 1769 he executed the leaders of the French rebellion that forced the first governor, Antonio de Ulloa, out of Louisiana. Those executions were carried out at Fort St. Charles, located on Esplanade Avenue, now the location of the Old US Mint (seen here in 1880). Once Spanish authority was firmly established, O'Reilly supervised the growth of Spanish Louisiana, particularly the rebuilding of New Orleans after the devastating fires of 1788 and 1794. (Courtesy LSM.)

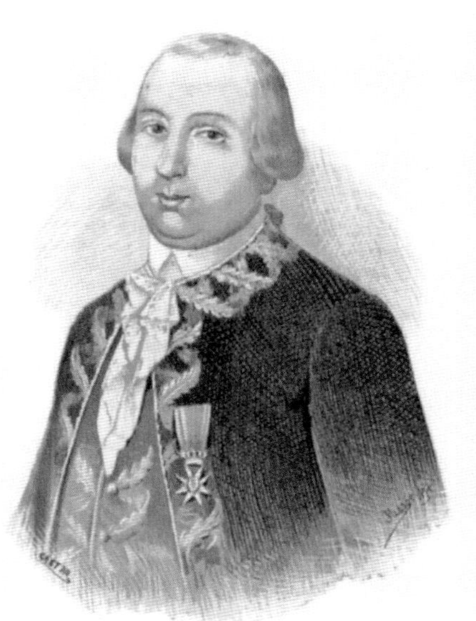

Revolutionary Hero

Bernardo de Gálvez y Madrid, the viscount of Galveston and count of Gálvez (1746–1786), became governor of Spanish Louisiana in 1777. Galvez was charged by King Charles III of Spain to continue assisting the Americans in their rebellion. He coordinated smuggling operations out of New Orleans and South Louisiana with Oliver Pollock. In 1781, Galvez led an expedition to Pensacola, Florida, laying siege to the British garrison occupying the colony. His victory led to the reconquest of Florida by Spain. (Courtesy LSM.)

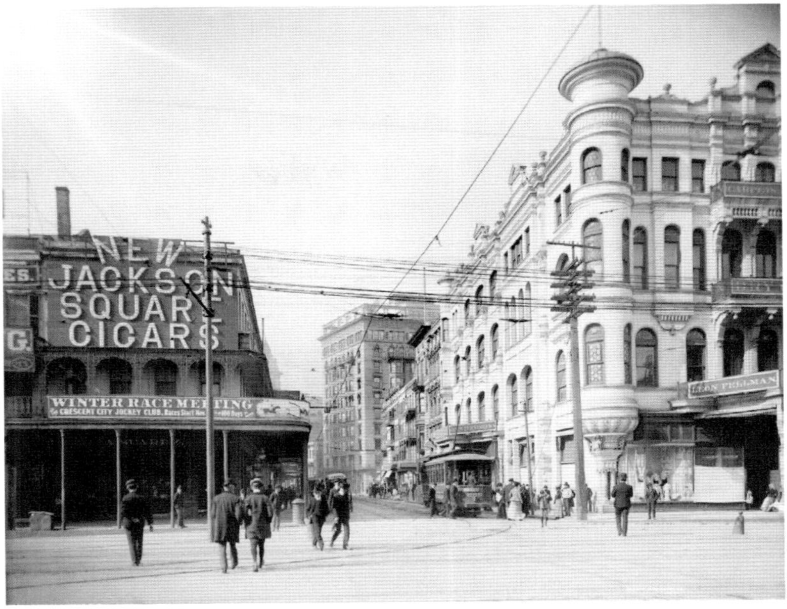

Administrator and Diplomat

Francisco Luis Hector, barón de Carondelet (1748–1807) was a professional administrator and politician of the Spanish crown. He assumed the governorship of Louisiana in 1794, succeeding Alejandro O'Reilly (see page 16). Carondelet (after whom the busy Faubourg Ste. Marie street, shown above in 1908, was named) continued the rebuilding of New Orleans after the 1794 fire. He also led the effort to build a canal connecting Bayou St. John with the city. The canal (pictured below), named in his honor, enabled boats and small ships to access New Orleans from the Gulf via Lakes Borgne, Pontchartrain, and the bayou. A skilled negotiator, Carondelet developed good relations with Native American tribes in Louisiana, helping prevent the Americans from gaining unfettered access to the Mississippi River. (Above, courtesy LSM; below, courtesy NOPL.)

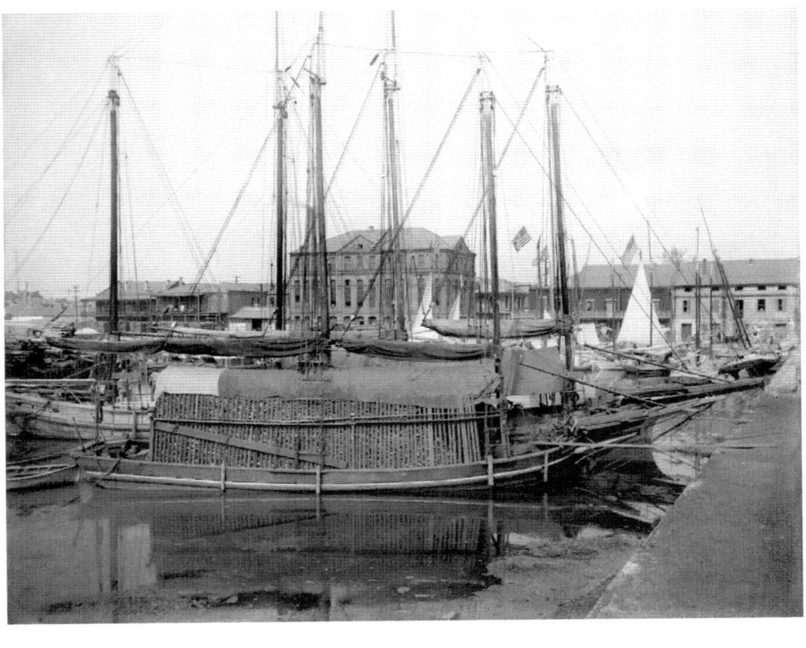

Bureaucrat and Philanthropist

Don Andres Almonaster y Rojas (1728–1798) was a younger son of a noble Andalusian house. Andres made his way to Louisiana after the Spanish assumed control and got Governor O'Reilly (see page 16) to appoint him as the colony's notary public. This was a lucrative position in New Spain, as doing business with the colonial government required a lot of papers to be certified. Almonaster's relationship with O'Reilly also enabled him to acquire a large tract of land in the center of the city that his daughter Micaela Almonaster de Pontalba later developed into what is now Jackson Square and the Pontalba Apartments. Don Andres used his wealth to finance the rebuilding of St. Louis Cathedral after the fire of 1794. He also financed the construction of several schools, as well as what is now St. Mary's Italian Church, next to the Old Ursuline Convent. Almonaster is buried under the altar in St. Louis Cathedral. (Right, courtesy LSM; below courtesy NOPL.)

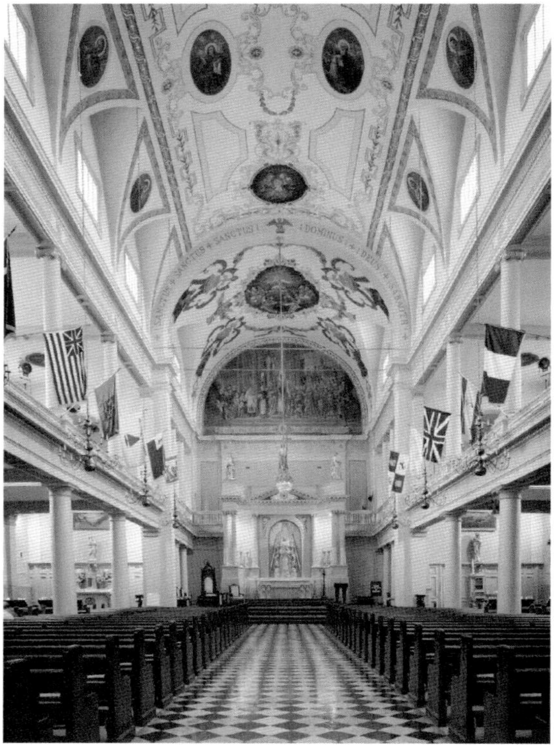

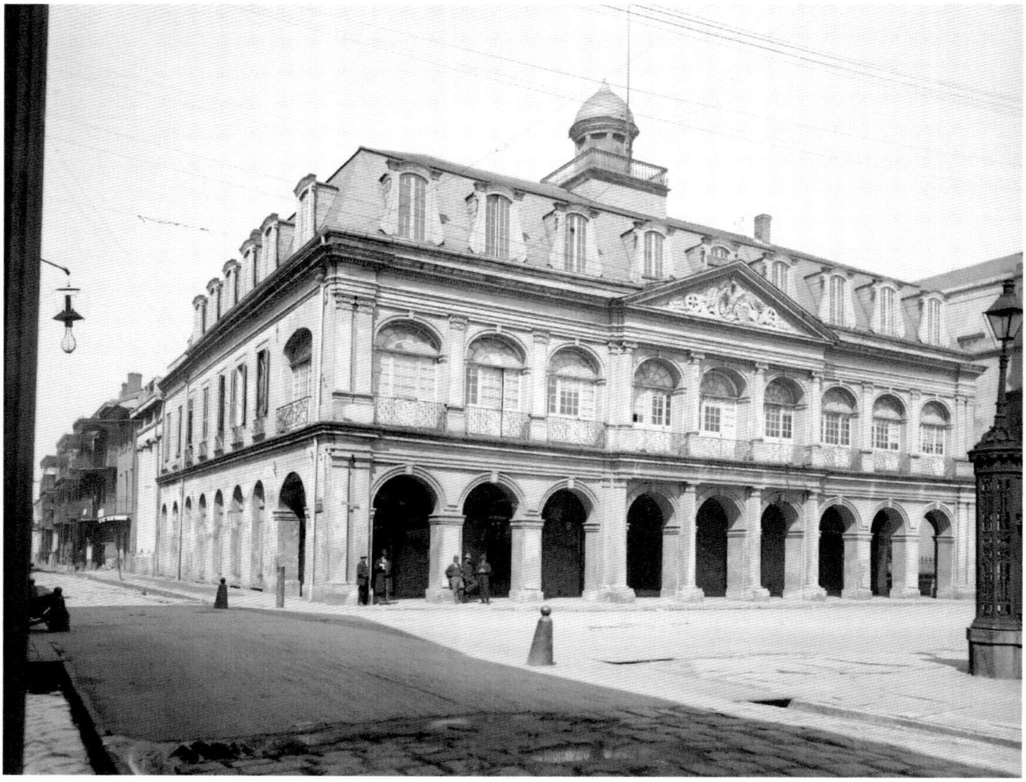

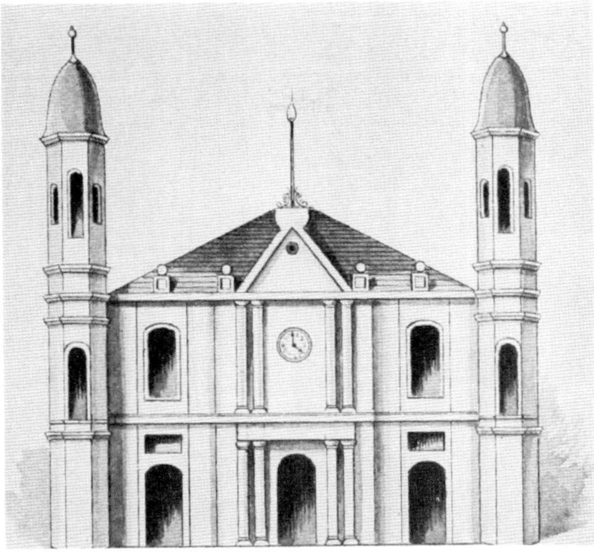

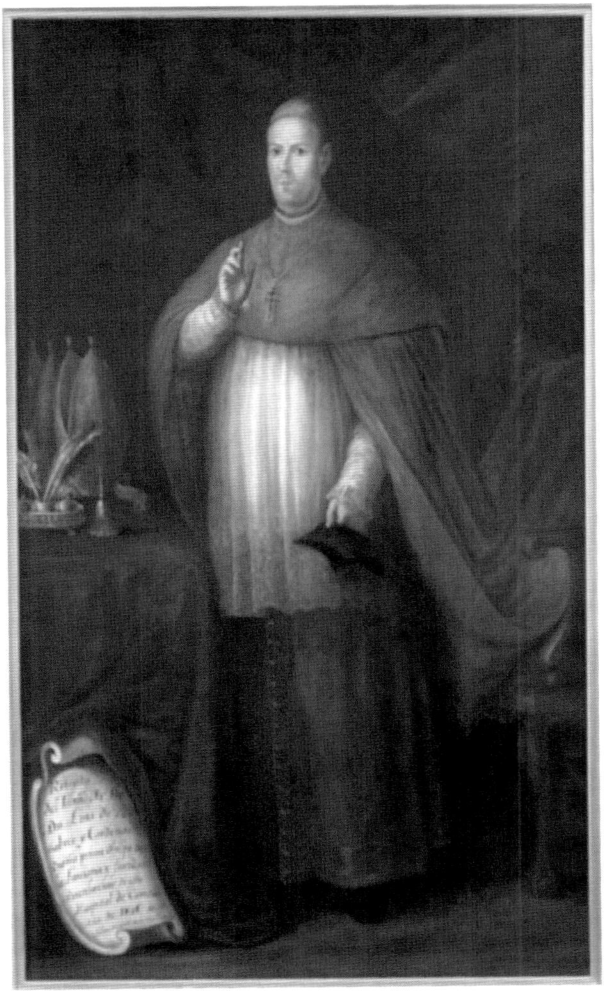

Bishop
Luis Peñalver y Cárdenas (1749–1810) was named the first bishop of the Diocese of Louisiana and the Floridas by Pope Pius VI in 1794. Peñalver arrived in New Orleans in July 1795. He designated the Church of St. Louis as his cathedral and seat, expanding the influence of the Catholic Church in what was to become the Louisiana Purchase territory. (Top, courtesy LSM; bottom, courtesy NOPL.)

American Control

W.C.C. Claiborne (1774–1817) was born in Virginia and moved to Tennessee in 1794. He ran for a seat in the US House of Representatives from Tennessee that had been vacated in 1797 by Andrew Jackson. This created controversy, as Claiborne was believed to only be 23 at the time, and the US Constitution requires members of the House to be at least 25. He resigned from Congress in 1801 to become governor of the Mississippi Territory. In 1803, he was appointed as the first US governor of the Louisiana Territory, supervising the transfer of New Orleans from the French to the Americans, as depicted by a series of paintings in the US Capitol. Claiborne held the post of territorial governor until 1812, when he became the first elected governor of the state of Louisiana. He was elected to the US Senate from Louisiana in 1817 but died before returning to Washington to assume the duties of that office. (Right, courtesy LSM; below, courtesy LOC.)

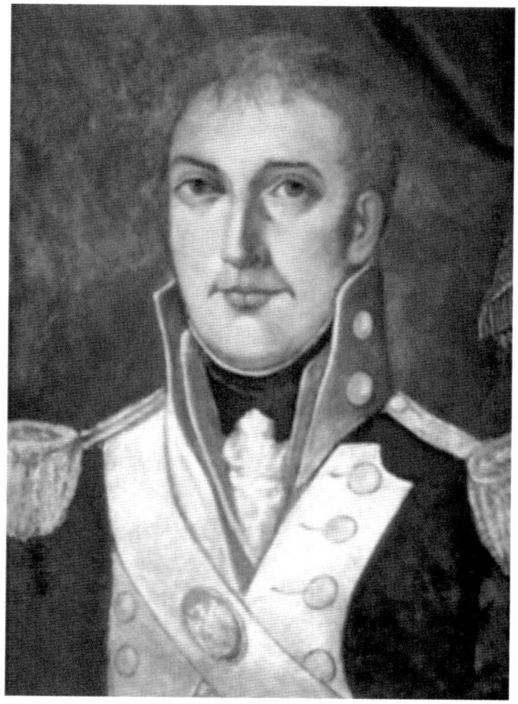

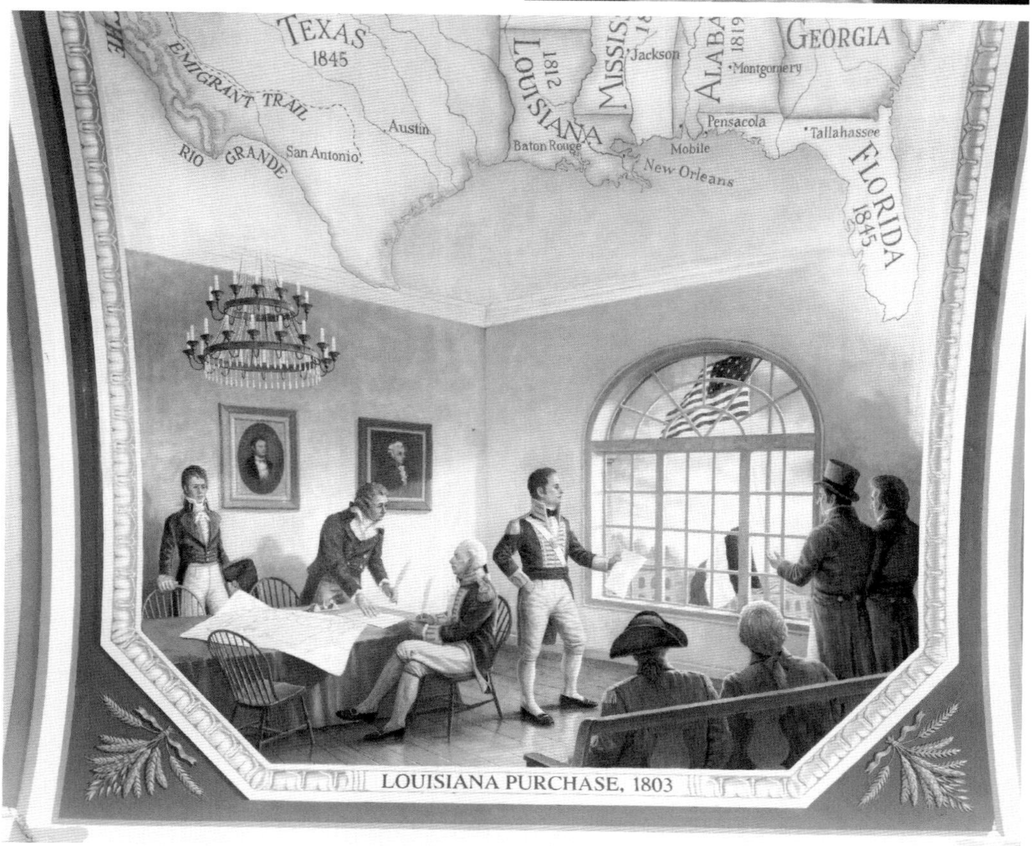

CHAPTER TWO

Music

Music is one of the major influences that binds New Orleanians together. The first music heard in New Orleans was the drumbeats and chants of Native Americans in the thousands of years before European explorers traveled down the Mississippi River. When the French established a base camp along the Mississippi at the end of the 17th century, those chants and songs were enhanced by the sailors' tunes and folk songs from France and Canada. These songs mingled with those of the Spanish, then the British, and other Europeans who made their way to the Port of New Orleans. Slaves brought involuntarily from Africa and the Caribbean contributed songs and musical instruments from their native lands, as well as the various songs they sang while in bondage in the islands.

This incredible mix of cultures gave New Orleans a unique sound that its people took with them when they left the city for other places. The continued integration of slaves and free people of color into New Orleans society transferred the native beats, dances, and songs into white, European households and entertainment establishments. That blending led to the musical form now called jazz, which spread like wildfire in the late 19th and early 20th centuries, going up the Mississippi to Chicago, or from New Orleans to New York City by train and ship.

Steeped in traditions of music and celebration, New Orleans recognizes and loves its musical legends and heroes, from the slaves whose music forms the roots of so much of the city's sound, to the early pioneers of jazz and those who developed jazz into a mature musical genre. The rhythms of the city's neighborhoods—Faubourg Treme and Congo Square, the French Quarter, Downtown and Uptown—flow from one street to another, into school band rooms, garage practice areas, and nightclubs. These musicians proclaim their love for the city when marching in Carnival parades, performing at family gatherings and on Sundays in church, even when escorting loved ones home to the cemetery after funerals. Music is the lifeblood of New Orleans.

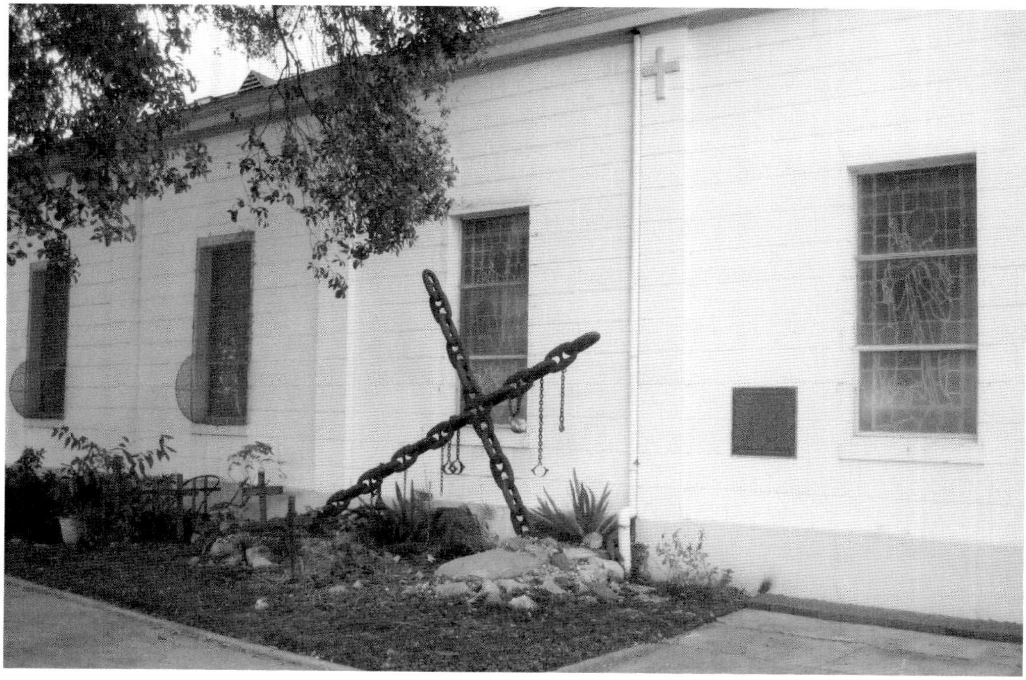

People of Color

Unlike slave owners in the British colonies of the United States, French and Spanish planters did not prohibit their slaves from making the music of their native lands. Slaves (commemorated in the Tomb of the Unknown Slave memorial at St. Augustine Catholic Church in Faubourg Treme) in and around New Orleans would gather on Sunday afternoons in an area just outside the boundaries of the original city, which became known as Place Congo, or Congo Square. Taking advantage of their afternoons off, slaves, joined by "free people of color," would drum, make music, sing, and dance in Congo Square. Their music was noted with curiosity by white people of the city; those rhythms and sounds naturally were picked up by others and spread all around town. (Above, courtesy St. Augustine Church; below, courtesy NOPL.)

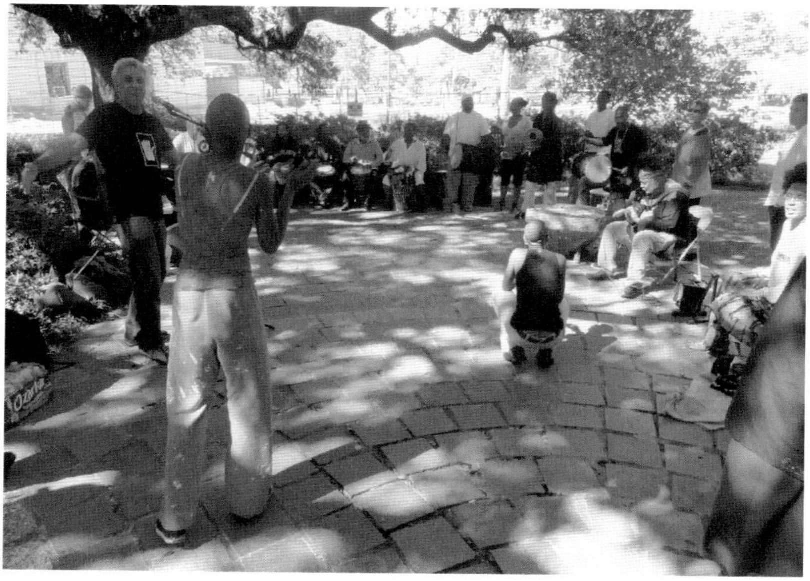

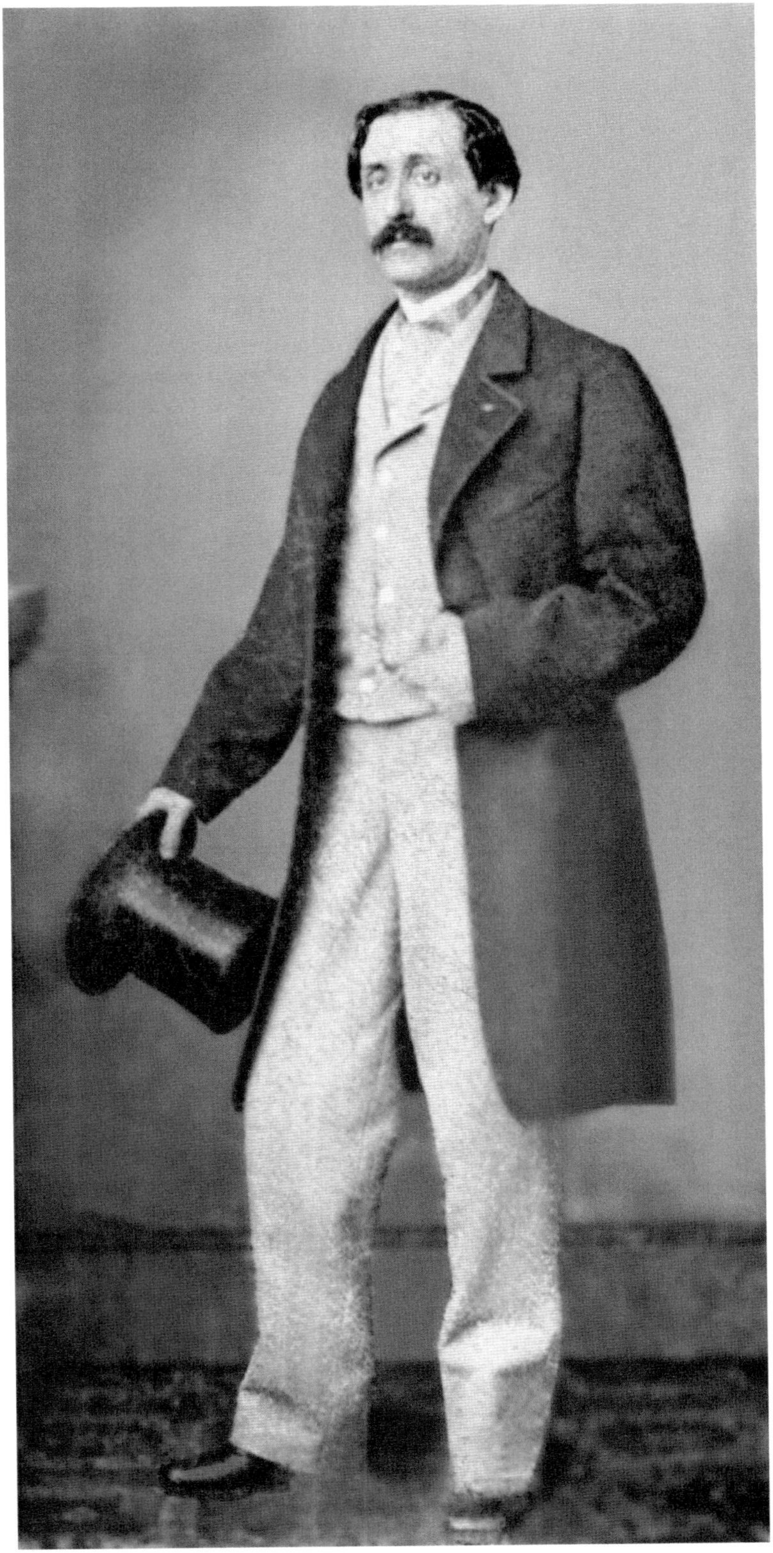

African Influence
Louis Moreau Gottschalk (1829–1869) grew up in New Orleans, listening to the rhythms of Place Congo. His mother's family was from Saint-Domingue (she was a New Orleans Creole). Gottschalk's father recognized early that Louis was a piano prodigy and sent him to Europe for classical training when he was 13. In 1845, Gottschalk wrote *Bamboula*, the first of three pieces for piano directly influenced by his New Orleans Creole upbringing. Louis toured the United States extensively upon his return from France but was forced to leave the country in 1865 because of a sex scandal involving a female student in San Francisco. (Courtesy NOPL.)

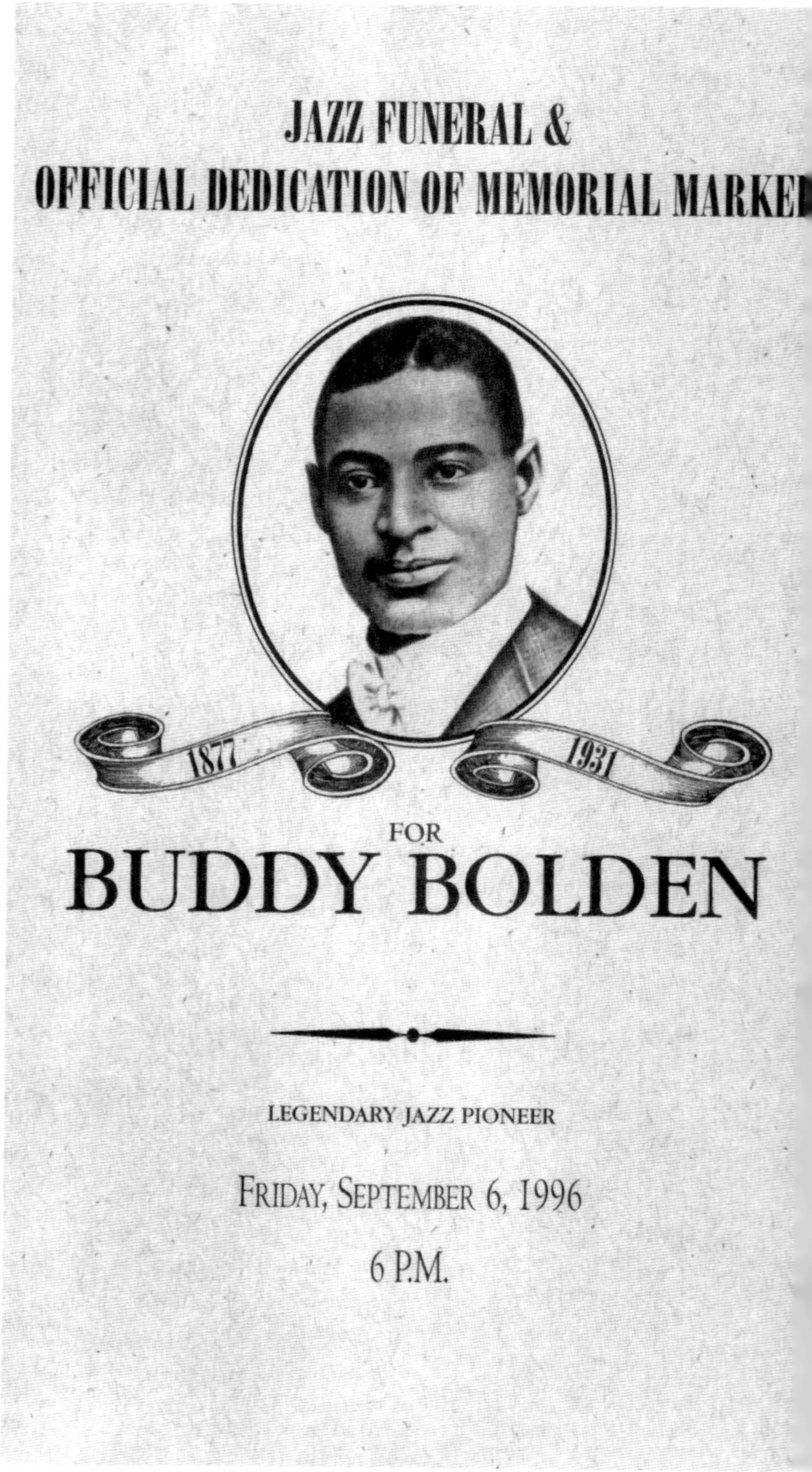

Tortured Genius
Charles "Buddy" Bolden (1877–1931) grew up in New Orleans, but little is known about his early life. He is credited with developing the "Big Four," a modification of the bass-drum patterns that Bolden, no doubt, heard on the streets of the city. This syncopated rhythm led to other improvisations, which is why many historians credit Bolden and his band as some of the originators of what is now know as jazz. While none of his musical recordings have survived, Bolden's tune "Funky Butt" (also known as "Buddy Bolden's Blues" is widely covered by jazz musicians. Bolden is also a critical character in New Orleans author Louis Maistros's novel *The Sound of Building Coffins*, which contains many scenes depicting Bolden playing his cornet. Bolden suffered from schizophrenia and was committed in 1907 to the Louisiana State Insane Asylum at Jackson, Louisiana, where he remained until his death. (Courtesy NOPL.)

Jelly Roll's Jazz

"Jelly Roll's Jazz" Ferdinand Joseph LaMothe (1885–1941) was a pianist and bandleader known professionally as "Jelly Roll Morton." A native, Morton grew up in this house in Faubourg Marigny. He is widely regarded as one of the originators of jazz, and Morton was arrogant enough to claim he invented the genre himself. As a bandleader, Morton was one of the first to actually morph jazz from merely an improvisational format into formally arranged music. He played many of the saloons and parlors of New Orleans's famous Storyville district at the beginning of the 20th century, eventually leaving the city to tour nationally. (Courtesy Carlos "Froggy" May.)

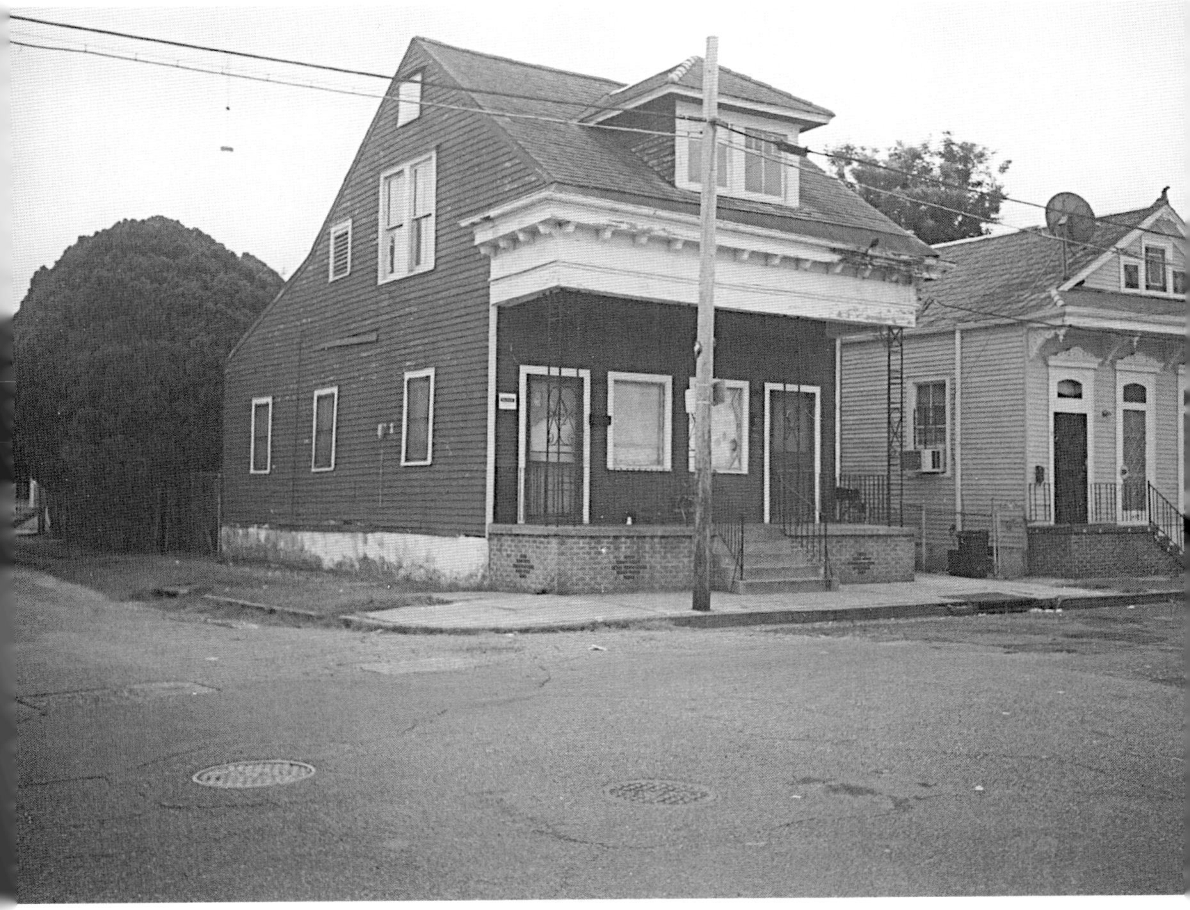

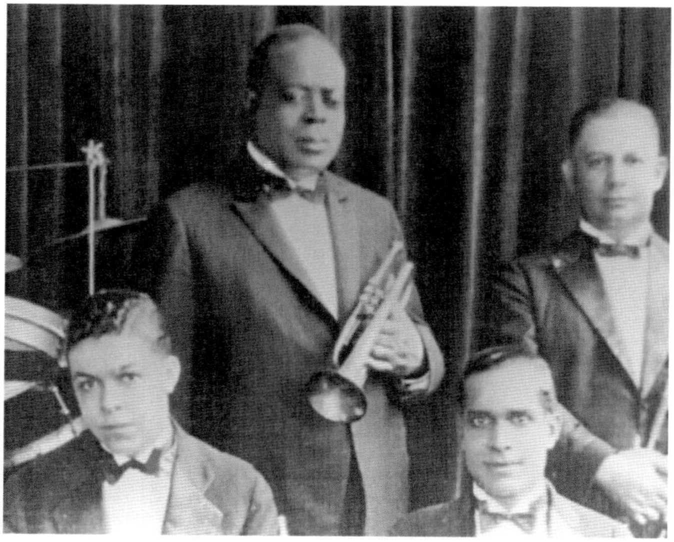

Creole Jazz

Joe "King" Oliver (1885–1938) was born in Donaldsonville, Louisiana, just north of New Orleans, and moved to the city as a boy. He played cornet extensively in the Storyville District but left New Orleans after an incident in 1919 when a fight broke out in a club and police arrested him and his band. Oliver mentored a young Louis Armstrong, who joined his band as second cornet in Chicago. Even though he never returned to New Orleans, Oliver's bands were shining examples of Dixieland jazz throughout the 1920s. (Courtesy State Library of Louisiana.)

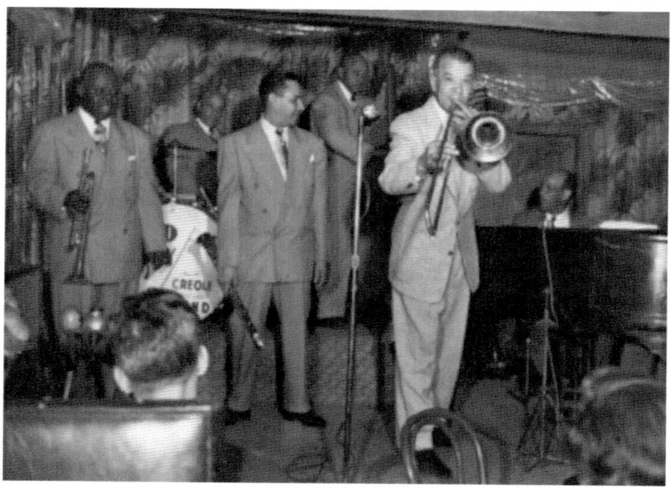

"Tailgate"

Edward "Kid" Ory (1886–1973) played banjo as a child, developing a style known as "tailgate," where the trombone player plays rhythm, under the lead of trumpets and cornets. Originally from LaPlace, Louisiana, legend is that Buddy Bolden discovered the 21-year-old Ory in Uptown New Orleans and brought him into the fledgling Storyville jazz scene, but his sister told Bolden her brother was too young to play the clubs. Ory did make it to Storyville in the 1910s, then moved to Los Angeles in 1919, eventually making his way to Chicago. In Chicago, he played with King Oliver, Jelly Roll, and Louis Armstrong. Ory took a long hiatus during the Great Depression, but his career enjoyed radio success from 1944 to 1961. (Courtesy NOPL.)

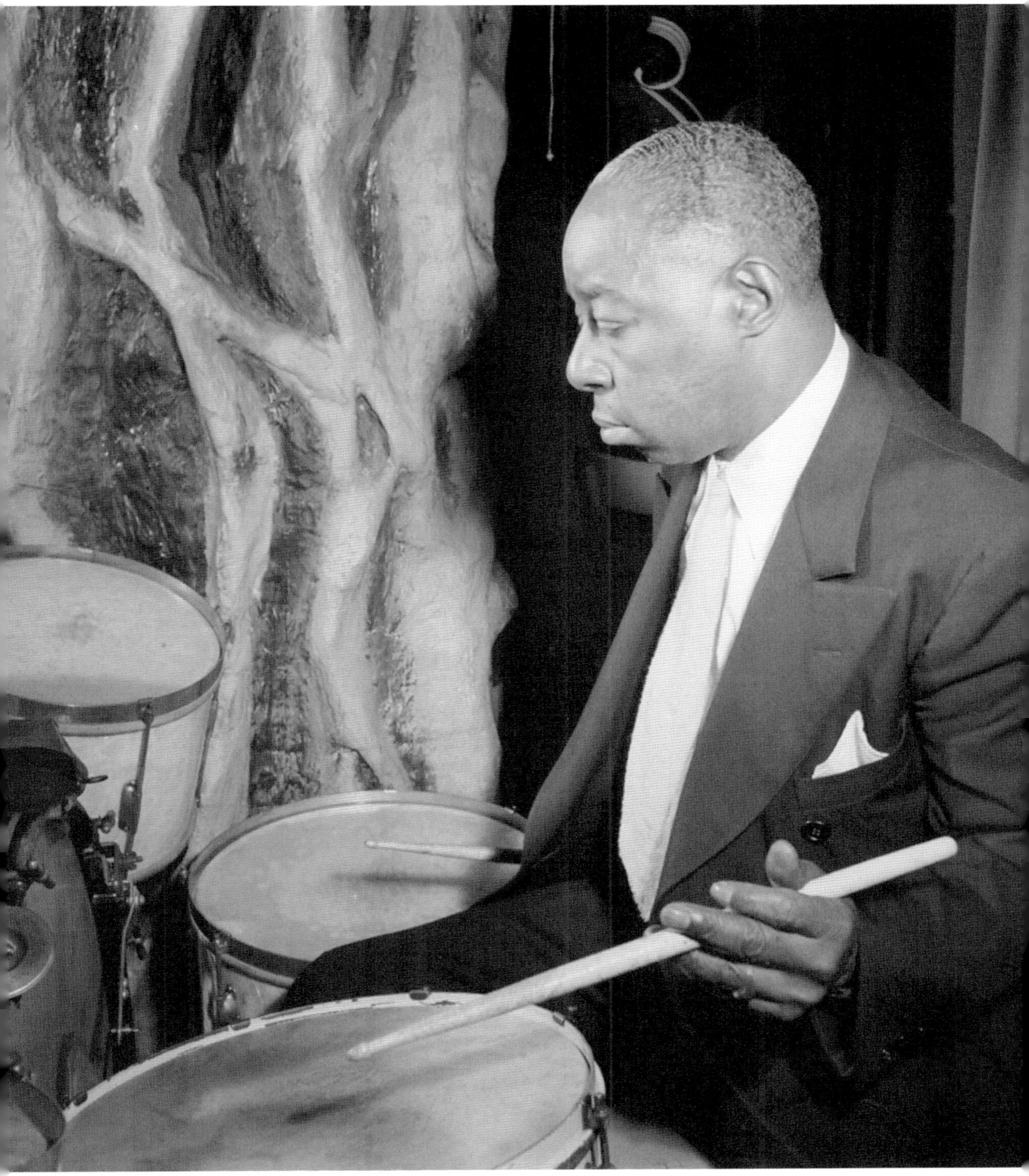

King's Drummer

Warren "Baby" Dodds (1898–1959), the younger brother of clarinetist Johnny Dodds, was one of the top drummers of the pre–Big Band era. "Baby" made his mark playing with Sonny Celestin and Fate Marable. After style disagreements, Dodds and Louis Armstrong left Marable's band to join up with his older brother in King Oliver's band. The Dodds brothers followed Oliver to Chicago, where they kept the Dixieland style alive. (Courtesy NOPL.)

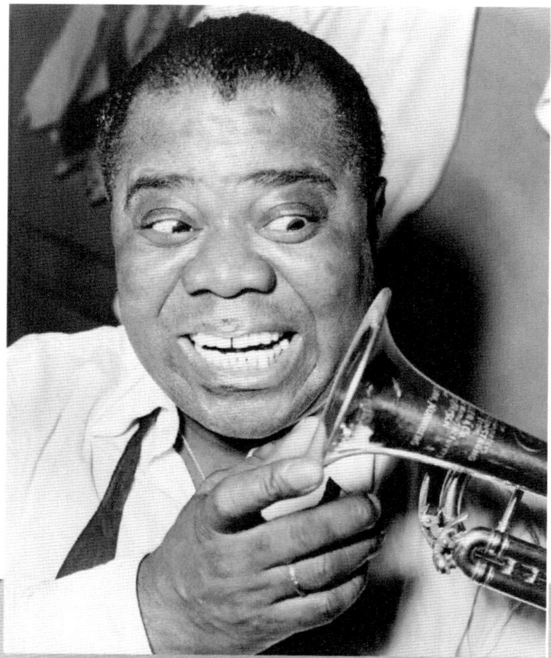

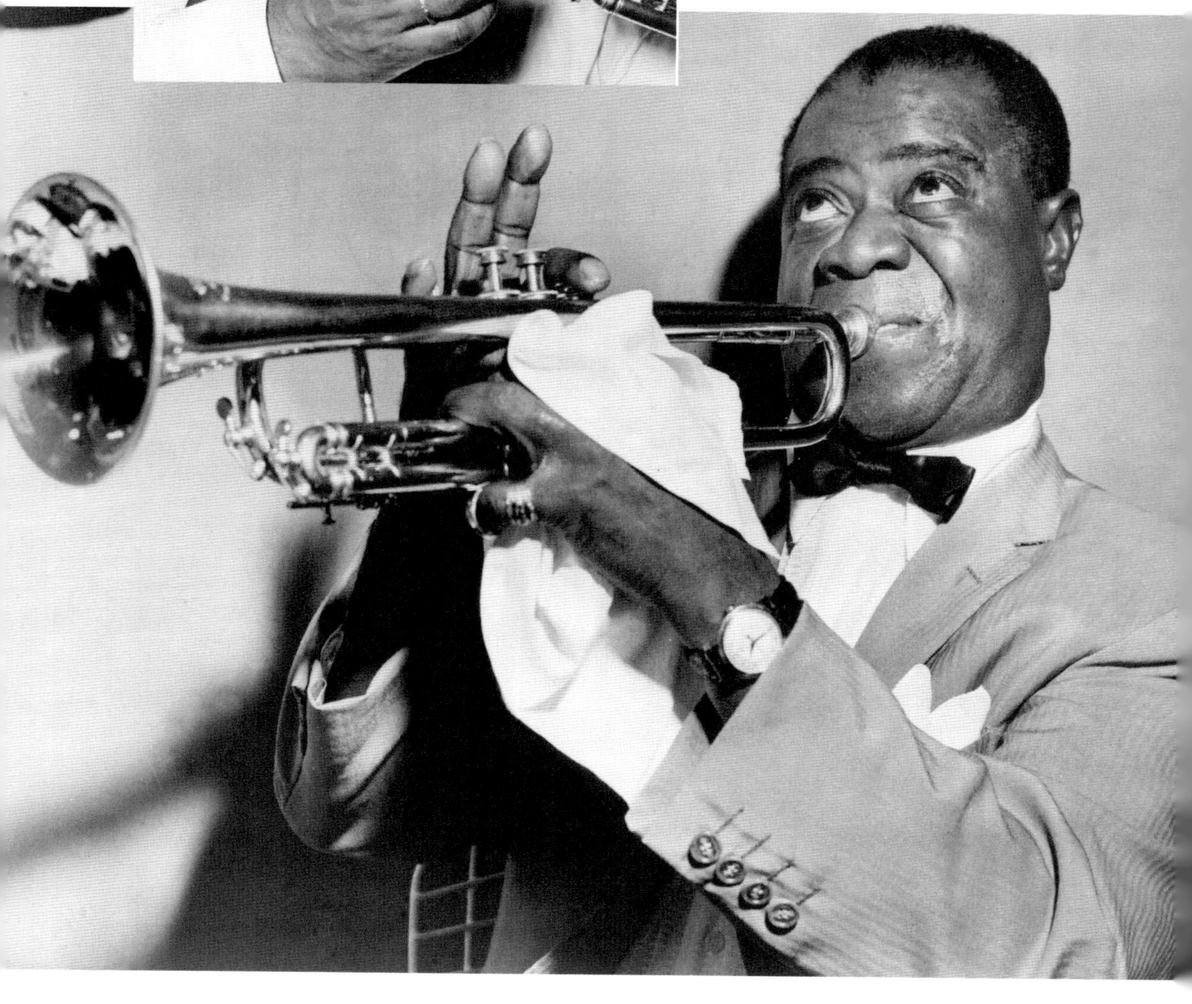

"Pops"

Louis Armstrong (1901–1971) is arguably the most "legendary" New Orleanian in the city's history. Armstrong began to play the cornet by ear at the age of 11, hanging out in Storyville at night after spending the day hauling coal to the clubs and brothels. He spent a good deal of time from ages 11 to 14 in the New Orleans Home for Colored Waifs (later known as Milne Boys' Home when it was moved to Gentilly). Armstrong joined the band at the home, learning how to read music and improving his technique. Upon his release from the home at the age of 14, he began to play with the Storyville bands. King Oliver was his mentor, but he was also influenced by Kid Ory, Buddy Petit, and Bunk Johnson. Armstrong played in bands on riverboats, eventually joining Kid Ory's band when King Oliver decided to leave New Orleans. He followed Oliver to Chicago in 1922 and then went to New York City, alternating between the two for most of the 1920s. Armstrong spent most of the Depression in Los Angeles, then toured the United States and Europe, eventually settling down in New York in 1943. He returned to New Orleans and a hero's welcome for Mardi Gras in 1949, when he was named king of the Zulu Social Aid and Pleasure Club. "Satchmo" (the nickname's origins are in the term "satchelmouth") played with a mix of big band groups and small combos during the 1950s. He enjoyed his greatest commercial success in 1964, when "Hello Dolly" knocked The Beatles off the charts. Armstrong, also nicknamed "Pops" because he called so many people by that name when he forgot their real names, died of a heart attack in New York in 1971. Even though "Pops" did not return often to New Orleans after he left in 1922, he was one of the leaders in keeping the Dixieland style thriving. "Pops" married Daisy Parker of Gretna, Louisiana, in 1918, but the relationship was short-lived. He then married Lil Hardin in 1923, then divorced her in 1938 to marry longtime girlfriend Alpha. He divorced his third wife when he moved to New York in 1942, marrying number four, Lucille Buchanan Wilson, whom he remained with until the end. Armstrong had no children of his own, but he cared for the boy he and his first wife adopted in 1918 at the age of three. The boy was mentally disabled, and Armstrong took care of him after the death of Daisy, doing so for the rest of his life. (Opposite page, both courtesy LOC; below, courtesy Carlos "Froggy" May.)

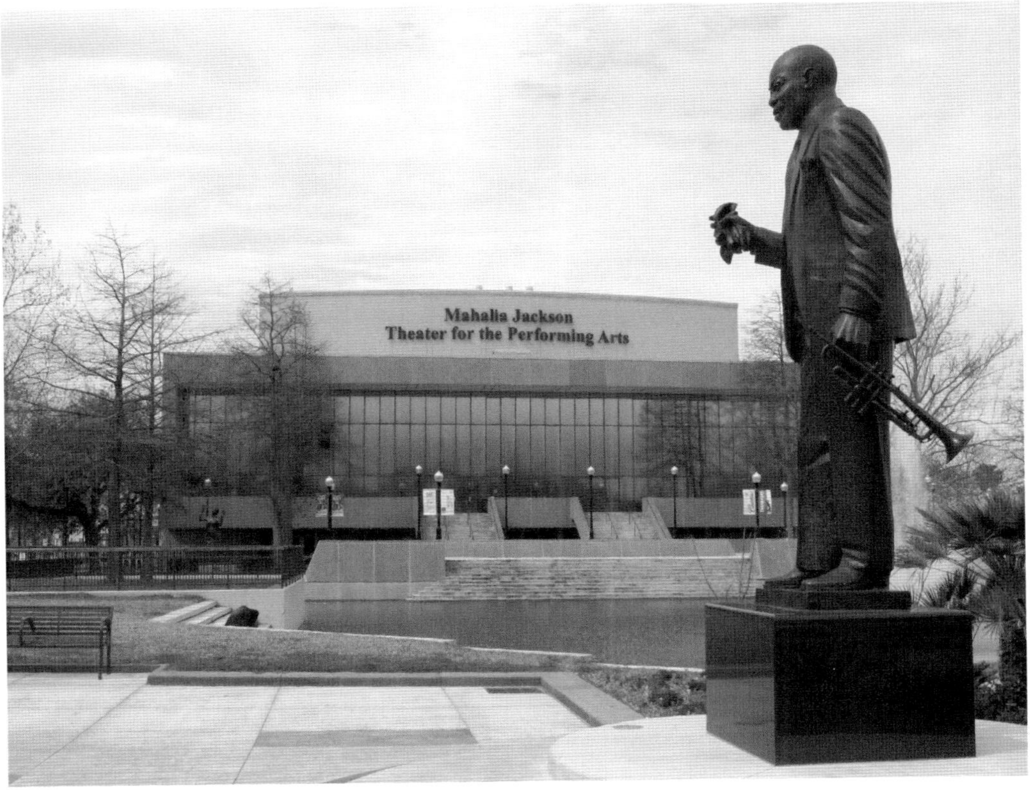

"Gonzo"

James Carroll Booker III (1939–1983) was a native New Orleans piano player and singer. Booker had commercial success with his 1960 tune "Gonzo," which reached No. 43 on the Billboard chart and No. 3 on the R&B chart. Booker's career was marred by drug problems. In spite of this, he still played regularly around New Orleans, touring some, most notably in 1976 with Jerry Garcia. Harry Connick Jr. was a student of his. (Courtesy NOPL.)

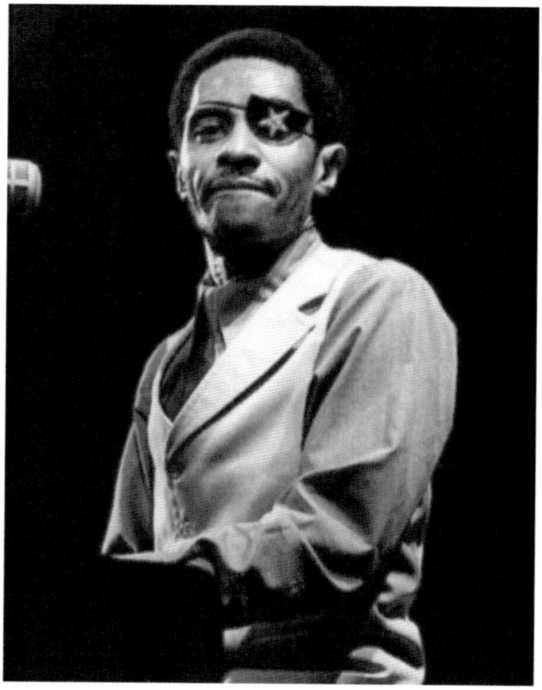

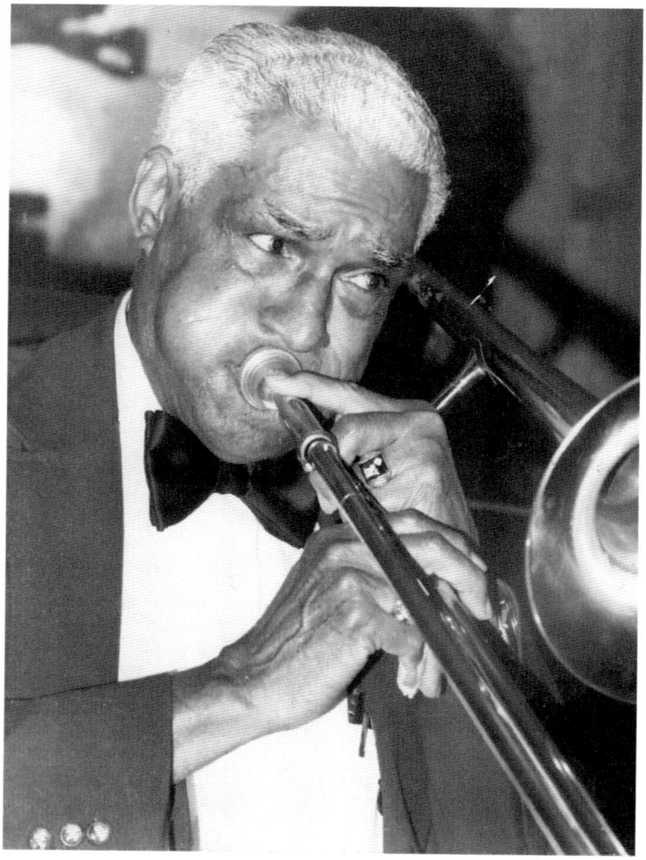

Preservation Hall

Louis Hall Nelson (1902–1990) began his career playing the trombone at the age of 15. He played with many of New Orleans's greats in the 1920s, then joined a Works Progress Administration band during the Depression. Enlisting in the US Navy during World War II, Nelson played in a Navy band in Memphis, becoming a musician first class. Upon returning to New Orleans, Nelson played with Sidney Desvigne's Orchestra, then with the Kid Thomas Valentine Band. He became a regular in the fledgling Preservation Hall venue in 1961 and was exposed to a new and younger audience. Offers to play and tour came in, and Nelson did just that right up to his tragic death, which was the result of a hit-and-run automobile accident. (Courtesy NOPL.)

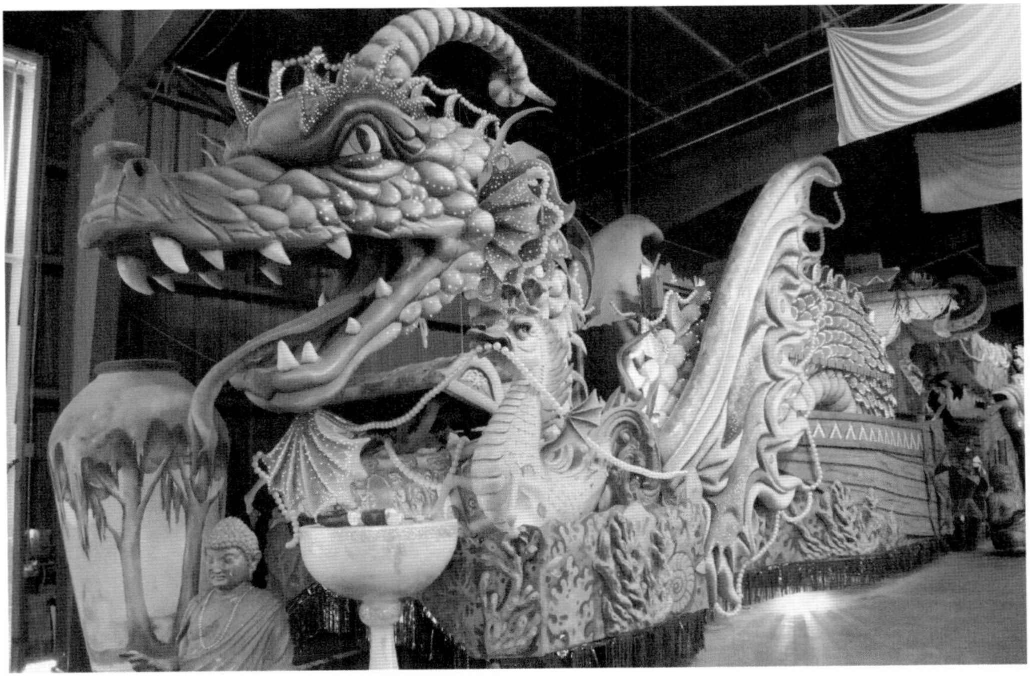

Orpheus Rising

Harry Connick Jr. (born 1967) is the son of former Orleans Parish district attorney Harry Connick Sr. At the age of nine, he performed with the New Orleans Symphony Orchestra. As a teen, Connick was mentored by Ellis Marsalis Sr. and James Booker at the New Orleans Center for Creative Arts (NOCCA). After high school and a brief period studying at Loyola University, Connick moved to New York, where he studied at the Manhattan School of Music and was signed by Columbia records. After recording his debut album and a follow-up, he received the opportunity to do the soundtrack for Rob Reiner's 1989 movie *When Harry Met Sally*. Connick made his acting debut in 1990 in the film *Memphis Belle* and has enjoyed critical acclaim as both an actor and a musician. Locally, Connick is lauded for founding the Krewe of Orpheus, whose signature Carnival float, the "Leviathan" is featured here. Orpheus, which parades on Lundi Gras, rapidly grew in popularity and is regarded as a "super-krewe." Connick has also been very active in the recovery of the Lower Ninth Ward neighborhood in the wake of Hurricane Katrina. (Above, courtesy Stephanie Schoyer; below, courtesy Carlos "Froggy" May.)

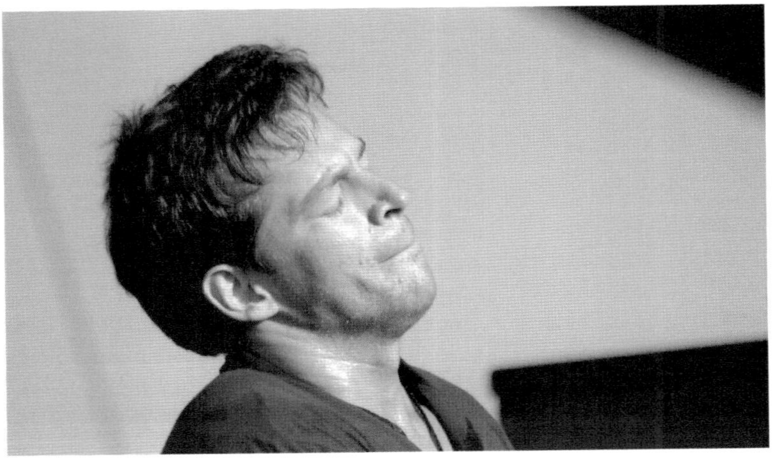

Studio Genius

Cosimo Matassa (born 1926) opened his first recording studio on Rampart Street in New Orleans when he was 18. By 1955, the business outgrew the Rampart Street location and he opened Cosimo's Recording Studio at 521 Governor Nicholls Street in the French Quarter. Cosimo (seated at right) engineered or produced numerous rock 'n' roll and R&B artists and is credited with the creation of what became known as the "New Orleans Sound." Cosimo was inducted into the Rock and Roll Hall of Fame in Cleveland in 2012. (Courtesy Carlos "Froggy" May.)

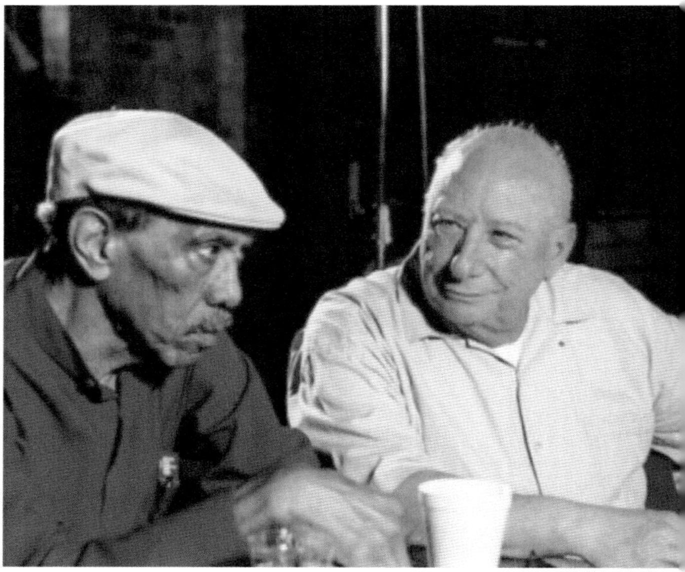

French Market Jazz

Danny Barker (1909–1994) is known best for his jazz banjo, guitar playing, and vocals, but his role as founder of the Fairview Baptist Church Marching Band is probably Barker's greatest contribution to New Orleans music. He played clarinet and drums in his youth but switched to guitar when he moved to New York in 1930. He remained in New York or touring for 35 years, returning to New Orleans in 1965. Seven years later, in 1972, Barker formed the Fairview Baptist Church Marching Band, which launched the careers of an entire generation of musicians including Wynton and Branford Marsalis, Kirk Joseph, Leroy Jones, and Nicholas Payton. (Courtesy NOPL.)

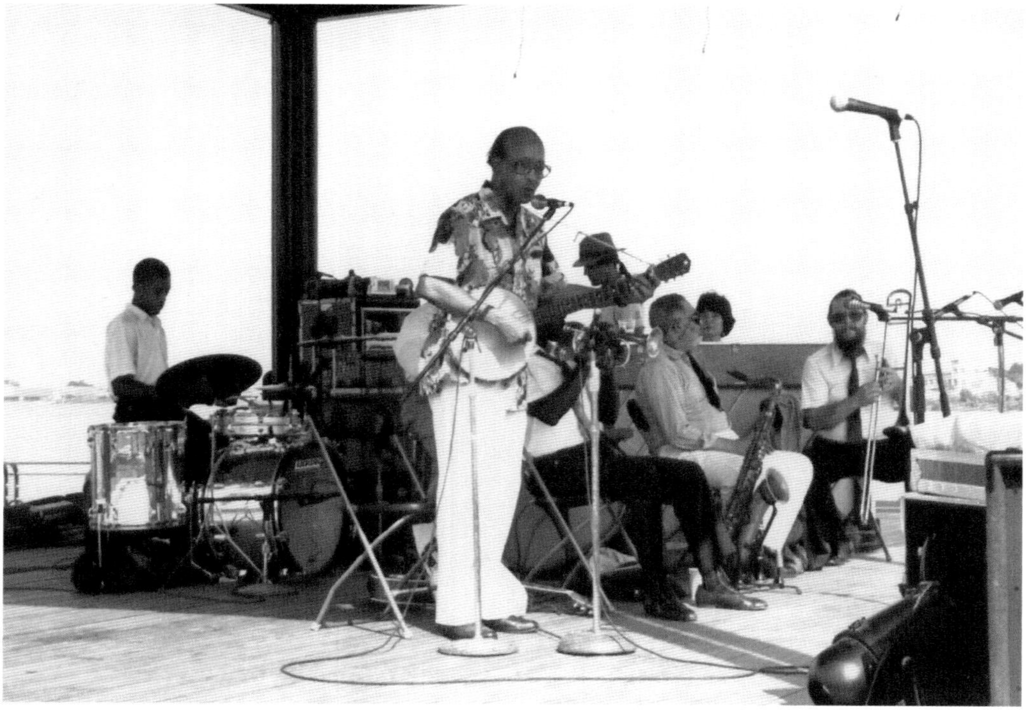

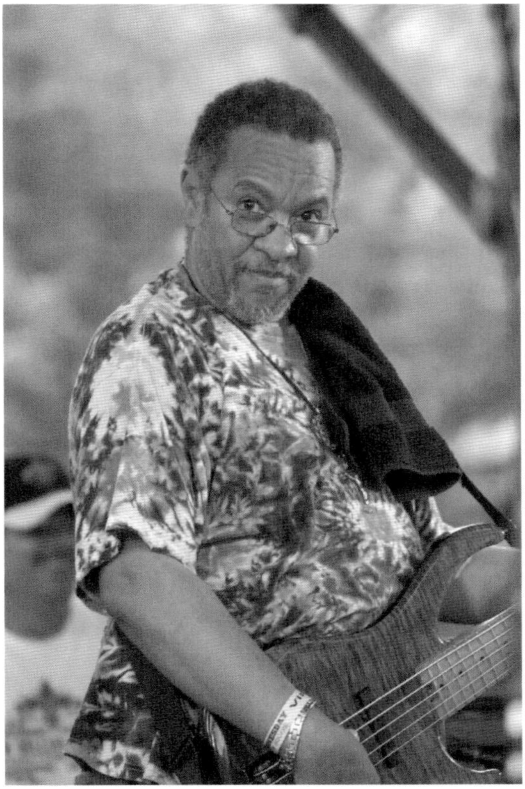

Funkify!

George Porter Jr. (born 1947) is, along with Art Neville, one of the founding members of The Meters, one of the groups that created the "New Orleans funk" sound. Porter continues to play with Neville in The Funky Meters as well as reunion gigs of the original group. He also plays around New Orleans and tours with his own band, Runnin' Pardners. Porter has played with a wide range of musicians, including Patti Labelle, Sir Paul McCartney, Jimmy Buffett, and David Byrne. (Courtesy Robbie Mendelson.)

Struttin'

Art Neville (born 1937), of the world-renowned Neville Brothers, is also a founding member (with George Porter Jr.) of The Meters. An accomplished keyboardist and singer, Neville (pictured at the keyboard with Porter on guitar) recorded his first successful single, "Mardi Gras Mambo," in 1954 with his band The Hawketts. (Courtesy Masahiro Sumori.)

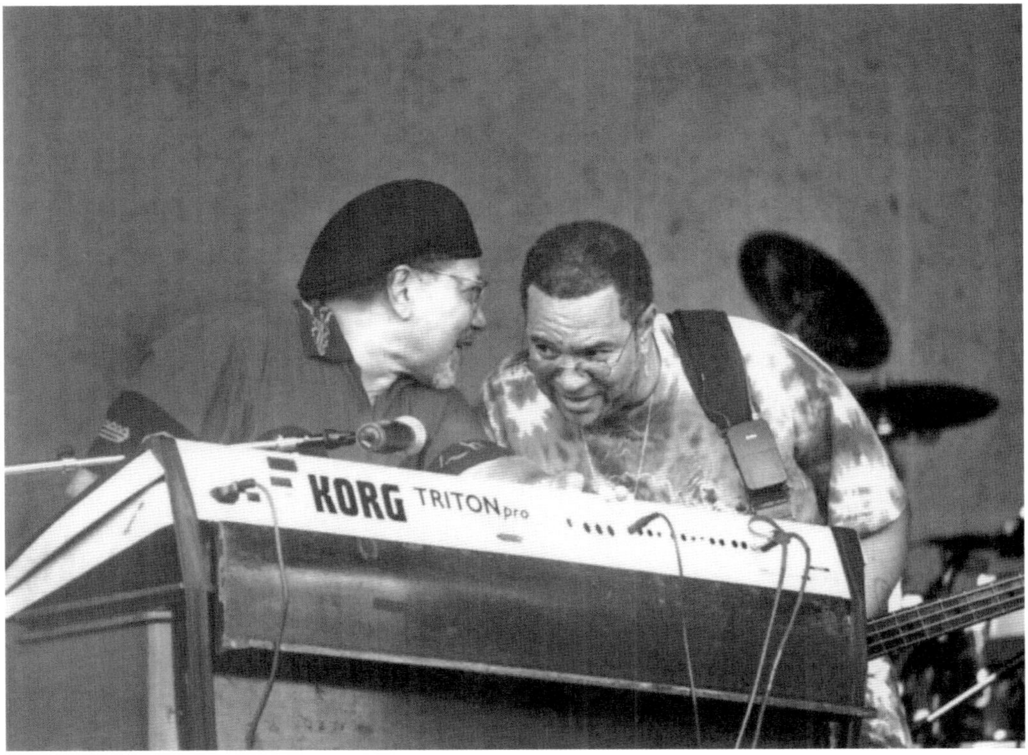

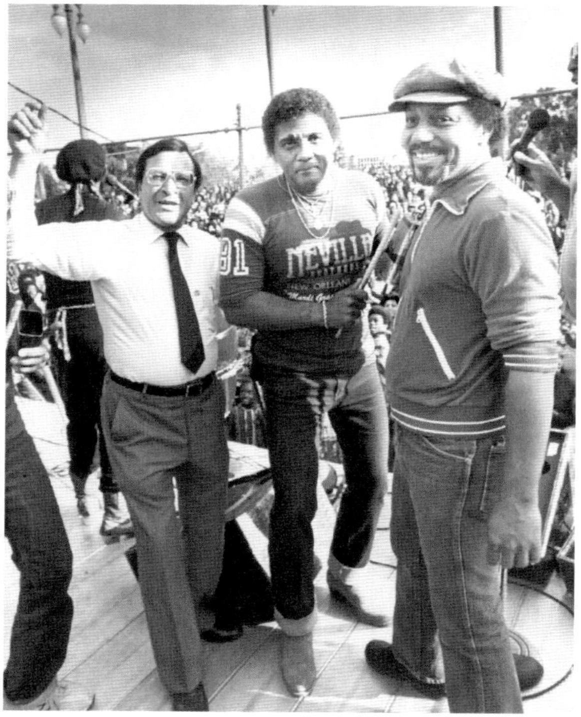

Soulful

Aaron Neville (born 1941) first broke out on the Billboard R&B chart in 1967 with his version of "Tell It Like It Is." Aaron is a member of the Neville Brothers, along with his brothers Art, Charles, and Cyril. He has had the most commercial and critical success of his siblings, winning a Grammy for a duet with Linda Ronstadt and four platinum-certified albums of his own. Here, Neville (center), poses with brother Art (right) and Mayor Ernest Morial in 1977. (Courtesy NOPL.)

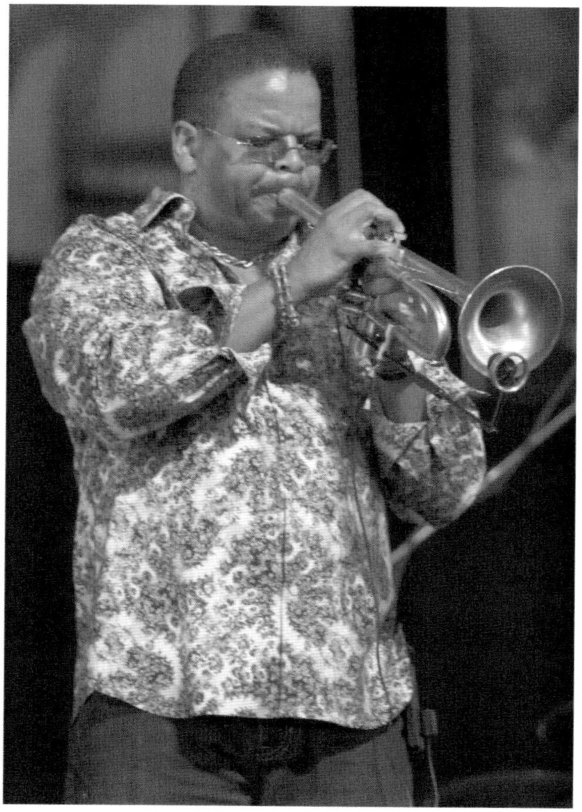

Hard Bop

Terence Blanchard (born 1962) was a childhood friend of Wynton Marsalis and studied under Ellis Marsalis Jr. at NOCCA. He replaced Wynton Marsalis as trumpet player in the Jazz Messengers. As artistic director at the Thelonious Monk Institute of Jazz at the University of Southern California, he successfully lobbied the institute to move to Loyola University of New Orleans after Katrina. Blanchard plays trumpet in the "hard bop" tradition. (Courtesy NOPL.)

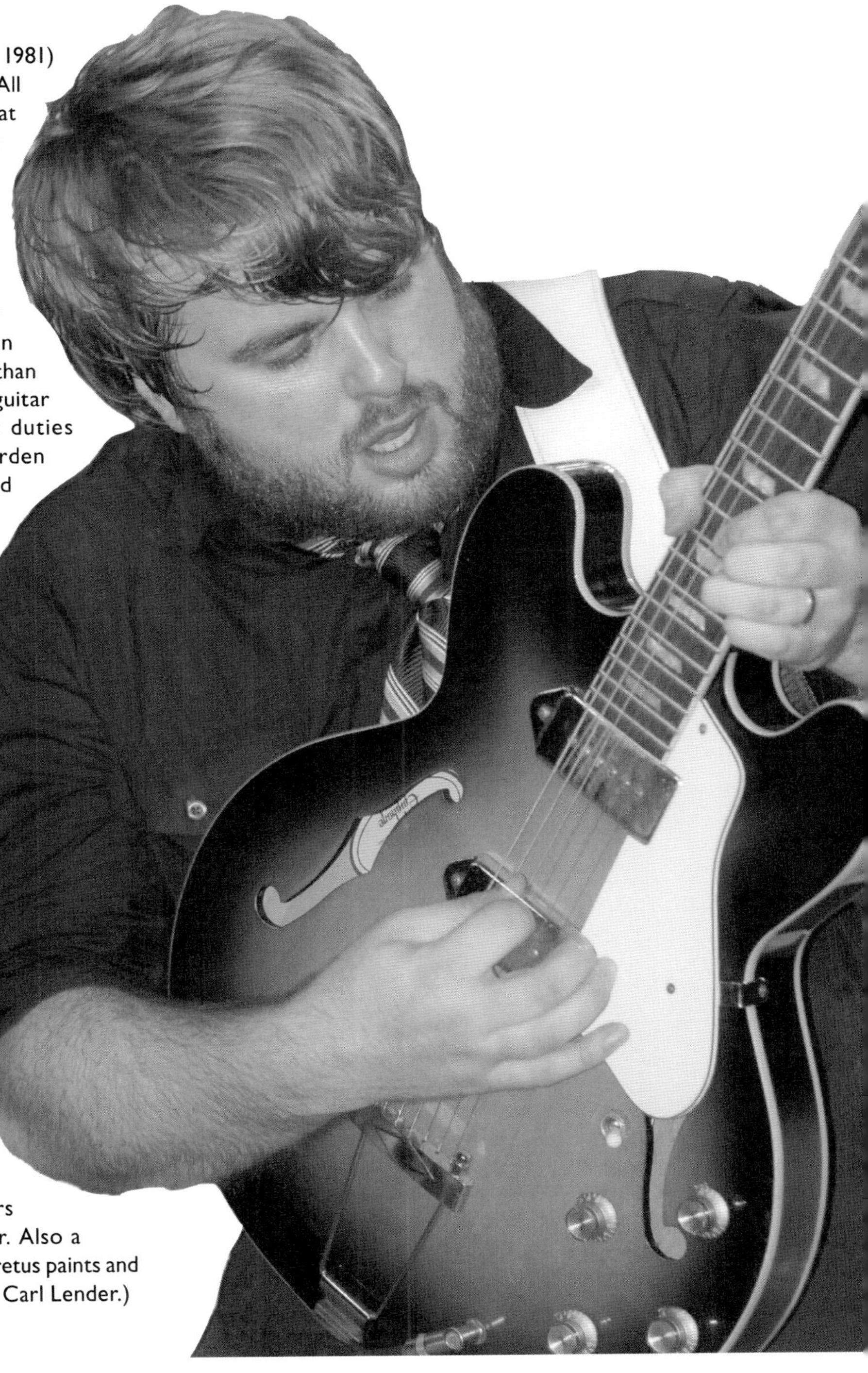

Garden District
Jonathan Pretus (born 1981) formed his first band, All She Wrote, in 1997 at the age of 16, playing drums. While at Louisiana State University, Pretus was the front man and guitar player for tWeezer, a Weezer cover band in Baton Rouge. In 2005, Jonathan was playing rhythm guitar and shared vocalist duties in the band The Garden District. The band toured extensively, and released an EP produced by Fred LeBlanc of Cowboy Mouth and Tom Drummond of Better than Ezra. Pretus toured for several weeks in 2007 with Cowboy Mouth, joining the band full-time that August. He left Cowboy Mouth after working on the band's most recent album. His latest band is The Breton Sound, in which Pretus partners with Stephen Turner. Also a skilled visual artist, Pretus paints and sketches. (Courtesy Carl Lender.)

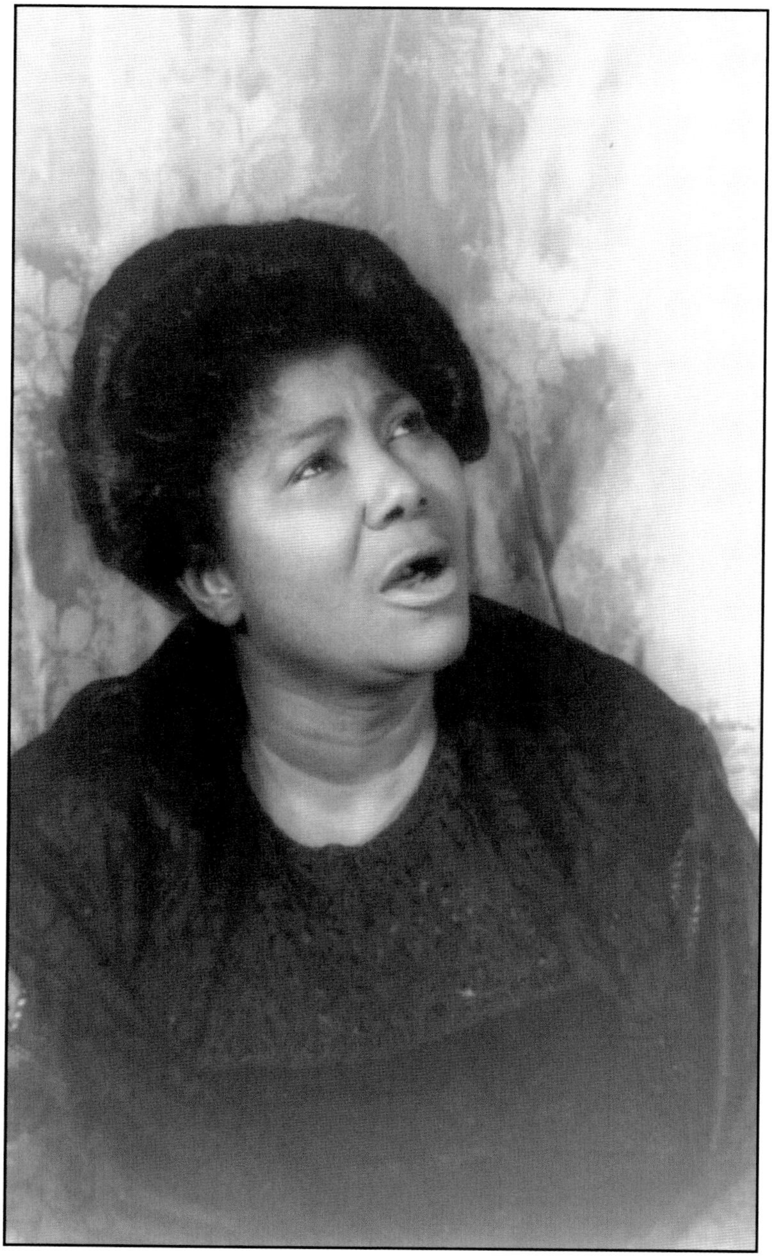

Queen

Mahalia Jackson (1911–1972) was often referred to as the "Queen of Gospel." Mahalia grew up in Uptown New Orleans and moved to Chicago when she was 16. She became a member of the Greater Salem Baptist Church Choir and toured Chicago's churches with the Johnson Gospel Singers. She made numerous recordings on the Apollo label and was the first gospel singer to play at Carnegie Hall in New York. Jackson sang at the March on Washington in 1963, before Martin Luther King Jr. spoke, and she sang at his funeral in 1968. The 2,100-seat New Orleans Theater for the Performing Arts—the long-term residence of the Louisiana Philharmonic Orchestra in Louis Armstrong Park—is named in her honor. (Courtesy LOC.)

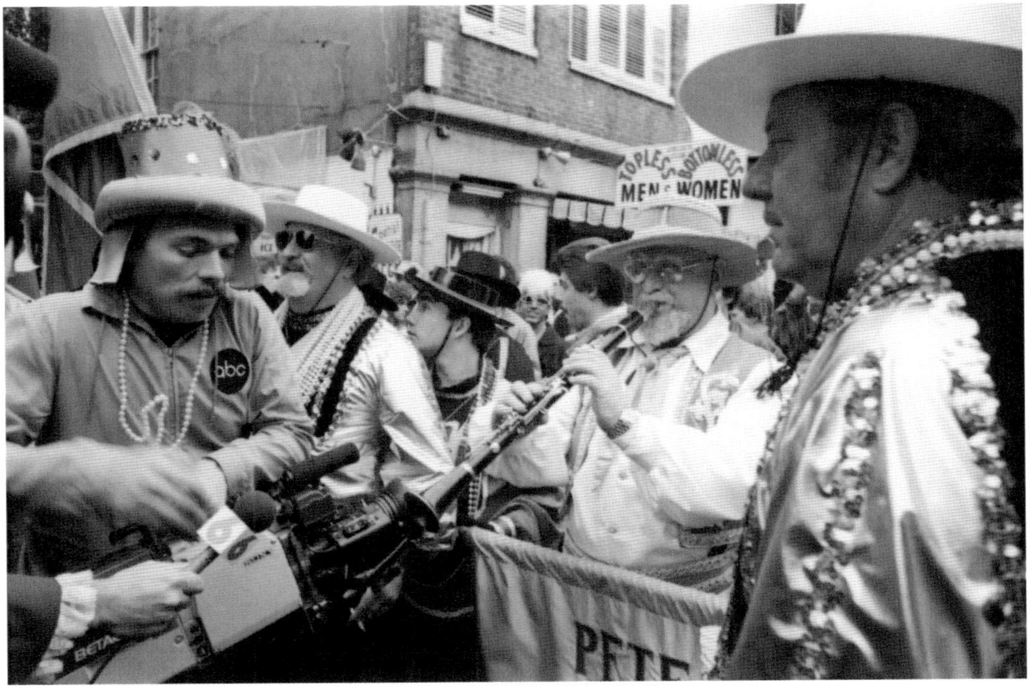

Half-Fast

Pete Fountain (born 1930) was born Pierre Dewey LaFontaine Jr. His father later changed his name to Peter Dewey Fountain, and son followed suit. After Pete was diagnosed with a weak lung condition, a doctor advised Fountain's father to get the boy a musical instrument to build up his lungs. Pete chose clarinet and learned to play jazz by listening to Benny Goodman recordings. His first band was The Basin Street Six, founded in 1950. Fountain joined the Lawrence Welk Orchestra in 1954 but soon returned to New Orleans, first playing with the Dukes of Dixieland, then with his own bands. In the late 1960s, Pete (pictured center-right, playing the clarinet) founded the "Half-Fast Walking Club," a Carnival organization that parades on Mardi Gras. (Courtesy Robert Avery.)

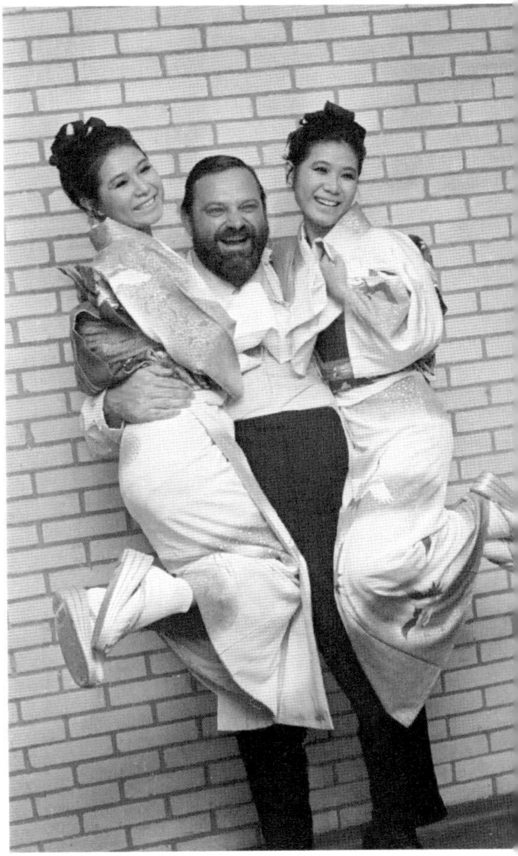

"Jumbo"

Al Hirt (1922–1999) was a trumpet player and Bourbon Street nightclub owner. He recorded the theme for the 1960s superhero show *The Green Hornet* and was a minority owner in the New Orleans Saints when the team was created in 1967. (Courtesy Netherlands National Archives.)

Gigolo

Louis Prima (1910–1978) was from a Sicilian family living in New Orleans. He played trumpet in a number of Italian-owned clubs in town, but his vocals garnered him much more recognition. Moving to New York in 1934, he organized the New Orleans Gang, combining scat and swing with traditional Dixieland. Prima moved to Los Angeles, mainly to avoid entanglements with the Italian mob. He opened The Famous Door nightclub, which led to movie appearances. In 1937, Prima returned to New York, where he began to record and perform Italian songs such as "Angelina." He met Keely Smith in 1951. They began to record together and married a short time thereafter. They divorced in 1961. Prima was chosen for the voice of King Louie in Disney's movie *The Jungle Book* in 1967. (Courtesy LOC.)

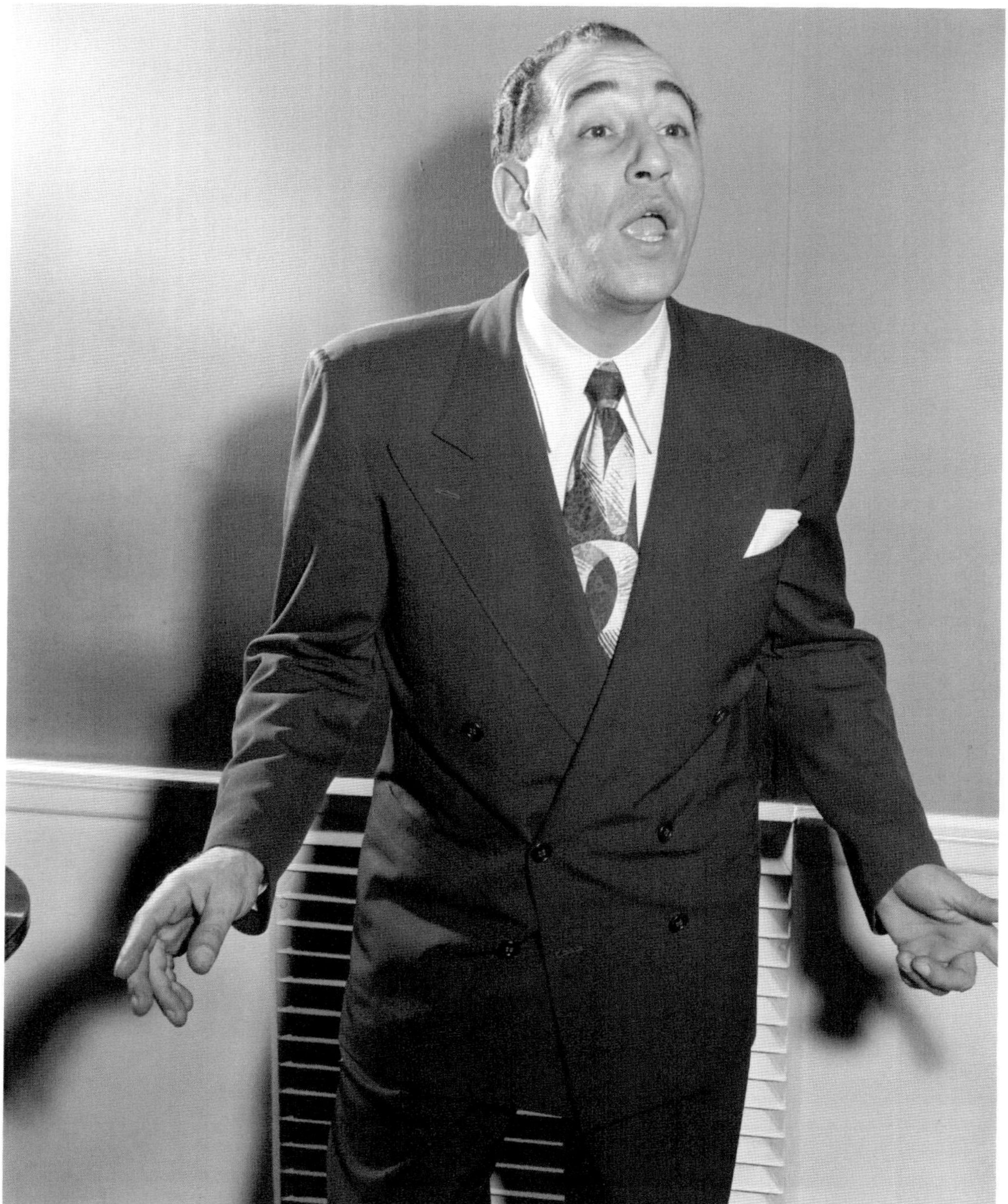

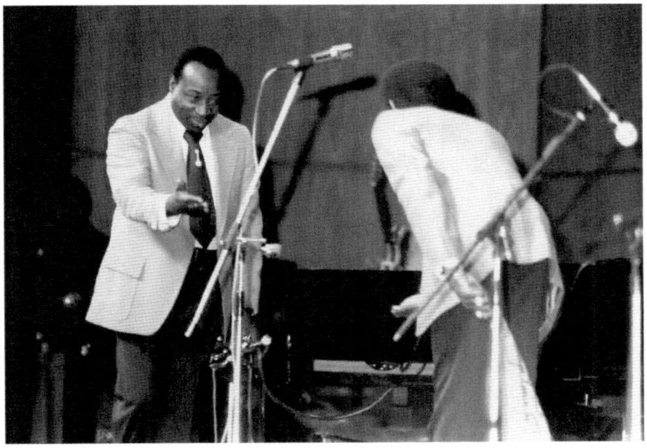

I'm Walkin'
Dave Bartholomew (born 1920) is a musician, band leader, composer, and arranger. As a trumpet player, Bartholomew's recording career began in 1947, but he is best known for producing numerous pop acts, and for cowriting (with Fats Domino) many hits, such as Domino's "Ain't That a Shame," "Blue Monday," and "I'm Walkin'." (Courtesy Klaus Hiltscher.)

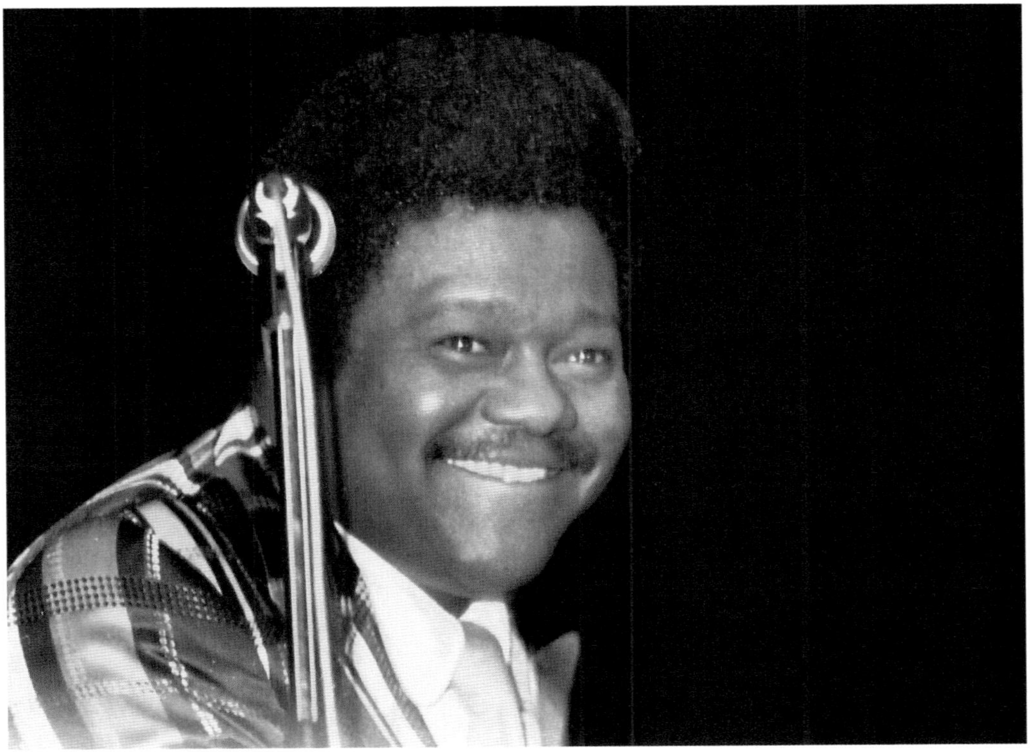

Blueberry Hill
Antoine Dominique "Fats" Domino Jr. (born 1928) is a true Ninth Ward legend. First breaking on the national scene in 1949, Domino had 35 Top 40 songs in his career. He collaborated with Dave Bartholomew throughout the 1950s on the Imperial label. He left Imperial in 1963, signing with ABC-Paramount, with whom he recorded for most of the 1960s to the 1970s. By the 1980s, Domino retired from national touring and stopped leaving New Orleans to record but remained a local favorite, playing clubs and events such as the New Orleans Jazz and Heritage Festival. When Hurricane Katrina struck on August 29, 2005, Domino was at his Ninth Ward home and had to be rescued by a Coast Guard helicopter. Because of the post-storm chaos in the city, many believed Domino had perished in the flooding. Domino lost almost all of his possessions when the water invaded his home. He moved to Harvey, Louisiana, but eventually rebuilt his home and office, and once again resides in "The Ninth." (Courtesy Klaus Hiltscher.)

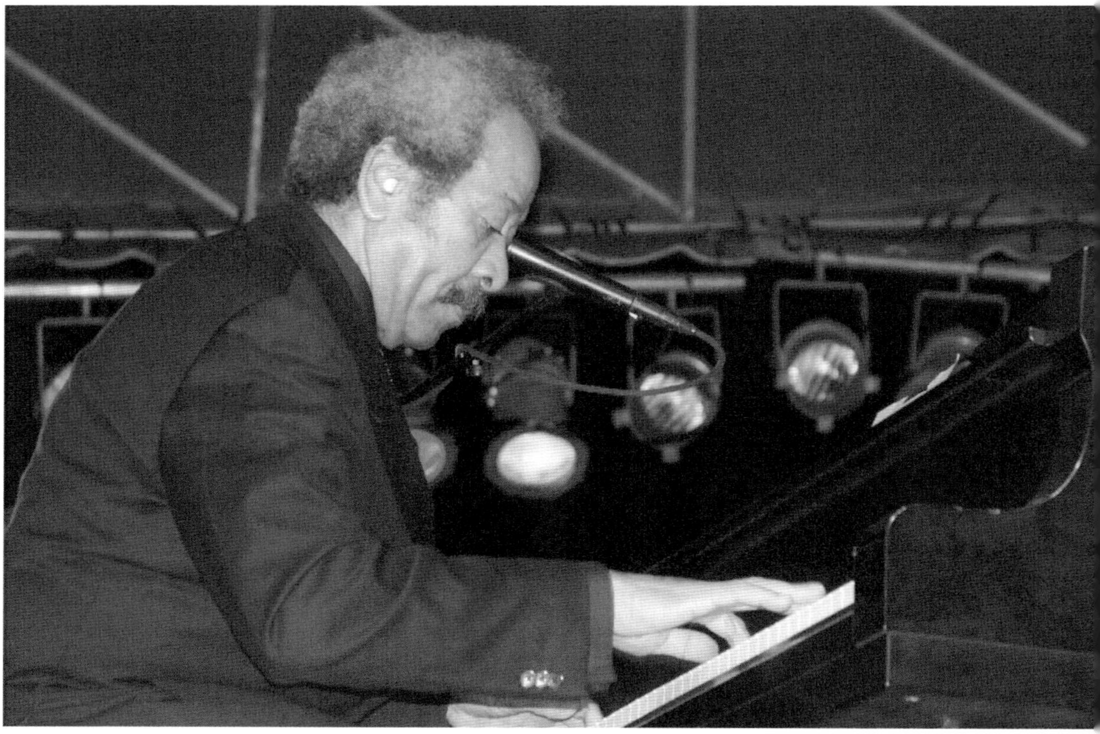

Composer
Allen Toussaint (born 1938) is best known as a songwriter and producer. Many artists have had great commercial success covering Toussaint's songs, most notably Glenn Campbell, who covered "Southern Nights" in 1977, riding it to the No. 1 spot on three charts: pop, adult contemporary, and country. Toussaint has produced artists as diverse as Robert Palmer, Elvis Costello, The Band, Paul McCartney, and countless local musicians, including The Meters, Ernie K-Doe, Dr. John, and the Wild Tchoupitoulas. Toussaint's house was destroyed in Hurricane Katrina, but he has remained active in the community and continues to perform and produce. (Courtesy Carl Lender.)

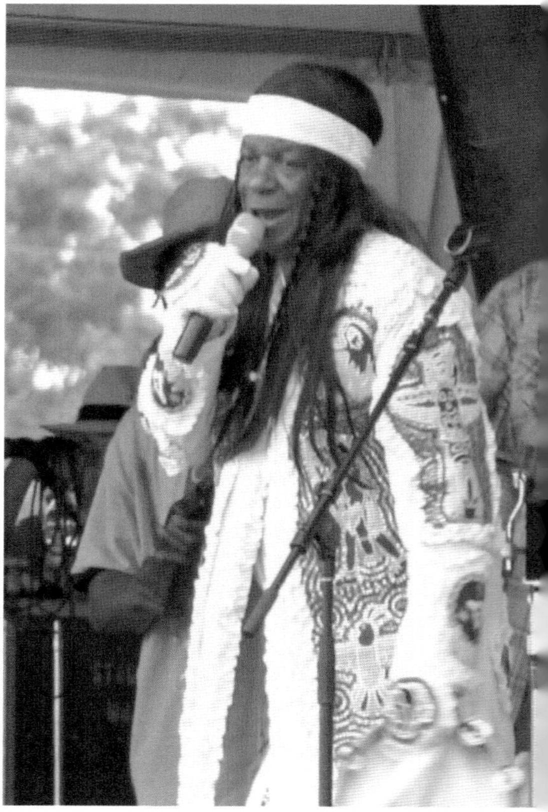

Big Chief
Monk Boudreaux is Big Chief of the Golden Eagles, one of the Mardi Gras Indian tribes of New Orleans. Boudreaux originally joined the Wild Magnolias tribe, performing with his friend Big Chief Bo Dollis for over 30 years. Boudreaux left the Wild Magnolias in 2001 over business disputes, forming the Golden Eagles and collaborating with a number of local bands and musicians. (Courtesy Carlos "Froggy" May.)

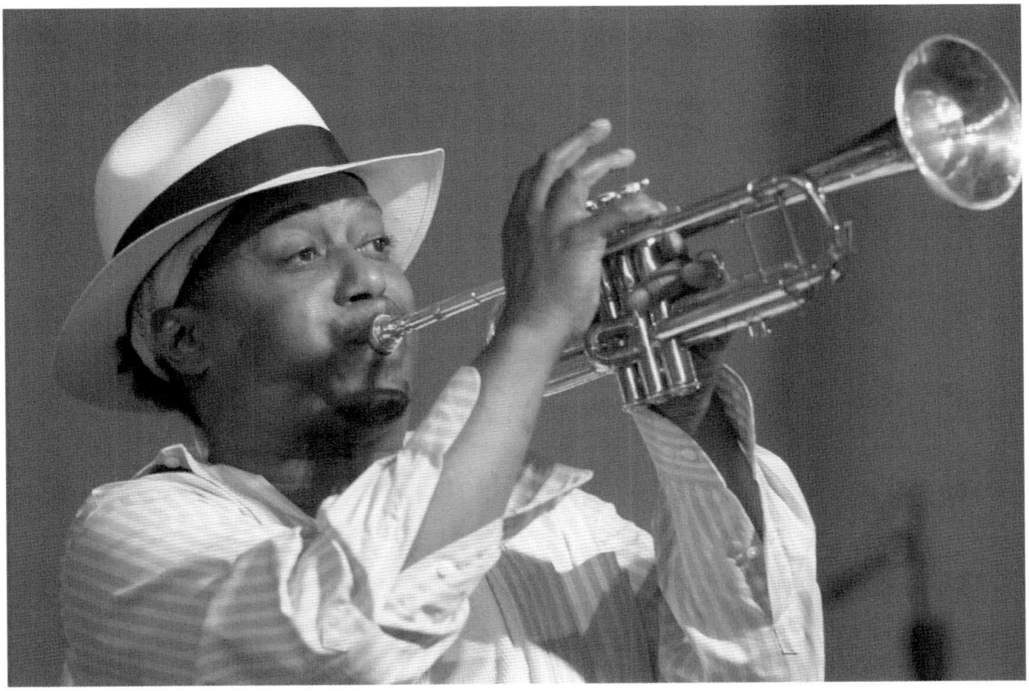

All Aboard!

Local trumpet player Kermit Ruffins (born 1964) cofounded the Rebirth Brass Band in 1983 while he was still attending Clark High School in Faubourg Treme. Inspired by the 1980s success of the Dirty Dozen Brass Band, Ruffins and Rebirth began recording in 1984. The band won a Grammy in 2012, and is a mainstay in local clubs, such as Rock 'n' Bowl. Ruffins is one of the musical stars of the popular HBO television series *Treme* and regularly plays with his jazz quintet the Barbecue Swingers at Vaughn's Bar in Bywater. (Above, courtesy Derek Bridges; below, Carlos "Froggy" May.)

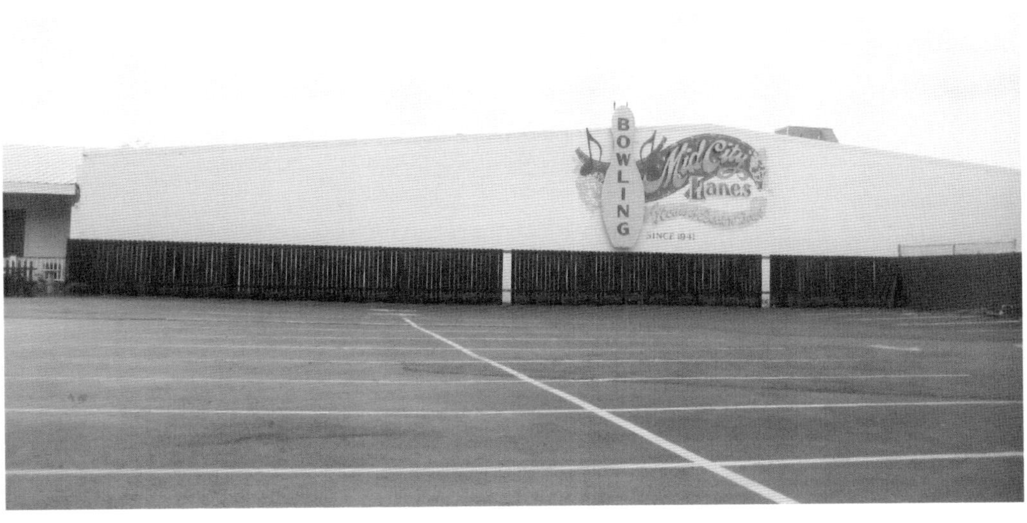

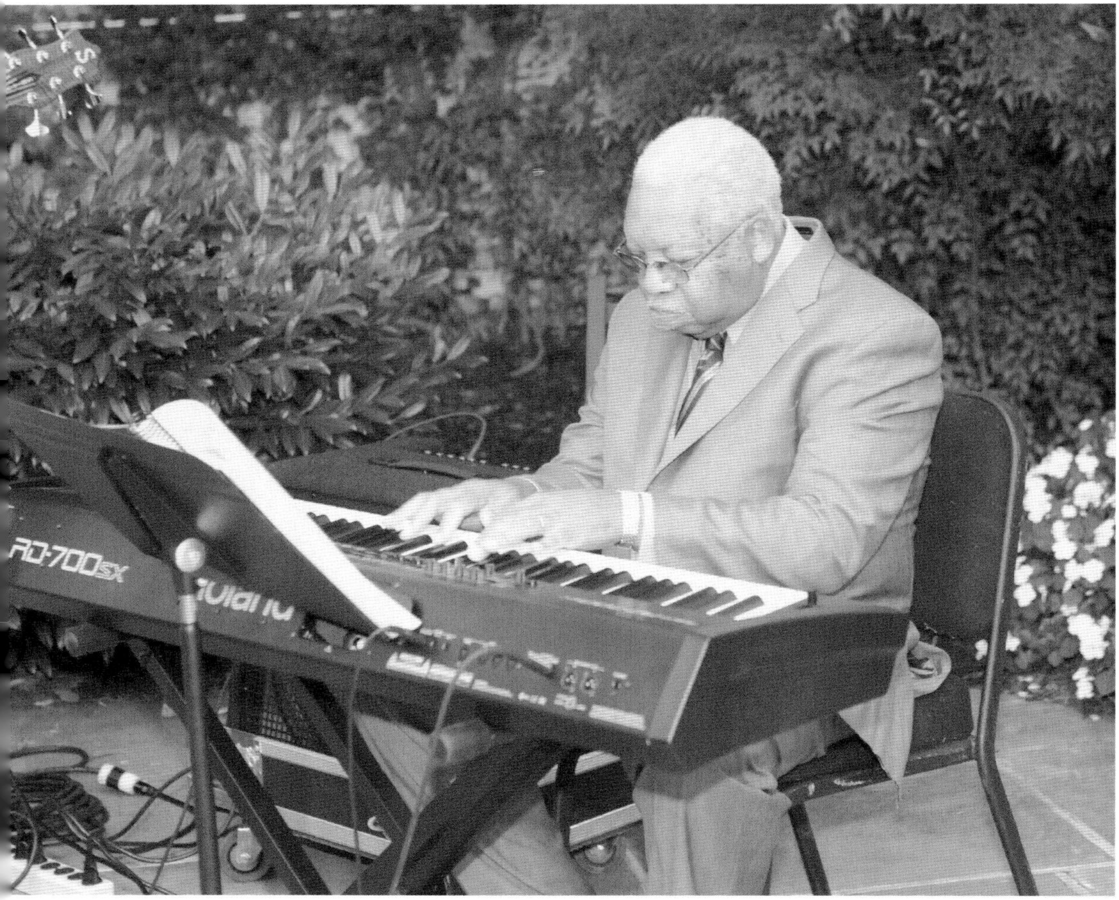

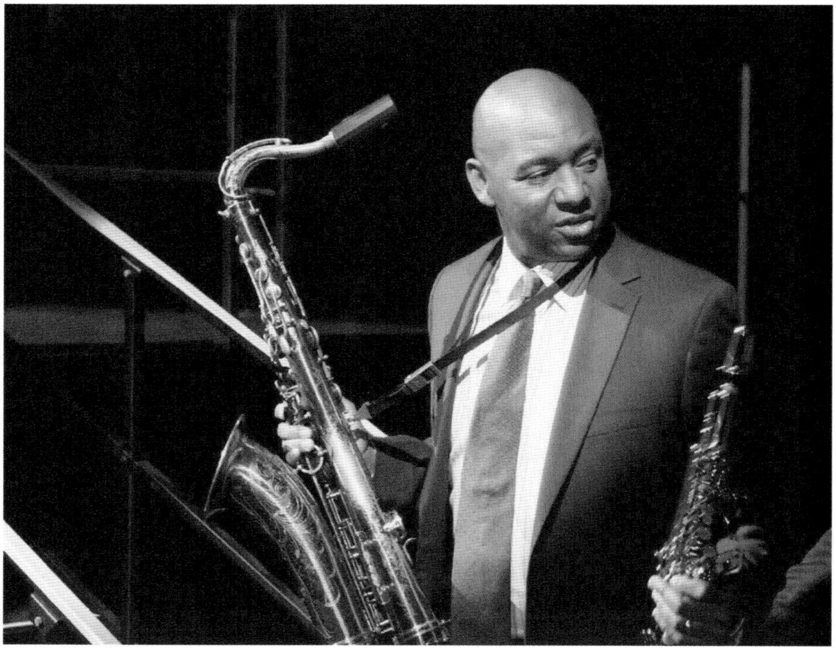

Royalty

Ellis Marsalis Jr. (born 1934) and his sons Branford (born 1960) and Wynton (born 1961) make up one of New Orleans's First Families of Music. Patriarch Ellis and his wife, Delores, have six sons total. Ellis began playing the saxophone as a child, switching to piano in high school. He has played with Cannonball Adderley, Al Hirt, and Eddie Harris but has never specialized in Dixieland. A true teacher, Ellis (opposite page, top) is affiliated with NOCCA, the University of New Orleans, and Xavier University of Louisiana. Ellis's oldest son, Branford (opposite page, bottom), plays saxophone and performed with his brother Wynton in the early 1980s. Branford worked with Sting on his solo The Dream of Blue Turtles in 1985. He was leader of the Tonight Show Band from 1992 to 1995. Wynton Marsalis (below) has had the most commercial success of the family and cofounded a jazz program at Lincoln Center in New York City. He has won nine Grammy Awards and notably gave a moving musical/poetic tribute to the New Orleans Saints during the pregame activities for Super Bowl XLIV. (Opposite page, top, courtesy of the US Marine Corps; opposite page, bottom, courtesy Darlene Susco; below, courtesy LOC.)

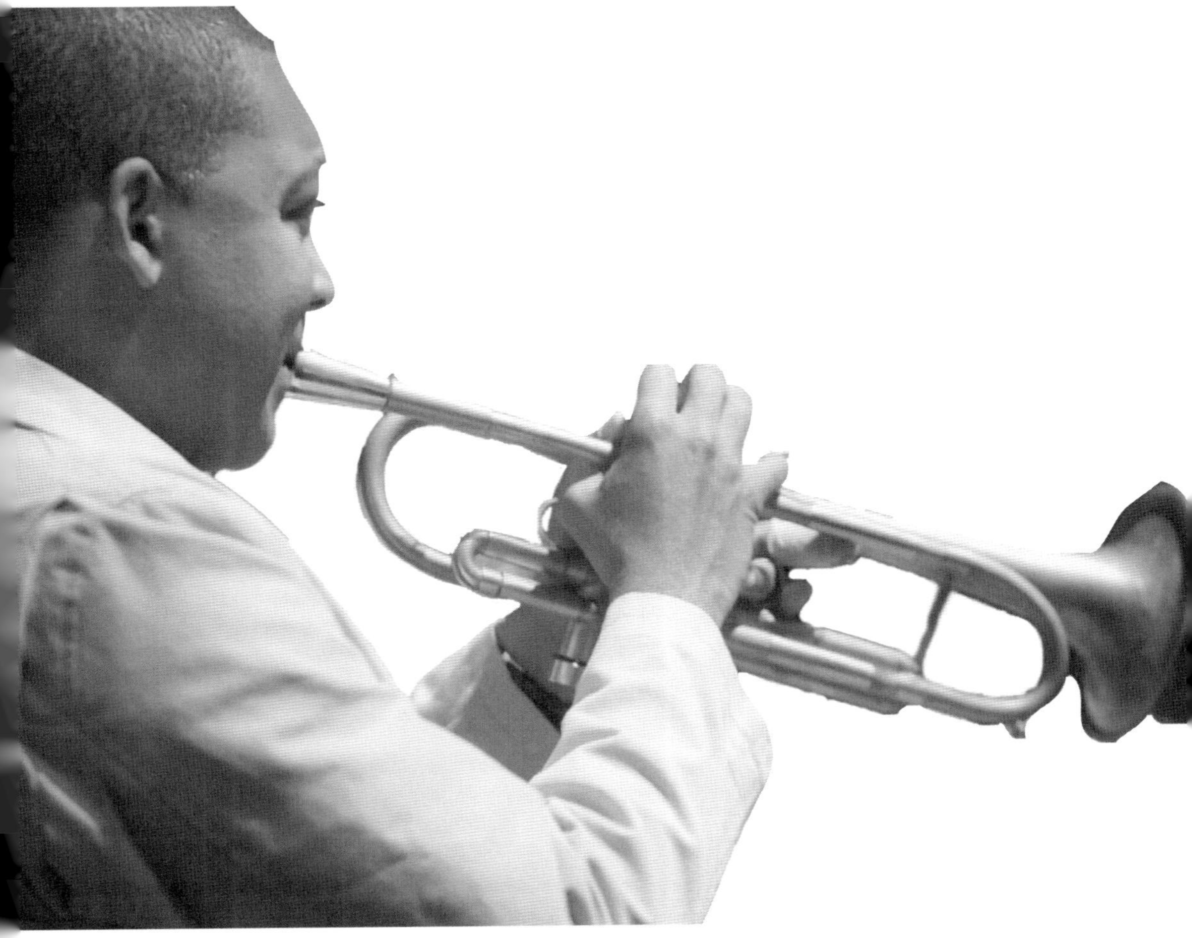

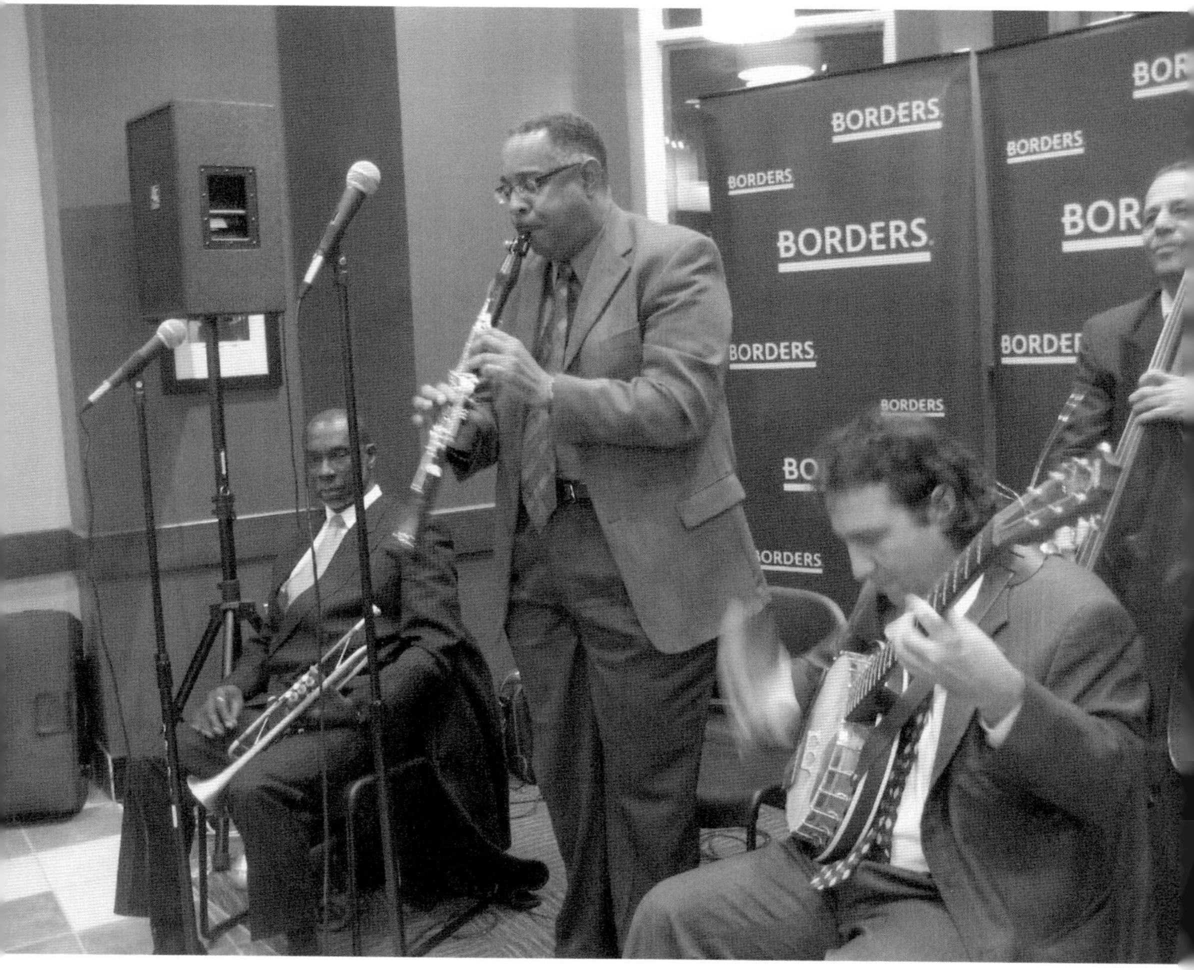

Liberty

Dr. Michael White (born 1954) is a professor of African American Music at Xavier University of Louisiana. He is a classically trained clarinetist who was a member of Danny Barker's Fairview Baptist Church Marching Band. Dr. White founded the Liberty Jazz Band in 1981 and plays with the Young Tuxedo Brass Band. He currently records for Basin Street Records and has served as guest director at several Jazz at Lincoln Center concerts featuring Wynton Marsalis. (Courtesy Carlos "Froggy" May.)

Shorty

Troy Andrews (born 1986) plays trombone and trumpet. His older brother James is a bandleader. Troy began playing trombone at the age of six, when he got his nickname, "Trombone Shorty." Andrews attended NOCCA and was a member of the Stooges Brass Band. He joined Lenny Kravitz's horn section in 2005, during Kravitz's world tour that year. Andrews and his band Orleans Avenue recorded their first CD, *Orleans and Claiborne*, in 2005, followed by the critically acclaimed *Backatown*, which hit Billboard's Contemporary Jazz Chart at No. 1 and stayed there for nine weeks. The band's latest CD is *For True*, released in 2011. Andrews has a recurring role as himself in the HBO series *Treme* and has received numerous awards for his community work and service. (Courtesy Carlos "Froggy" May.)

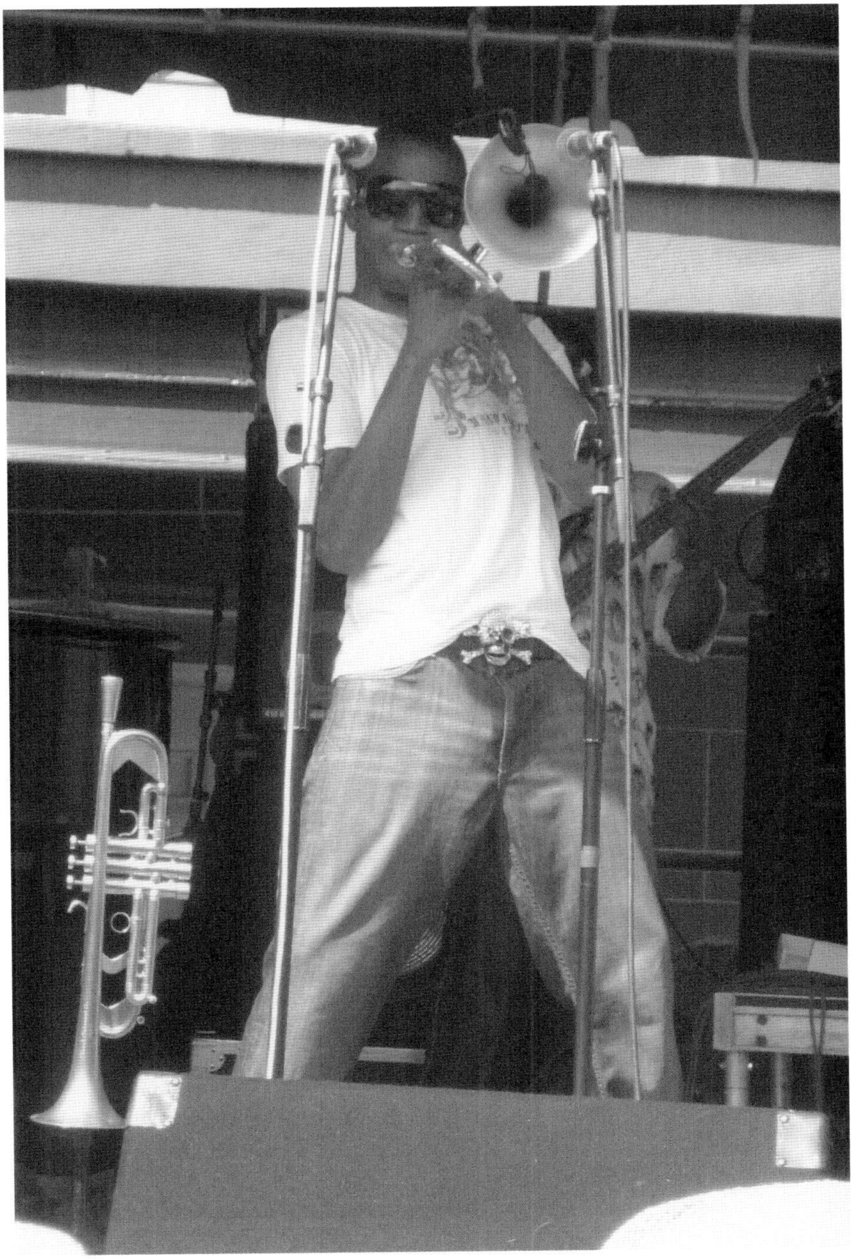

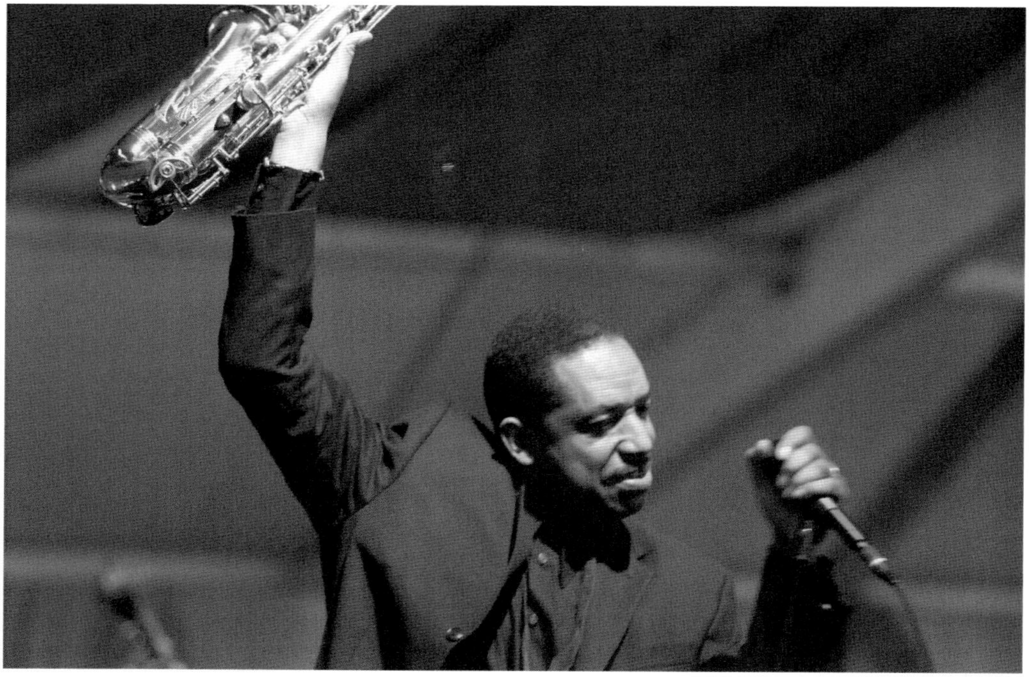

"Nouveau Swing"
Donald Harrison Jr. is a saxophonist and Big Chief of the Congo Nation Mardi Gras Indian Tribe, which keeps alive the secret traditions of Congo Square. He studied at NOCCA and created the "Nouveau Swing" style. The Donald Harrison Electric Band has charted on Billboard. Harrison has appeared as himself in numerous episodes of HBO's series *Treme*. Many believe the *Treme* characters of Albert and Delmond Lambreaux are based on Harrison and his father, Donald Sr. (Courtesy Derek Bridges.)

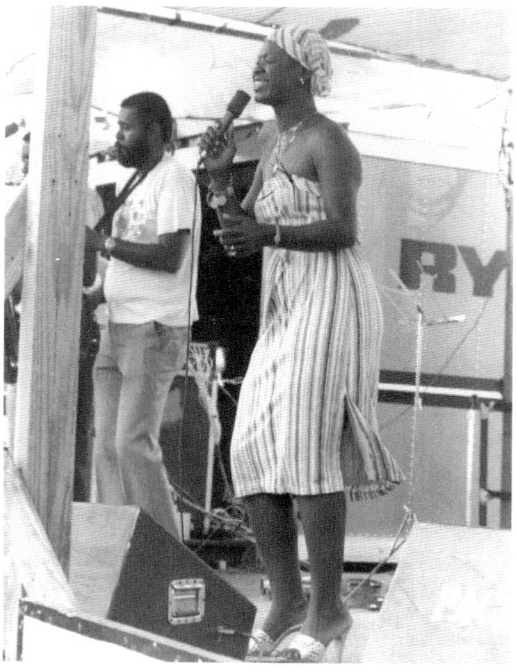

"Break-a-Way"
Irma Thomas (born 1941) grew up singing in church and sang for Tommy Ridgely in 1960. Ridgely helped her get signed with a local label, where she recorded "Don't Mess with My Man." That single hit No. 22 on the Billboard R&B chart. She then signed with Minit (which later became Imperial Records) and worked with Allen Toussaint on several of his songs. Her first singles for Imperial were promising, but follow-ups failed to generate a national audience for Irma. Still, she developed a serious local following and continued to national tours and cross-over gigs. Hurricane Katrina forced Thomas to close her club, but she still plays at various festivals and clubs in the metro area. (Courtesy Robert Avery.)

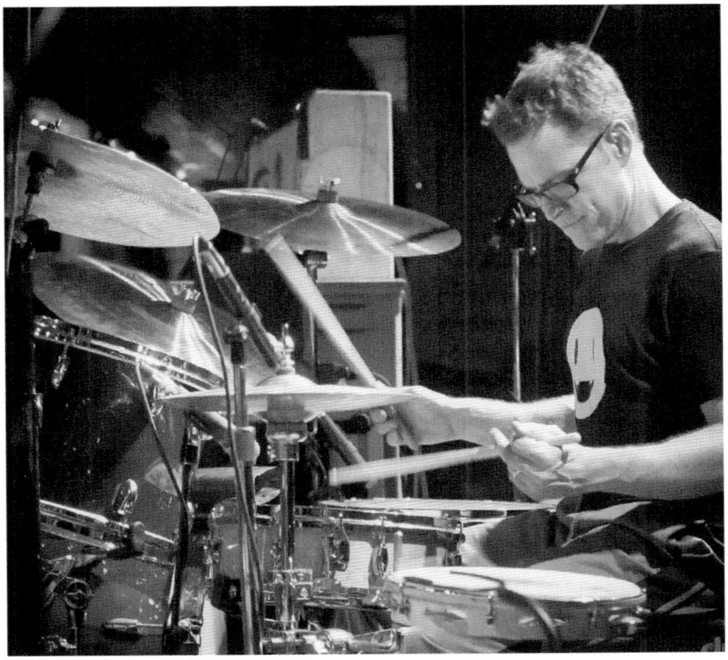

All Kooked Out!
Stanton Moore (born 1972) is one of the cofounders of the funk band Galactic. Playing with the band since the early 1990s, Moore and Galactic have toured extensively, both locally and nationally. In addition to anchoring Galactic, Moore played in bands he led, such as Moore and More, and Garage A Trois, with Galactic colleagues Skerik and Charlie Hunter. Stanton also travels internationally to teach New Orleans–style drumming. (Courtesy Mike & Ali Kerr, Southern Exposure Photography.)

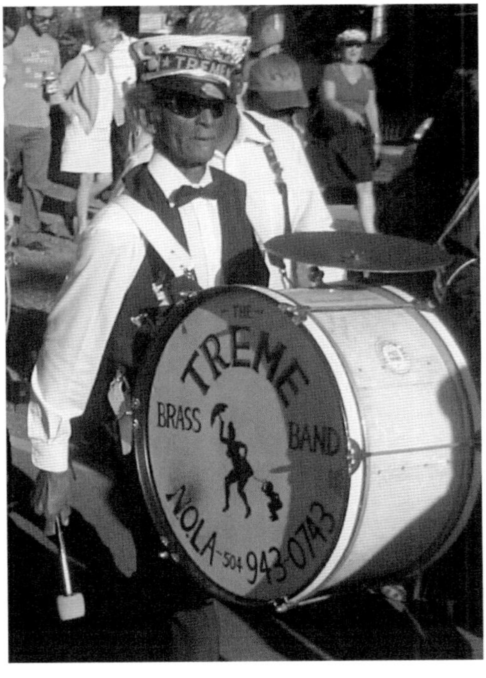

Influence
"Uncle" Lionel Batiste (1932–2012) was the bass drummer for the Treme Brass Band, and an inspiration and role model to several generations of New Orleans jazz musicians. He was king of the Krewe de Vieux parade for Carnival, 2003, and appeared in the pilot episode of HBO's *Treme*. (Courtesy Carlos "Froggy" May.)

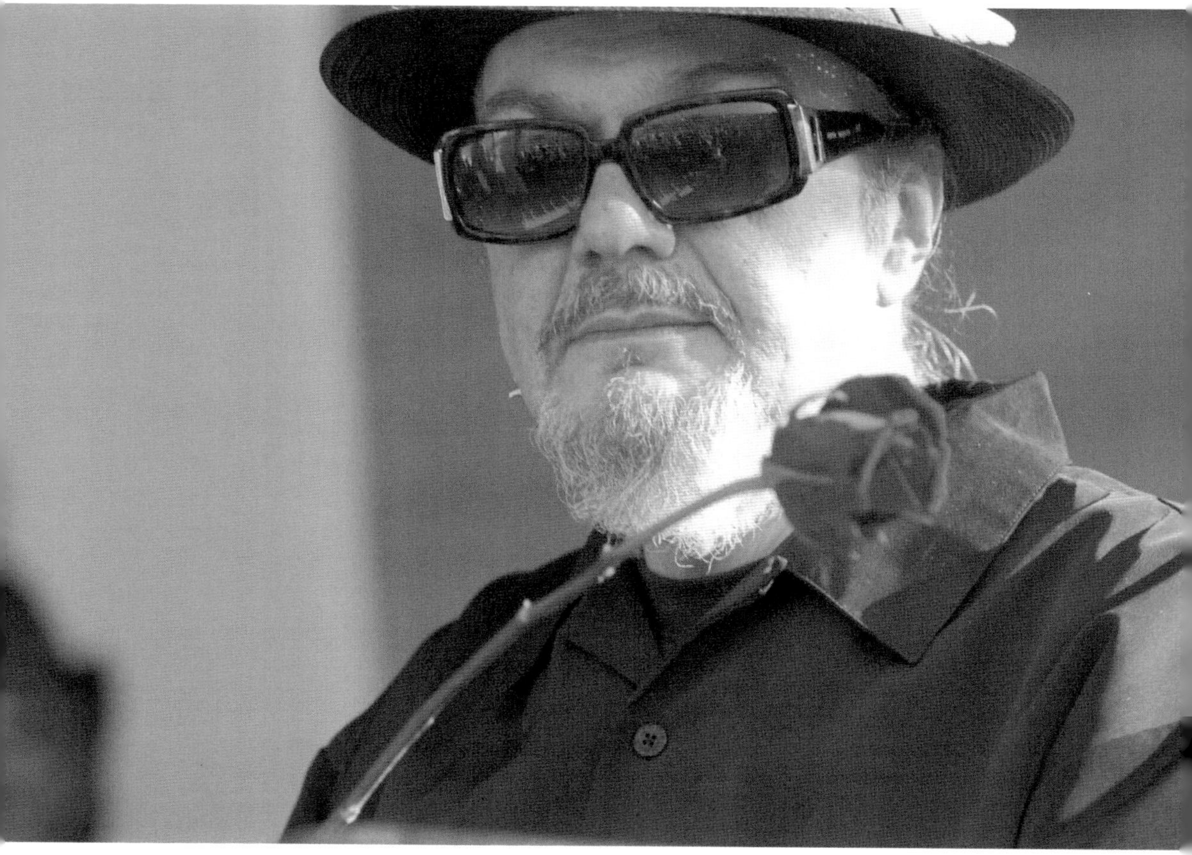

Night Tripper

Malcolm John "Mac" Rebennack Jr. (born 1940) is best known by his stage name, Dr. John. He has also called himself "The Night Tripper." A multitalented artist, Mac met Professor Longhair when he was 13 or 14 and became fascinated with his style. Dr. John played guitar and gigged locally with a number of different bands and groups, until his left ring finger was injured by a gunshot. He moved to Los Angeles in 1963, playing bass guitar. Professor Longhair's influence ultimately took over, and he switched to piano. Mac's fascination with voodoo helped him develop the "Dr. John" persona while working in California. By the late 1960s, he was doing the full "Night Tripper" stage act but softened it in the early 1970s, starting with his album *Dr. John's Gumbo* in 1972. He followed up that album with the Toussaint-produced album *In the Right Place*, backed by The Meters. He released a second Toussaint/Meters album, *Desitively Bonnaroo*, in 1974. Since the 1970s, Dr. John has been in demand as a session musician and to write the scores and soundtracks of several movies. Mac has been a tireless supporter of New Orleans since Hurricane Katrina, appearing at countless fundraisers and collaborating on benefit recordings. He has appeared as himself in several episodes of *Treme*, and his latest release is *Locked Down*, a collaboration with Dan Auerback of The Black Keys. (Courtesy Derek Bridges.)

CHAPTER THREE

Sports, Entertainment, and Cuisine

For all of New Orleans prominence in the history of the United States, the city was late to the major league sports scene. Minor-league baseball made its way to New Orleans at the beginning of the 20th century, but it wasn't until 1967 and the admission of the New Orleans Saints into the National Football League that the city moved up. The Saints were followed in 1974 by the New Orleans Jazz, a National Basketball Association team that moved to Salt Lake City, Utah, in 1979. In spite of this lack of top-tier sports teams, they city still produced a number of world-class athletes. Professional basketball returned to the city in 2002, in the form of the re-located Charlotte Hornets.

Much of the success of professional sports in New Orleans since the 1960s can be attributed to the development and construction of the Louisiana Superdome. In an age of "if you build it, they will come," the Dome has proven time and again that it is a solid venue for major sporting events. The Superdome can easily handle events ranging from a Super Bowl or the Sugar Bowl, to the NCAA's "Final Four" basketball tournaments. The Superdome's presence directly led to the construction of the New Orleans Arena next door, which enticed the NBA to return after the New Orleans Jazz defected to Utah in 1979.

In addition to sports legends, New Orleans has produced actors and entertainers, some serious, some funny, all guaranteed to take their audience to the realms of imagination, thought-provoking dialogue, and just plain fun. While many actors and actresses have to leave New Orleans to make their mark, they always carry the influences of the city with them.

In many parts of the country, the people "eat to live." But in New Orleans, people "live to eat." Instead of the classic dinner-and-a-show format for an evening out, New Orleanians go out to dinner, and sometimes never even making it to the show! The European tradition of the grand meal lives on in the city's Creole-French, Creole-Italian, and nouvelle restaurants. As a result of over a century and a half of restaurant service in the city, New Orleans has produced many top-notch chefs. Their cuisine helps get people through anything from the minor complications of the work day to major adversity like the aftermath of a world-changing hurricane.

"Boogie"

Tom Benson (born 1927) graduated from Treme's St. Aloysius High School in 1944. He eventually bought auto dealerships in metro New Orleans as well as San Antonio, Texas. In 1985, with a personal net worth in excess of $1billion, Benson stepped in and made an offer to the original owner of the New Orleans Saints, John Mecom of Houston, Texas, to keep Mecom from selling the team to out-of-town interests. Benson took control of the team in May 1985. Benson lifted fans' spirits with his local flavor; after victories in the Superdome, Benson would take to the field and second-line. His dances became known as the "Benson Boogie." Benson's hiring of head coach Sean Payton (and Payton's subsequent hiring of quarterback Drew Brees) led to the team's 2010 victory in Super Bowl XLIV. In 2012, with the New Orleans Hornets on the brink of leaving the city, Benson once again stepped in and acquired that franchise as well. (Courtesy NOPL.)

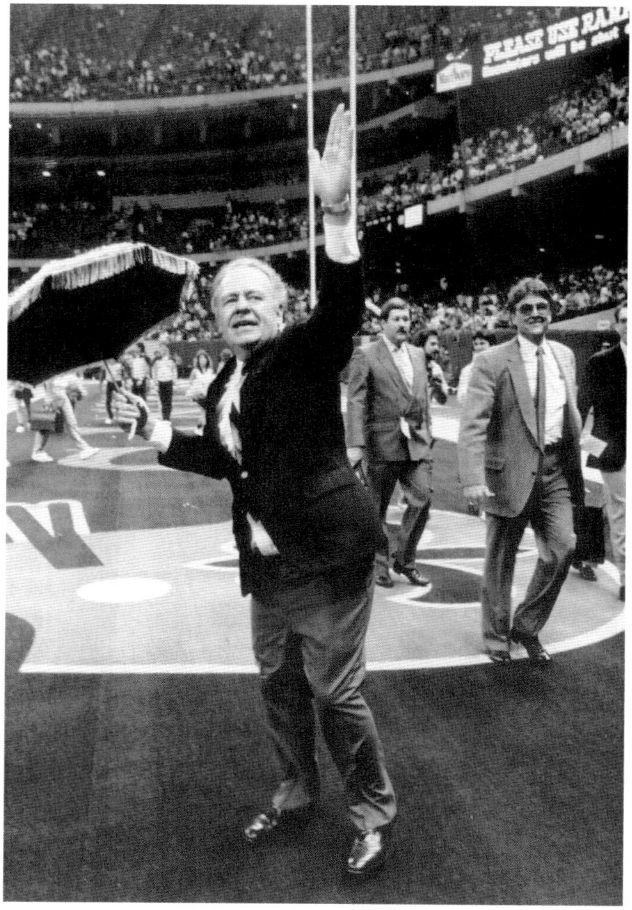

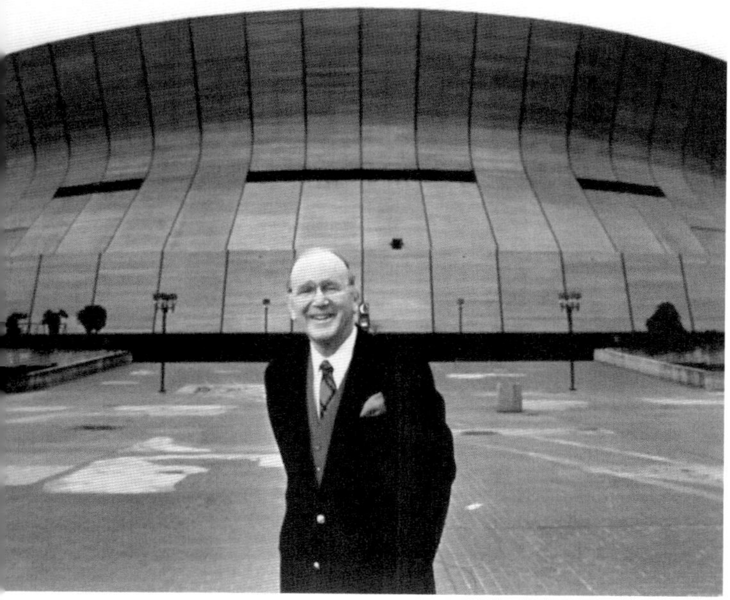

WCT/USFL

David Dixon (1923–2010) was the driving force behind the Louisiana Superdome. A Tulane graduate and the owner of a French Quarter art gallery, Dixon knew the NFL would only approve a team for New Orleans if the city would build a domed stadium. Dixon convinced then-governor John McKeithen of this, and the governor backed the financing plan that made the Superdome a reality. In addition to his role in bringing the Saints to New Orleans, Dixon was the founder of World Champion Tennis, and the 12-team US Football League, which played its games in the spring and summer in 1982. (Courtesy NOPL.)

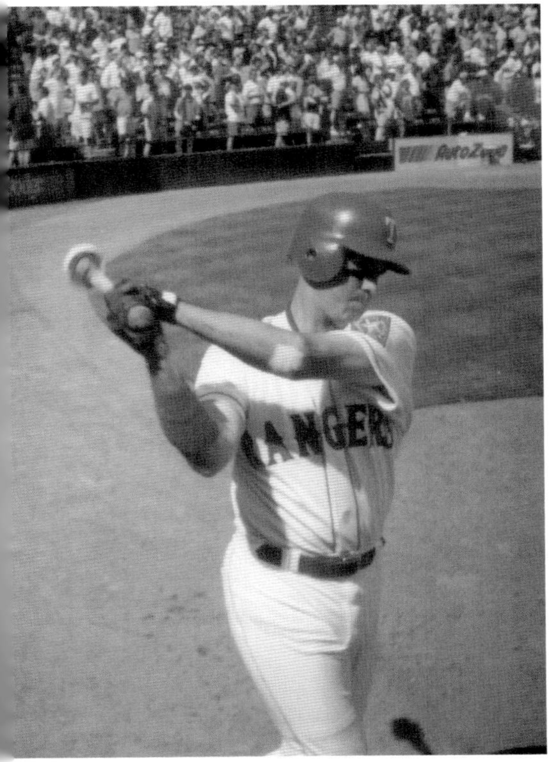

Giant

William Nuschler Clark Jr. (born 1964) attended Jesuit High School in New Orleans and Mississippi State University. His baseball prowess earned Will a spot on the 1984 US Olympic team. Clark was one of the team's stars but did not win a gold medal, since baseball was only an "exhibition" sport that year. He was the second overall pick in the 1985 MLB draft, chosen by the San Francisco Giants. The six-time All-Star also played for the Rangers, Orioles, and Cardinals, but the majority of his accomplishments and accolades came when he played for the Giants. (Courtesy John Bonzo.)

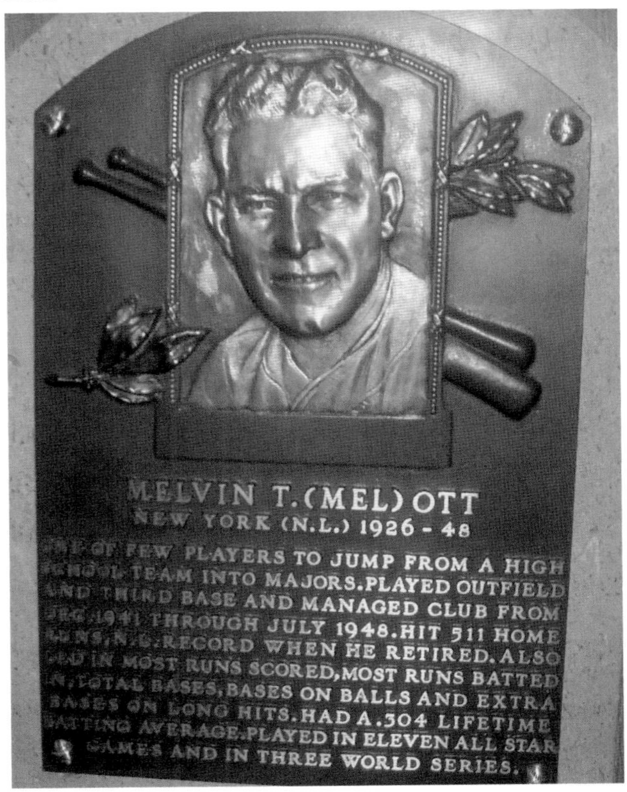

Slugger

Melvin T. "Mel" Ott (1909–1958) was born in Gretna, Louisiana, across the river from New Orleans. His baseball skills earned him a spot on the New York Giants team in 1926, starting a career that spanned 21 years. Ott was a 12-time All-Star and played in three World Series, sharing in the Giants' victory in the 1933 season. Ott spent his entire career with the Giants, and regularly returned to New Orleans to visit and help the community. Mel's number (4) was retired by the Giants in 1949, and he was named to the Baseball Hall of Fame in 1951. He died in a car accident in 1958, but his legacy lived on; Gretna developed a park and recreational area in his name, and the US Postal Service chose Ott to be one of four baseball players featured on a block of postage stamps in 2006. (Courtesy Justin M. Branley.)

Hall of Fame

William Layton Roaf (born 1970) is known as "Willie," even though his mother (Andree Layton Roaf, the first African American woman to serve on the Arkansas Supreme Court) insisted his name was "William." He was drafted out of Louisiana Tech University in the first round by the New Orleans Saints in 1993. The 11-time Pro Bowler played for nine seasons with the Saints, then three with the Kansas City Chiefs. Roaf (seen here on a USO tour in Iraq in 2009) retired from the NFL in 2006 and was elected to the NFL Hall of Fame in 2012. (Courtesy US Army.)

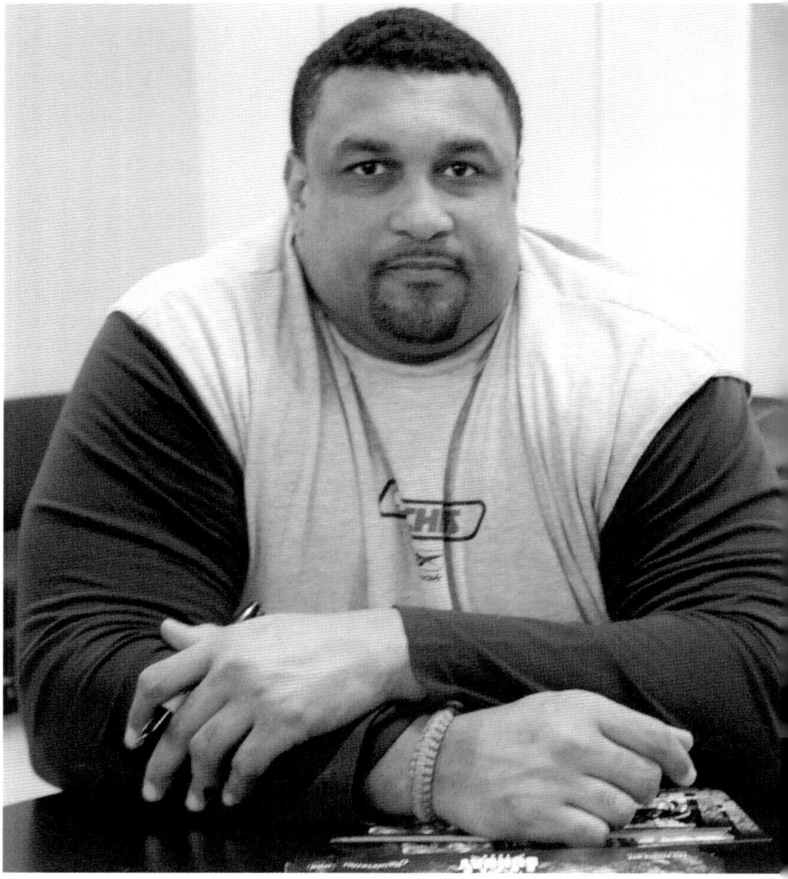

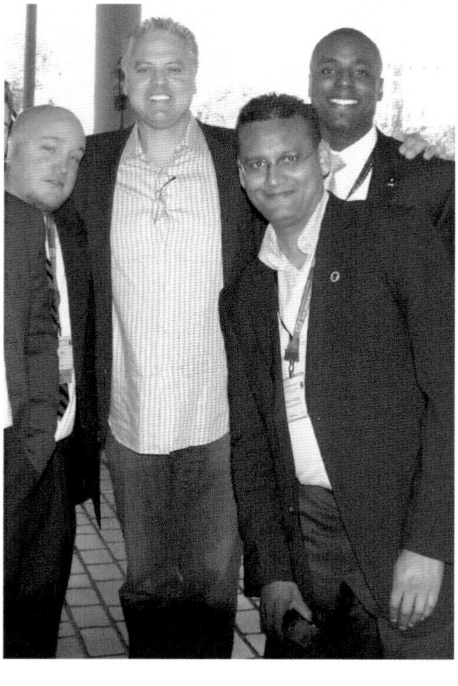

Quarterback

Bobby Joseph Hebert Jr. began his professional football career in Dave Dixon's USFL, playing for the Michigan Panthers and the Oakland Invaders, winning the league championship with Michigan in 1983. When the league folded, he was signed by the New Orleans Saints, giving him a chance to play in his native South Louisiana. He played for seven seasons with the Saints and three with the Atlanta Falcons, earning the nickname, the "Cajun Cannon." He retired from the NFL after the 1996 season, returning to New Orleans from Atlanta, and began a career in radio. Upon the passing of sportscaster Buddy Diliberto, Hebert (second from left, posing with fans from the US Army Corps of Engineers in 2011), took over "Buddy D's" evening show on WWL-Radio. In 2010, Hebert fulfilled Diliberto's pledge to wear a dress and parade around the Superdome if the Saints won the Super Bowl. The event became a huge parade of men wearing dresses, all celebrating the Super Bowl XLIV win. (Courtesy US Army.)

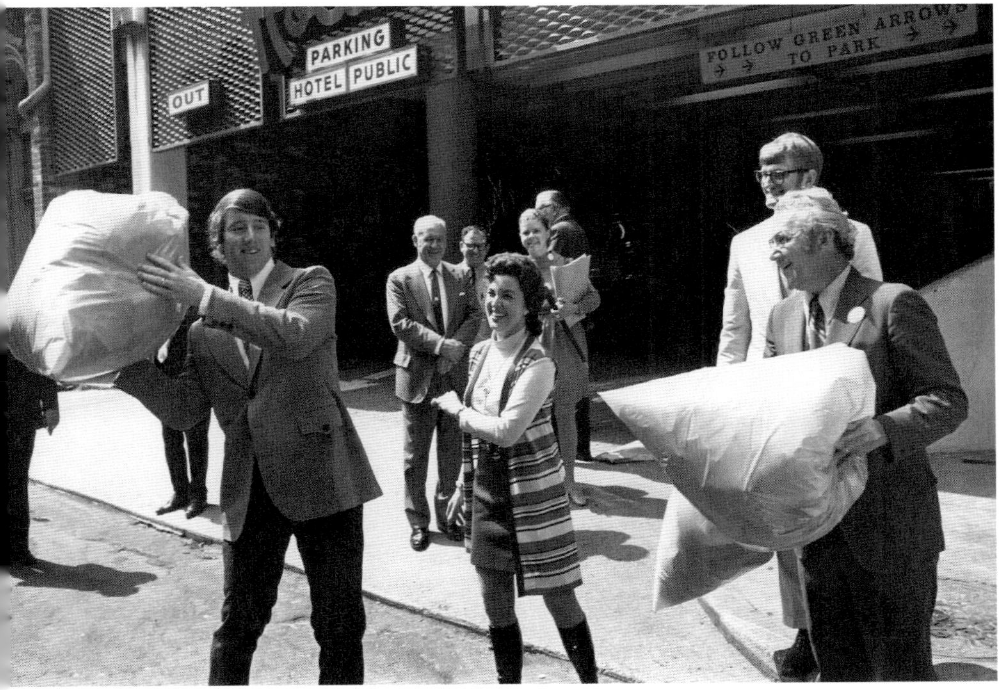

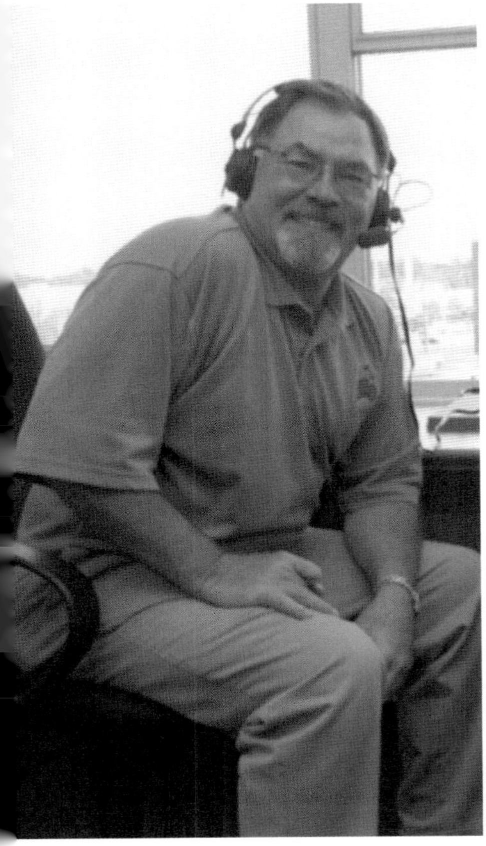

Dynasty
Elisha Archibald "Archie" Manning III (born 1949) came to New Orleans in 1971, as the Saints' first-round (second overall) pick in the NFL draft. He played for 10 seasons with the Saints and is considered almost universally to be one of the team's heroes, even though only one of those 10 teams had a break-even (.500) record. He played in the Pro Bowl twice and retired in New Orleans, having played for the Minnesota Vikings and Houston Oilers after the Saints. Archie (seen here in community service promotion photograph with Mayor Moon Landrieu in 1972) is the father of current NFL quarterbacks and Super Bowl winners Peyton and Eli. His oldest son, Cooper, is a local businessman. (Courtesy NOPL.)

"The Catch"
Ron Swoboda (born 1944) was a member of the "Amazin' Mets" team of 1969, and is known for making a diving catch of a ball hit by Brooks Robinson in game four of the 1969 World Series against the Baltimore Orioles. After retiring from baseball in 1973, Swoboda began a broadcasting career that brought him to WVUE-TV in New Orleans in the 1980s as the station's evening sportscaster. After leaving WVUE, Ron worked at Cox Sports Television, and he is currently the color commentator for the New Orleans Zephyrs, the city's AAA baseball team. (Courtesy New Orleans Zephyrs.)

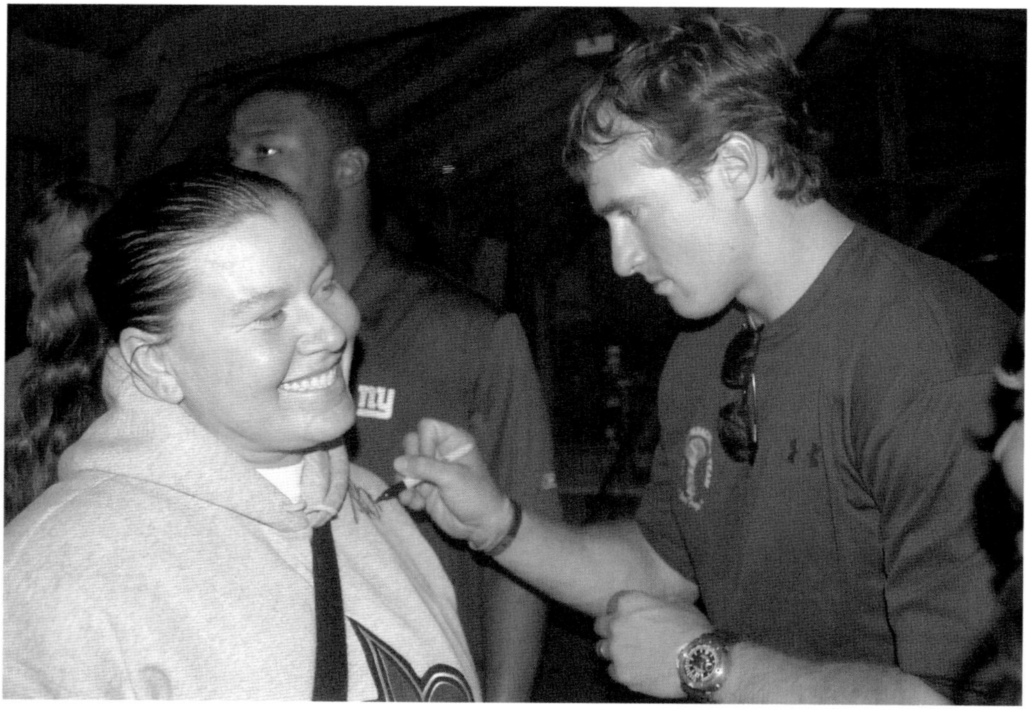
ny

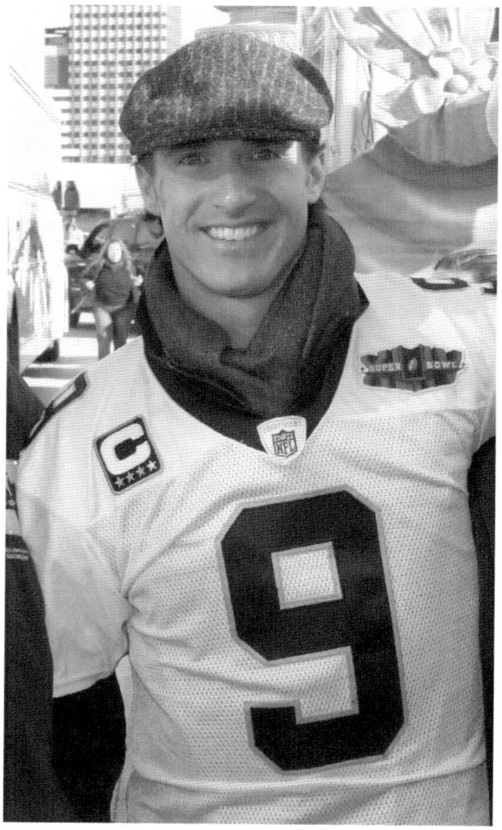
SUPER BOWL
C
9

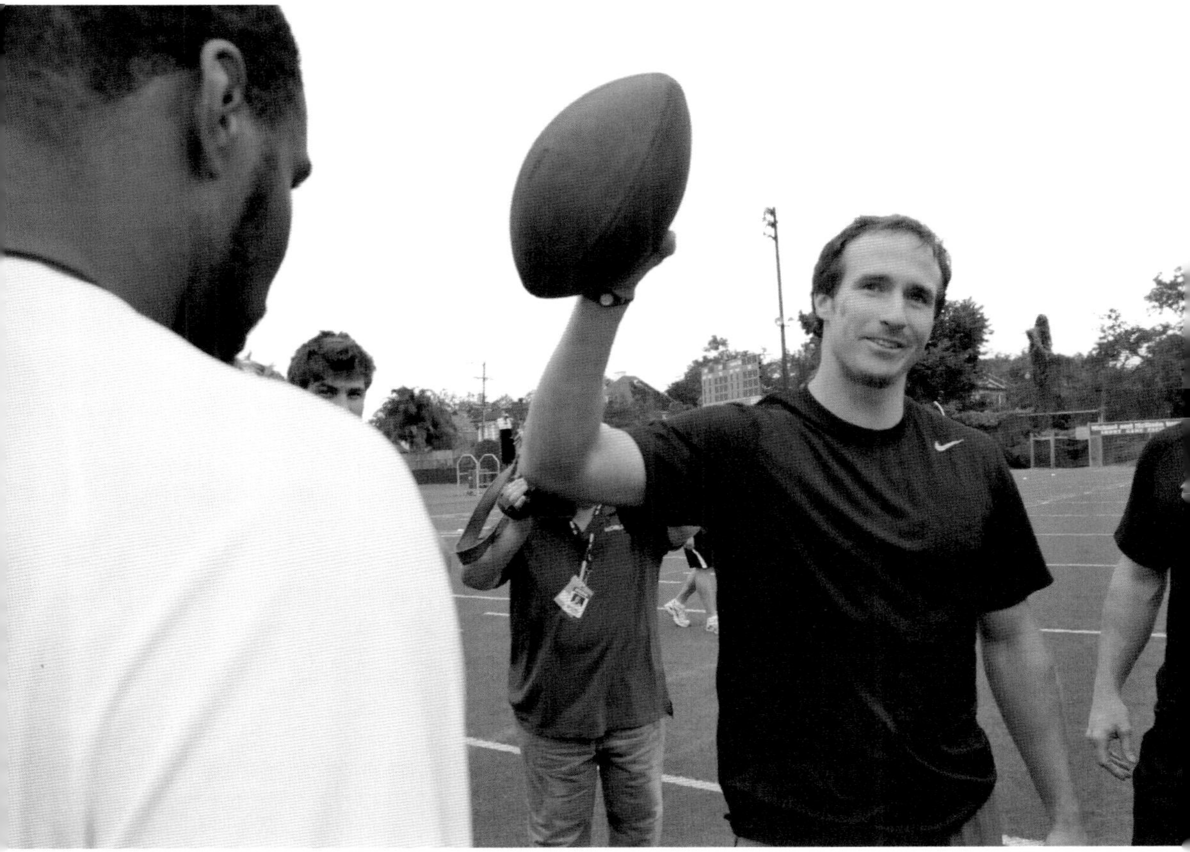

"Breesus"

Andrew Christopher Brees (born 1979) was drafted in the second round of the 2001 NFL draft by the San Diego Chargers. Originally from Austin, Texas, Drew played for the Chargers from 2001 to 2005 but was unable to come to terms with the team for the 2006 season. Brees was signed by the New Orleans Saints for the 2006 season, arriving in post-Katrina New Orleans with first-year head coach Sean Payton. Brees (pictured on the opposite page, top, signing PO1 Jennifer Crimm's sweatshirt in Afghanistan in 2008; bottom, in the Super Bowl XLIV victory parade in 2010; and above on Tulane's campus when Brees used Tulane's Westfeldlt practice facility to run practices during the NFL lockout in 2011) totally committed himself to the Saints on the field and the city when away from the Saints facilities. Brees took the Saints to their first conference championship game in January of 2007. The Saints lost that game to the Chicago Bears, but Payton, Brees, and the Saints continued to grow and develop as a team. That development climaxed in the 2009–2010 season, with the team's victory in Super Bowl XLIV. Drew and his wife, Brittany (his college sweetheart), live in Uptown New Orleans, with their two sons, Baylen (born in 2009) and Bowen (born in 2010). After Super Bowl XLIV in Miami, Brittany handed Baylen (who was wearing ear protectors) up to Drew on the podium in the center of the stadium, and they became the subjects of some of the game's most iconic photographs. An avid Twitter user, Drew solicited tweets from fans as input for naming Bowen during Brittany's pregnancy. Brees is also a published author and was named king of the Krewe of Bacchus for Carnival in 2010. He is extremely active in local charities, particularly assisting groups still struggling with post-Katrina recovery in the city. Drew is also cochair of Pres. Barack Obama's President's Council on Physical Fitness and Sports. (All, courtesy of Tulane University.)

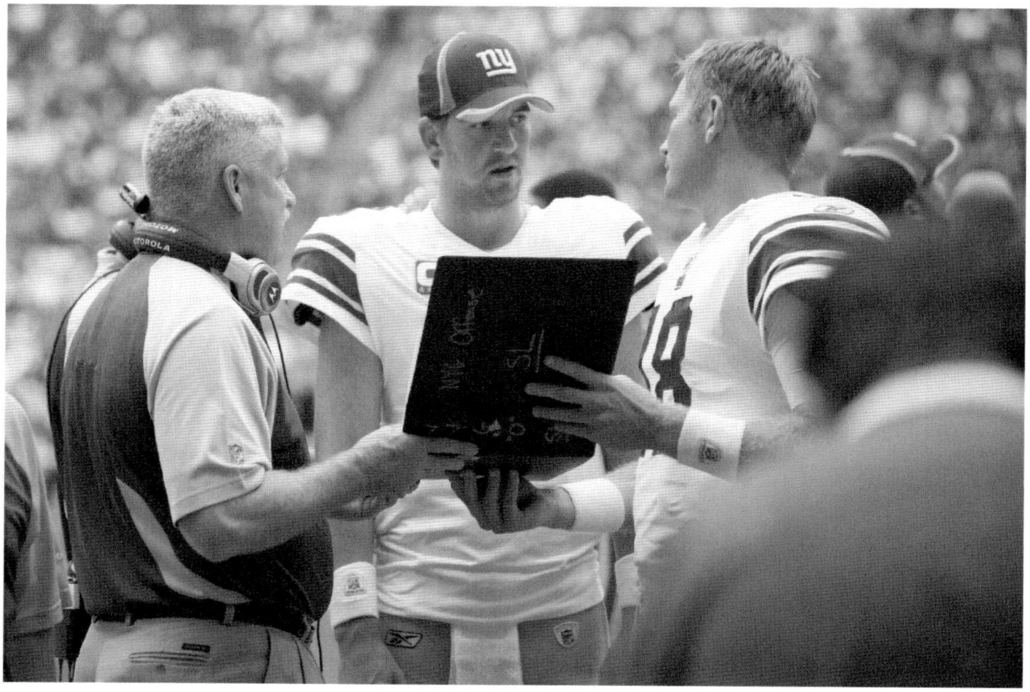

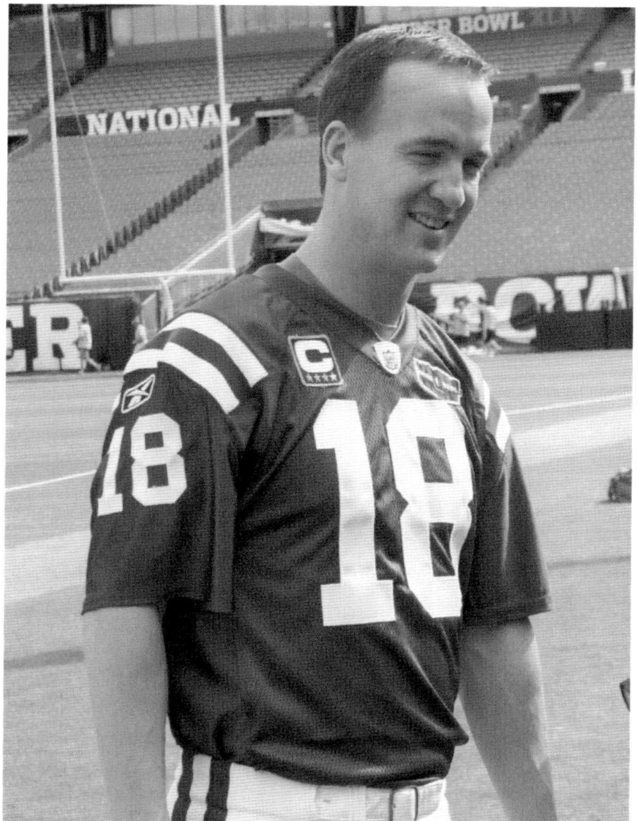

Brothers

Born in 1976, Peyton Manning (pictured left), is the oldest son of New Orleans Saints legend Archie Manning and his wife, Olivia. Peyton, who grew up in New Orleans, attending Isidore Newman School, then the University of Tennessee, was drafted first (first overall) by the Indianapolis Colts in 1998 and led the team as its quarterback to victory in Super Bowl XLI, but the Colts lost to the New Orleans Saints in Super Bowl XLIV. The 11-time Pro Bowler currently plays for the Denver Broncos. Peyton's younger brother Elisha Nelson Manning (born 1981) also attended Newman School but attended and played football at Ole Miss. Eli led the New York Giants to victory in Super Bowl XLII (the year after his brother), then again in Super Bowl XLVI. Eli (above, center) was named MVP of both games, holds several NFL records, and is still the Giants' starting quarterback. (Courtesy Ian Ransley and A.J. Guel.)

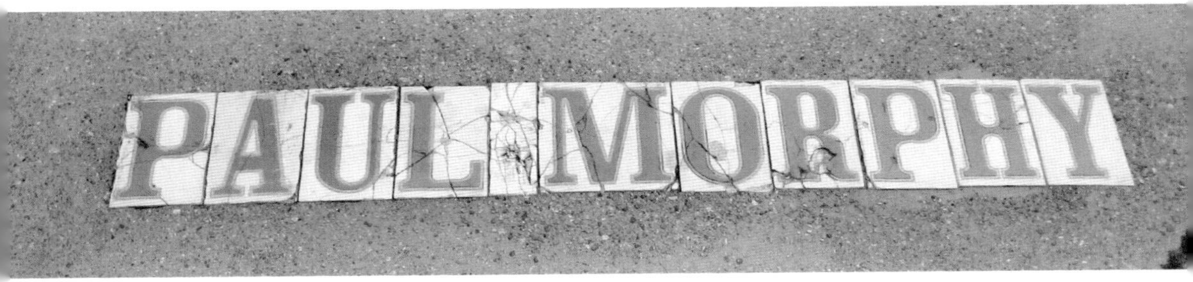

Chessman

Paul Charles Morphy (1837–1884) was regarded as the world champion of chess in his time, even though there was no official designation as such for the game. Born and raised in New Orleans, Morphy's family was wealthy and able to support his development as a chess player. (The Morphy family home on Royal Street in the French Quarter was later sold to Owen Brennan, where he opened the world-famous Brennan's Restaurant.) Morphy toured Europe in 1858–1859, playing and beating that continent's best players. He retired from chess competition upon his return from Europe in 1958. (Courtesy Carlos "Froggy" May.)

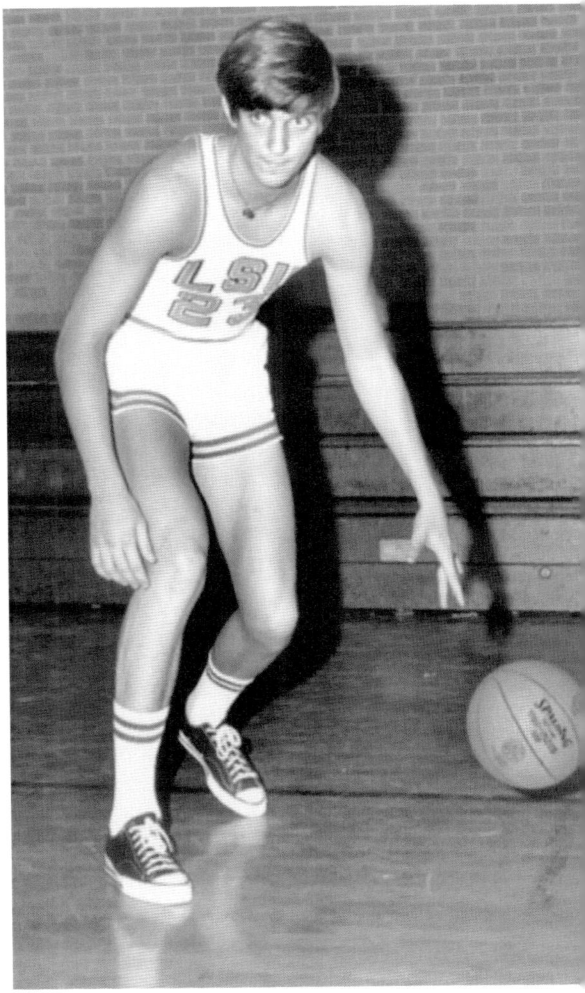

"Pistol"

Peter Press Maravich (1947–1988) was widely regarded as the best basketball point guard of his time. Maravich got the nickname "Pistol Pete" in high school because he would shoot the ball from his side, literally shooting from the hip. The motion left him looking as if he was holding a revolver. Born in Western Pennsylvania, Pete's original intention was to attend West Virginia University, but his father, "Press" Maravich, was head basketball coach at LSU. Pete followed his dad to Baton Rouge after high school and immediately earned a place on the Tiger basketball team, setting many NCAA records. Even though Maravich played before the NCAA adopted the three-point shot, Press Maravich's successor at LSU, Dale Brown, charted Pete's games, and calculated that, had the three-pointer been around, Maravich would have averaged 57 points per game. After LSU, Pete was drafted by the Atlanta Hawks in 1970. He was acquired by the new-franchise New Orleans Jazz in 1974, where he played until the team moved to Utah in 1979. Pete played one season for Utah, then a part-time season for the Boston Celtics, before being forced into retirement by knee injuries. He collapsed and died during a pickup game in 1988; an autopsy revealed a rare congenital heart defect. The LSU Assembly Center, home court for Tiger Basketball, was renamed in Maravich's honor, and his number was retired and hung up in the Superdome. (Courtesy NOPL.)

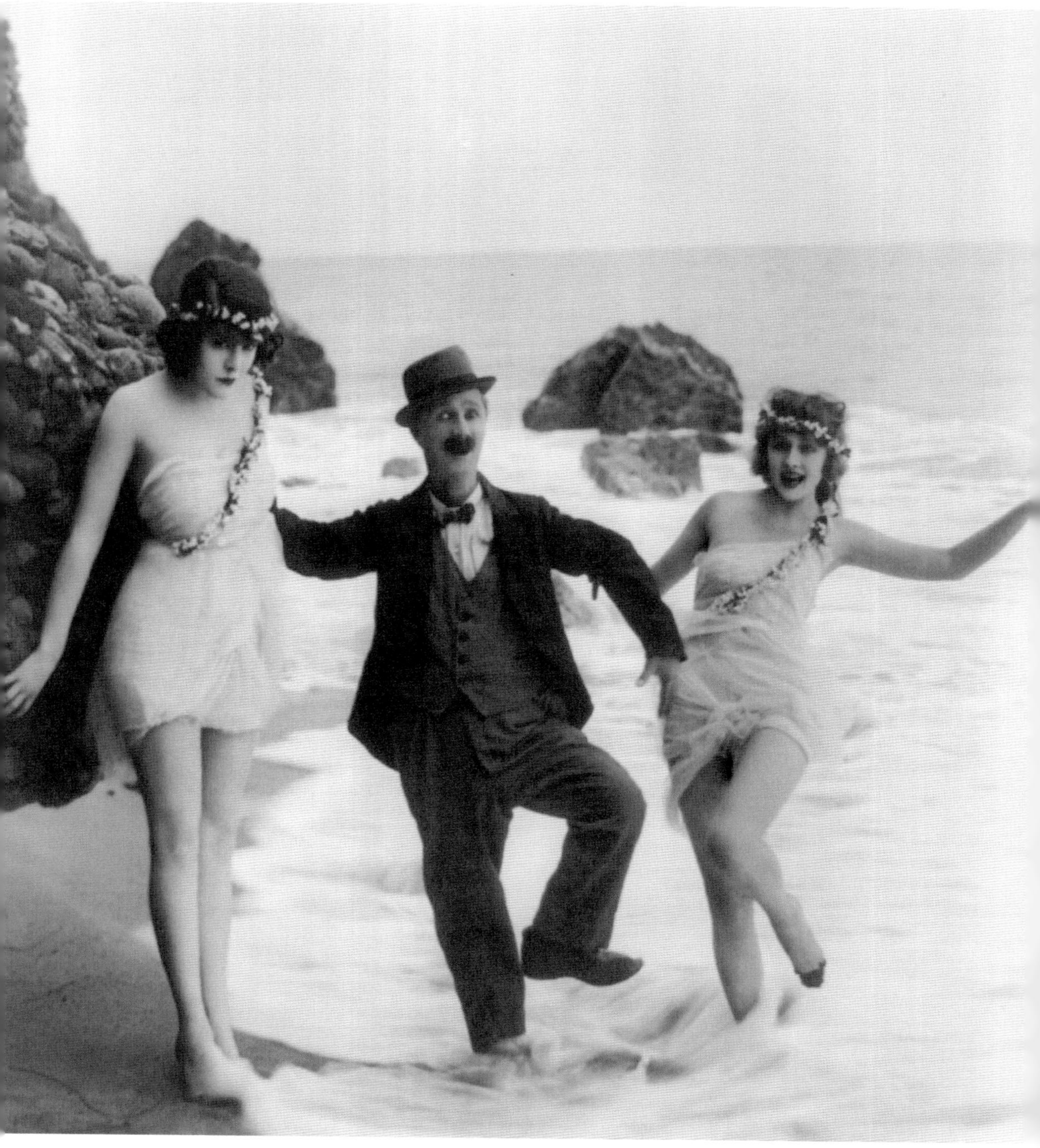

Silent Clown

Ben Turpin (1869–1940) began his career in vaudeville and burlesque as a slapstick comedian. His right eye was cross-eyed, so he would cross the left, adopting the look as his trademark. He made his first silent film in 1907, before joining the Mack Sennett studio in 1917. Turpin was a good fit with the Sennett studio, and he made a number of feature films and shorts. Even though he moved to Chicago and then Hollywood, Turpin still spoke like a New Orleanian. His "yat" accent helped him bridge the transition into talking pictures. (Courtesy NOPL.)

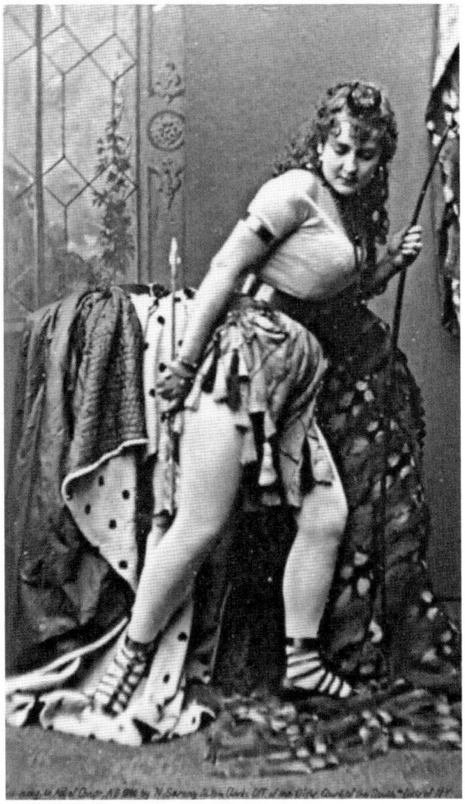

Dancer, Actress, Poetess

Adah Isaacs Menken (1835–1868) began her career as a ballet dancer at the French Opera House in the French Quarter. Her family made their way from New Orleans to Havana, where she continued her dancing career, eventually getting a role on Broadway in 1859. Unfortunately, the critics of the time did not believe her dance talent translated into quality acting, and the play, *The French Spy*, was roundly panned. Barely getting by in New York, Menken moved to Europe, touring, performing, and writing poetry. Her health took a turn for the worse, however, and she died in Paris at the age of 33. (Courtesy Charles D. Fredricks & Co.)

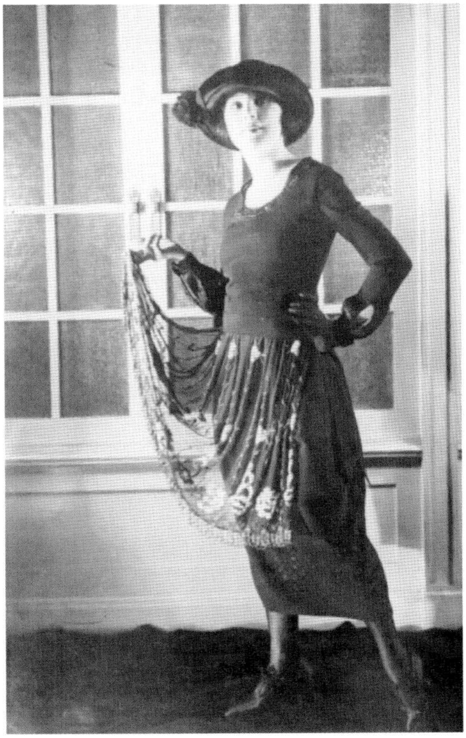

Silent and Southern

Another silent film performer named Leatrice Joy (1893–1985) made her first movie for the NOLA Film Company in 1915. She moved to Hollywood in 1917 and was signed by Samuel Goldwyn. Joy's career soared but then crashed with the advent of talkies. Her Southern drawl held her back from speaking parts. She was all but retired by 1930, taking the occasional small role over the years. (Courtesy LOC.)

"The Higher Order"

Momus Alexander Morgus is a scientist, esotericist, and sometimes television personality. He made his first appearance on New Orleans television in 1959, hosting *House of Shock*. The program would show horror films, with interludes originating from Morgus's laboratory. With help from his assistant, Chopsley, and his computer, E.R.I.C., Dr. Morgus has enjoyed a 50-year career, hosting several shows and making public appearances, such as this one, giving an "injection" to then-mayor Chep Morrison at an event at Tad Gormley Stadium in 1959. Possessing knowledge from a " 'Higher Order' of humanitarians devoted to the preservation of our planet through scientific means," Dr. Morgus strives to use nontraditional educational techniques and experiments to further science . . . and show old horror movies. (Courtesy NOPL.)

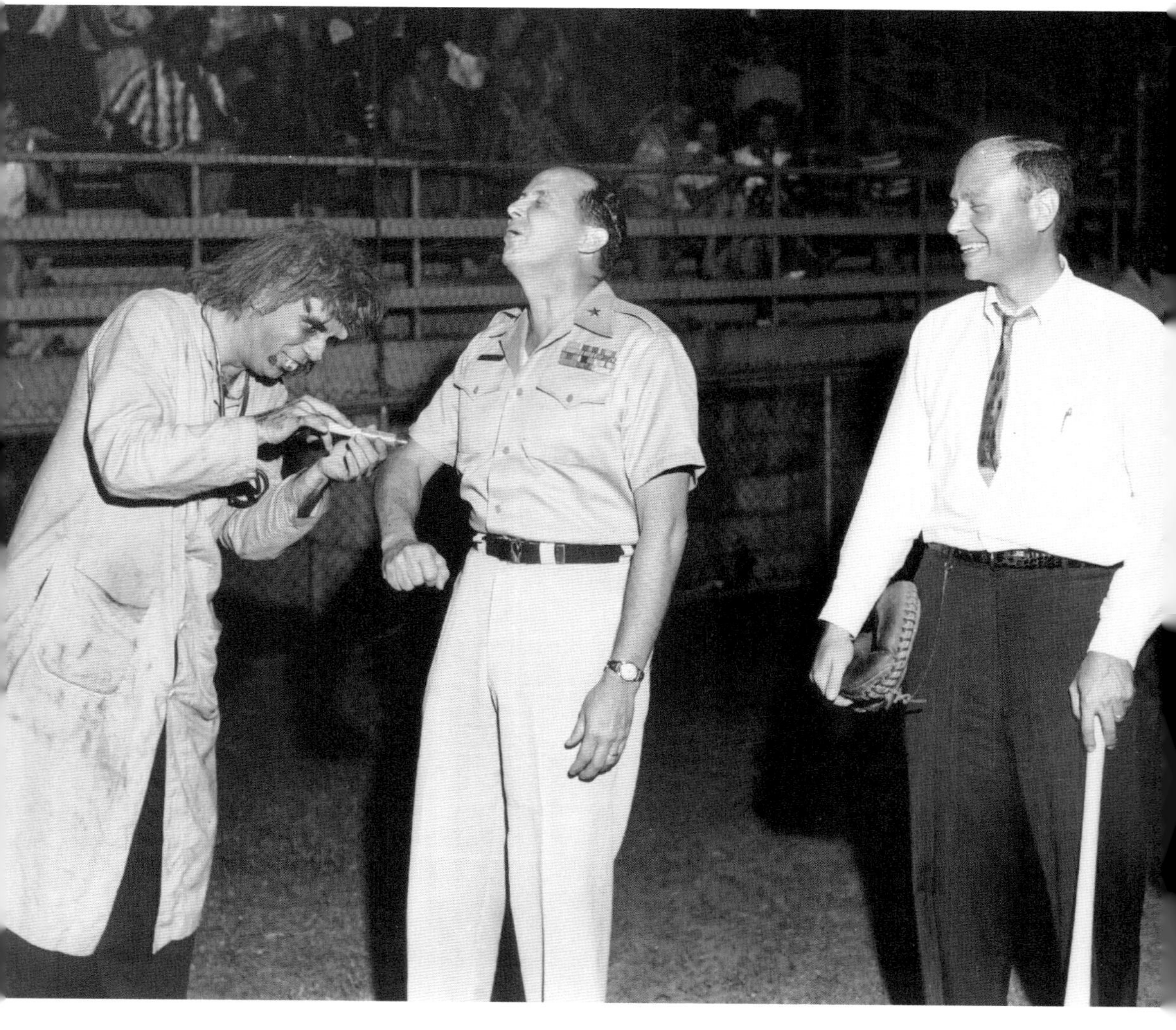

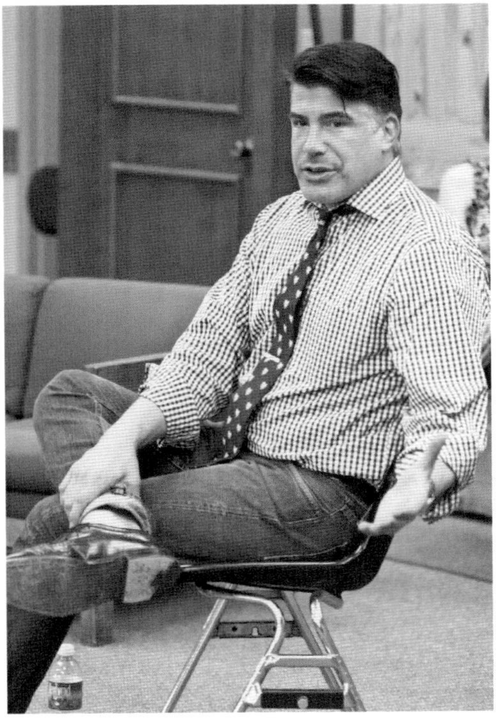

Mad Man

A scion of the family who owned and operated the Pontchartrain Beach amusement park, Bryan Batt (born 1963) is a successful actor, known best so far for his award-winning performances on AMC's *Mad Men*. Batt has also performed in several Broadway productions, such as *Sunset Boulevard*. Batt also wrote a memoir of his mother, *She Ain't Heavy, She's My Mother*. Even though his career takes him away from New Orleans, Batt has not forgotten his roots; he and his partner, Tom Cianfichi, own a home furnishings store on Magazine Street called Hazelnut. (Courtesy Tulane University.)

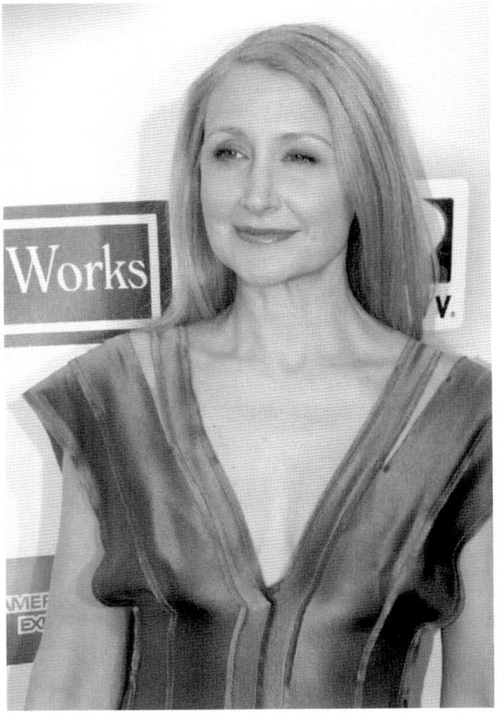

NOLA Defender

Patricia Clarkson, (born 1959) is the daughter of New Orleans councilwoman Jacquelyn Brechtel Clarkson. Patricia, who holds a master of fine arts degree from Yale, landed her first movie role in 1987, as Catherine Ness in *The Untouchables*. Her portrayal of "Aunt Sarah" in the HBO series *Six Feet Under* earned her an Emmy in 2002. Clarkson is in demand for both films and television, guest-starring on the NBC show *Parks and Recreation*, as well as doing "SNL Digital Short" performances for *Saturday Night Live*. Clarkson was very active in support of the Gulf Coast after the 2010 Deepwater Horizon oil spill. (Courtesy David Shankbone.)

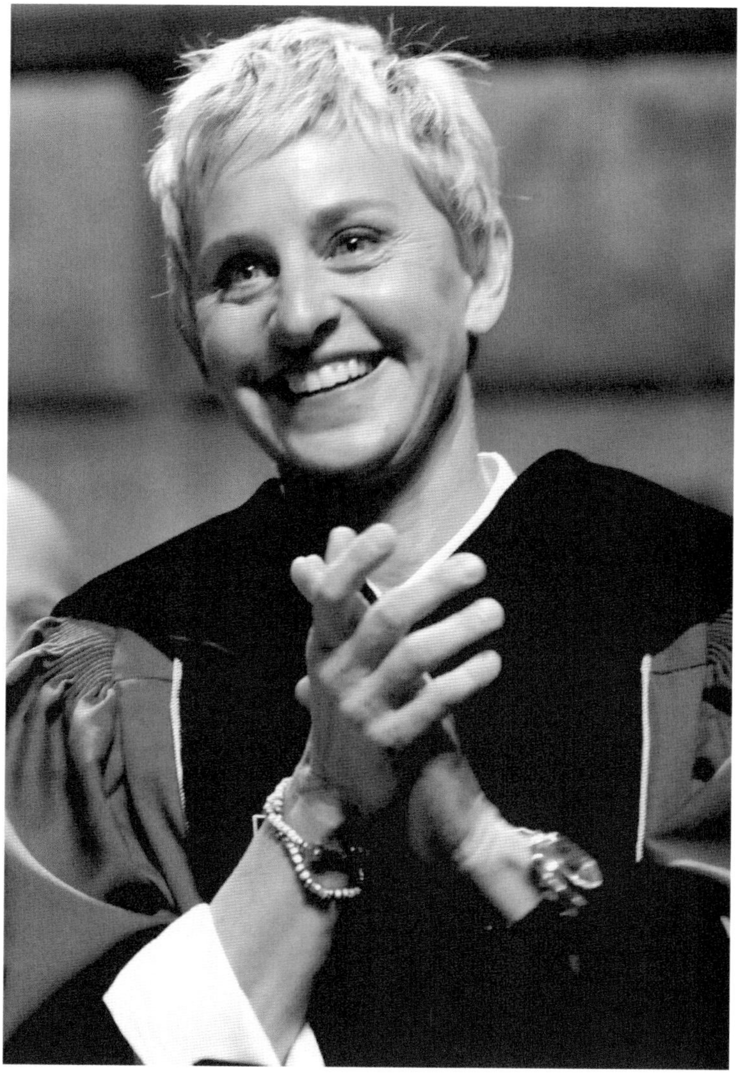

Ellen

Ellen DeGeneres (born 1958), star of the talk show that bears her name, was born and raised in suburban New Orleans. She began her comedy career in 1981, performing locally. She then moved to Los Angeles, where she continued to perform stand-up. In 1986, she was invited on *The Tonight Show Starring Johnny Carson*. Ellen impressed Carson, and she became the first female comedienne to sit in with the panel rather than just doing her routine. After that appearance, other bookings followed. Ellen transitioned from stand-up to sitcom acting when her first show, *Ellen*, debuted in 1994. The show gained huge notoriety in 1997 when Ellen's character came out as homosexual. Several sponsors dropped the show, and it was canceled in 1998, in spite of DeGeneres winning an Emmy for the coming-out episode. She left sitcom television and began a career in film (among Ellen's roles was as the voice of "Dory" in *Finding Nemo*), eventually returning to television in 2003. This time, DeGeneres took on the task of hosting a talk show, also with the title *Ellen*. Another NOLA actor who has not lost her roots, DeGeneres regularly (and fondly) remembers her hometown. Ellen kicked off her tenure as a spokesman for JC Penney, by returning to the Penney's store in Lakeside Mall in Metairie, where she worked while getting her comedy career going. (Courtesy Tulane University.)

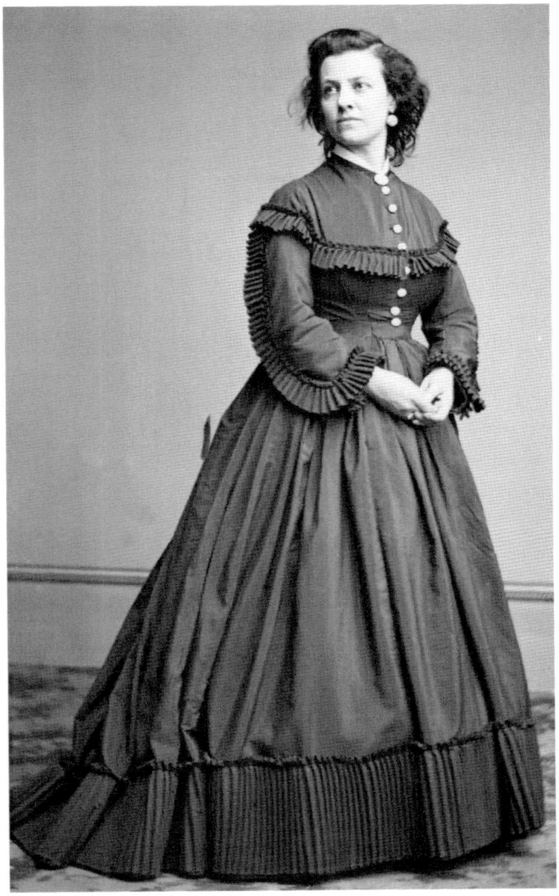

Spy

Pauline Cushman (1833–1897) was considered the "greatest heroine of the age." Born Harriet Wood in New Orleans, Cushman's family moved to Grand Rapids, Michigan, but she returned to New Orleans in 1851 to join a variety group, where she took her stage name. While part of a traveling troupe in the 1860s, she ingratiated herself with Confederate officers, even though she totally supported the Union cause. She acquired military intelligence, hiding plans and drawings in her shoes. She was caught and sentenced to hang, but the collapse of the Confederacy and Union troops approaching combined to spare her life. After the Civil War, Cushman was hired by P.T. Barnum, who billed her as a war hero. (Courtesy LOC.)

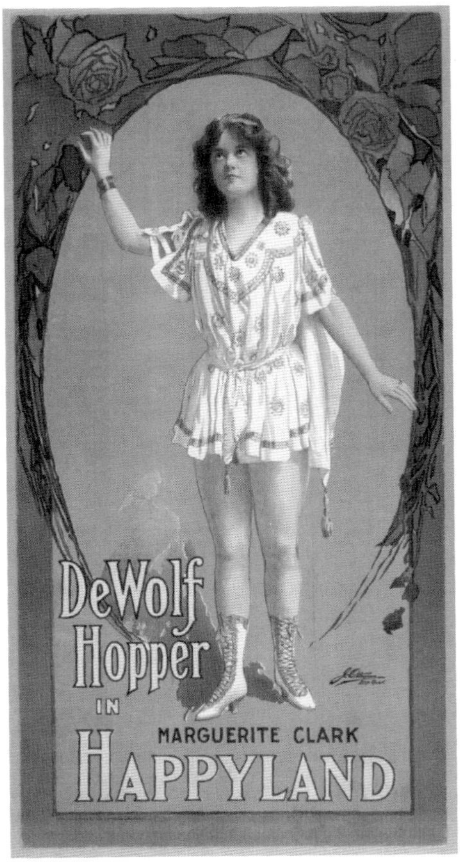

Silent

Marguerite Clark (1883–1940) was born in Cincinnati, Ohio, and debuted as an actress on Broadway at the age of 17. After over a decade in the theater, she began performing in short silent films. She went on to act in more than 40 films. In 1918, Clark (who was only 4 feet, 10 inches tall and had very youthful features) married businessman Harry Palmerston Williams from New Orleans. She moved into a mansion on St. Charles Avenue with Williams and continued to travel to make movies. She took over her husband's aircraft construction/service company upon his death in 1936, moving to New York, where she passed away in 1940. (Courtesy LOC.)

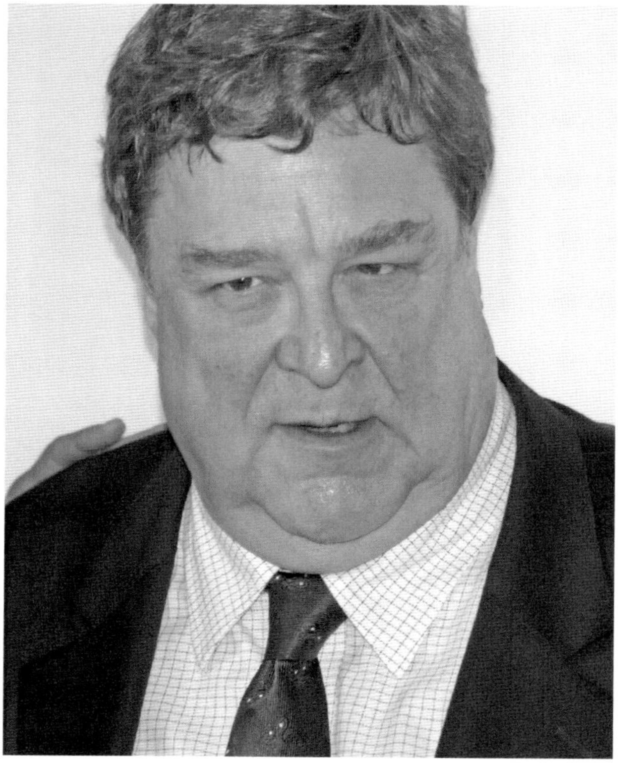

Dan

John Stephen Goodman (born 1952) was born in St. Louis, Missouri, but has been a longtime resident of New Orleans. He is best known as Dan Connor on the television show *Roseanne* but has played a wide range of roles on stage, in films, and on television. He has hosted *Saturday Night Live* 12 times and was the voice of Big Daddy in the 2009 Disney animated film *The Princess and the Frog* (set in New Orleans). An Emmy and Golden Globe award winner, Goodman is passionate about New Orleans's recovery in the wake of Hurricane Katrina. (Courtesy David Shankbone.)

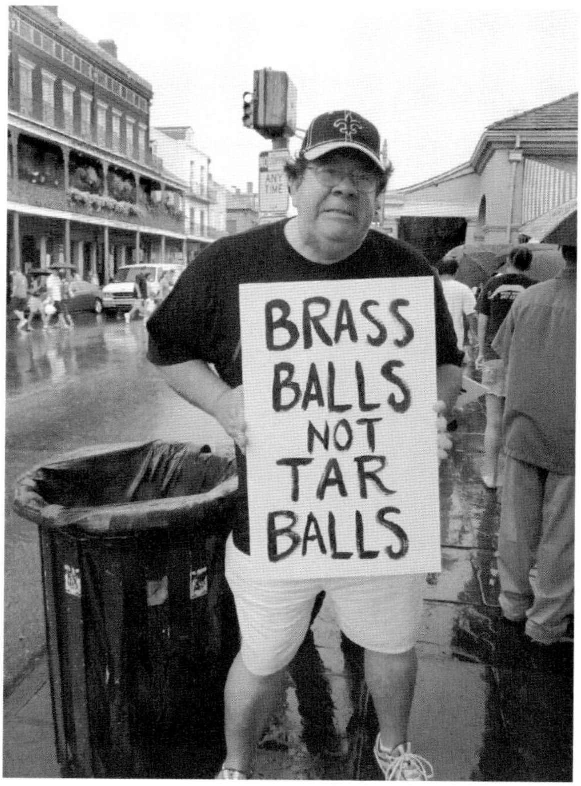

Ignatius

John "Spud" McConnell is a character actor and popular talk show host on WWL-AM, one of the nation's clear-channel stations (no other station in the country uses 870AM). Besides his radio show, "Spud" is best known for his portrayal of Ignatius J. Reilly, the central character of John Kennedy Toole's novel *A Confederacy of Dunces*. McConnell's one-man performances as Ignatius inspired the bronze statue of the character that stands "under the clock at Holmes" on Canal Street. He also has a recurring role on the HBO series *Treme*, as a WWOZ disc jockey. (Courtesy Carlos "Froggy" May.)

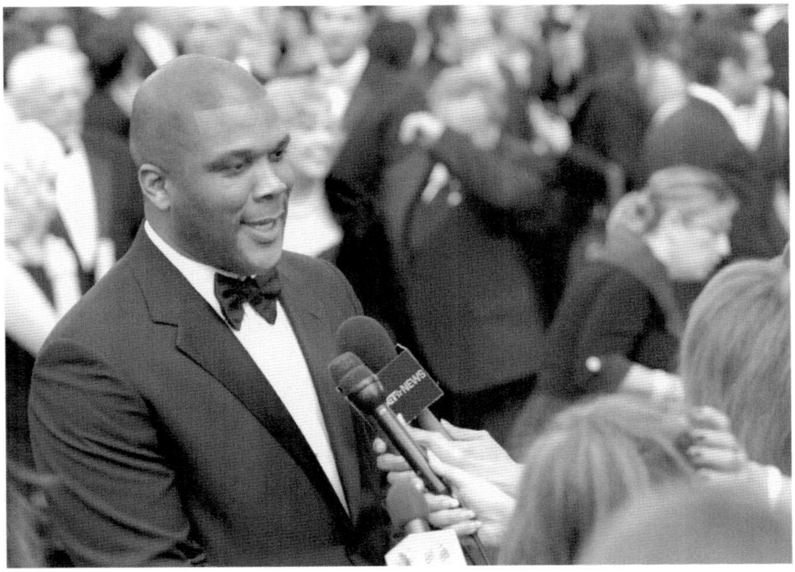

Madea

Tyler Perry (born 1969) grew up in an abusive household, but he "put it into the writing" and rose above the abuse to become an acclaimed actor, author, producer, and director. Tyler (who was born Emmitt Perry Jr. but legally changed his name at 16) moved to Atlanta from New Orleans when he was 21 and produced his first play two years later. He has been involved in 17 movies, including 2009's *Star Trek*. (Courtesy Sgt. Michael Connors, 302nd Mobile Public Affairs Detachment, US Army.)

"Antoine"

Wendell Pierce, was Detective Bunk Moreland in HBO's *The Wire*. A graduate of Benjamin Franklin High School and Julliard's Drama Division, Pierce's first on-screen role was in the 1986 film *The Money Pit*. He earned critical acclaim in Spike Lee's 1996 *Get on the Bus* and had a recurring role in the television drama *NUMB3RS*. In 2010, producer and writer David Simon once again turned to Pierce (who grew up in Gentilly) for his HBO drama *Treme*, in which he plays Antoine Batiste, a journeyman trombone player who makes his way through post-Katrina New Orleans. In addition to being one of the dramatic faces of modern New Orleans, Pierce is working to give back to his community, financing and promoting a chain of grocery stores in low-income neighborhoods. (Courtesy Mr. Pierce.)

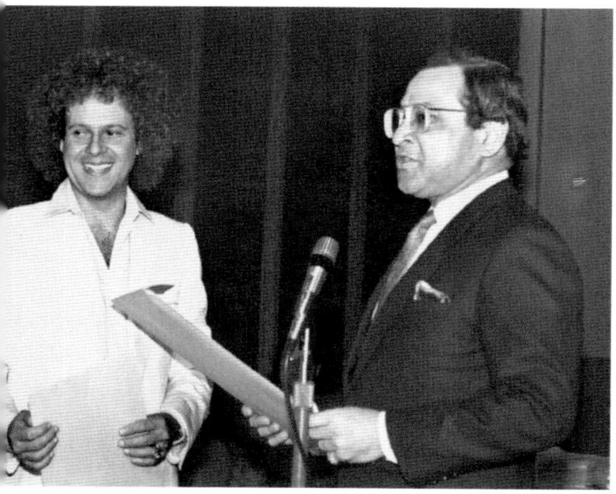

Guru

When Richard Simmons (born 1948) attended Cor Jesu High School in New Orleans, he was the fat kid who got picked on all the time. After graduating from Florida State University, Simmons moved to New York and then Los Angeles. Taking an interest in fitness, he opened his own exercise studio, losing a significant portion of the 268 pounds he weighed in high school. His focus on healthy diet, motivational speaking, and aerobics exercise led to him developing a following in Los Angeles, which led him to a role on the soap *General Hospital*. This acting role helped boost his media profile, opening up opportunities for appearances on a wide variety of shows including Howard Stern's radio program as well as *Late Night with David Letterman*. Simmons regularly returns to New Orleans; on one trip in the early 1980s, he was honored by Mayor "Dutch" Morial. He actively works to promote New Orleans in the wake of the storm. (Courtesy NOPL.)

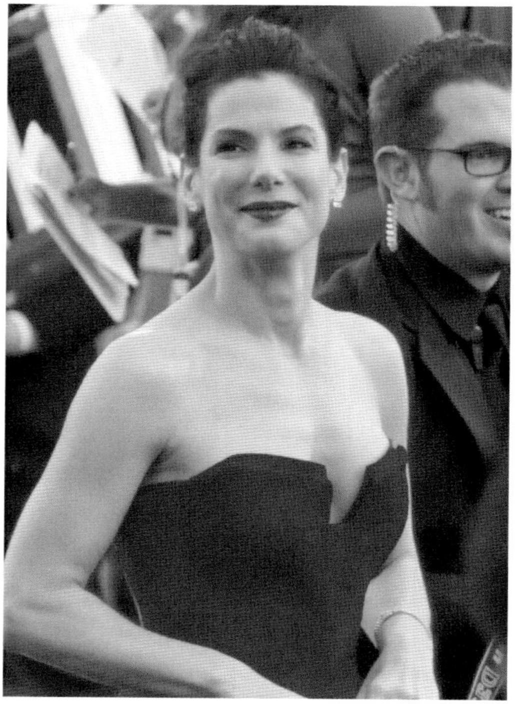

Congenial

Sandra Bullock (born 1964) used the New Orleans premiere of the movie *The Blind Side* as a fundraiser for one of her favorite causes: Warren Easton Charter High School. The school, which has been a fixture on Canal Street in Mid City since the beginning of the 20th century, was severely damaged in Hurricane Katrina. So moved by the destruction of the storm (Easton alone suffered over $4 million in damages), Bullock donated over $100,000 to the school, which went to, among other things, new uniforms and instruments for the band. After purchasing a house in the Garden District, Sandra announced she believed she would "find her child" in New Orleans, and eventually adopted her son, Louis. In spite of a busy acting career (she won an Academy Award for her performance in *The Blind Side*) and entrepreneurial interests across the country, Bullock considers herself a New Orleanian and is committed to the city. The faculty and board at Warren Easton firmly believe that Sandra actually has over 800 children: their students. (Courtesy David Torcivia.)

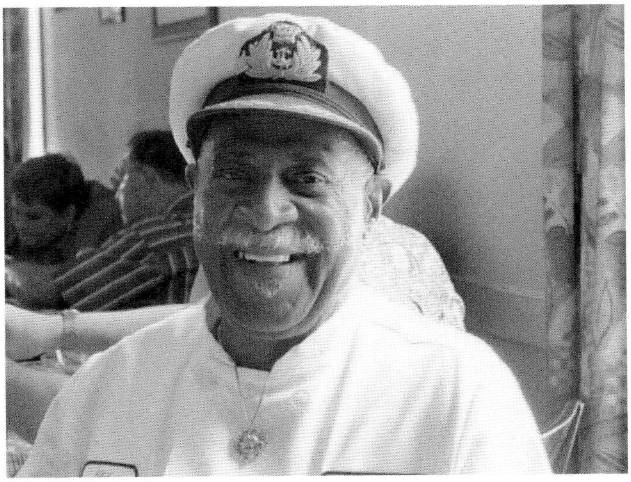

"Creole Soul"
Austin Leslie (1934–2005) started his cooking career at Portia's Fountain on Rampart Street, delivering Portia's popular fried chicken by bicycle. He apprenticed at the restaurant inside the D.H. Holmes department store on Canal Street. When his Aunt Helen opened Chez Helene in 1964, Austin joined the staff as the chef. "The Chez" took off, and Leslie's food received favorable reviews from critics, who rated it on the same level as Antoine's, Brennan's, and Commander's Palace. Austin bought the restaurant from his aunt in 1975. His trademark smile and captain's cap became Chez Helene's brand, along with his recipe for fried chicken. Leslie attempted to expand Chez Helene into other cities, as well as entering the fast-food fried chicken business, but none of these ventures were successful. Leslie closed Chez Helene and did a six-month stint in Denmark, cooking at a New Orleans–themed restaurant in that city. Upon his return home, he joined the staff at Jacques-Imo's on Oak Street. His fried chicken was an instant Jacques-Imo's hit. Leslie's story of surviving Hurricane Katrina is a common New Orleans hurricane-rescue tale: He climbed into his attic, cut a hole in his roof, and was rescued by helicopter. (Courtesy Jason Perlow.)

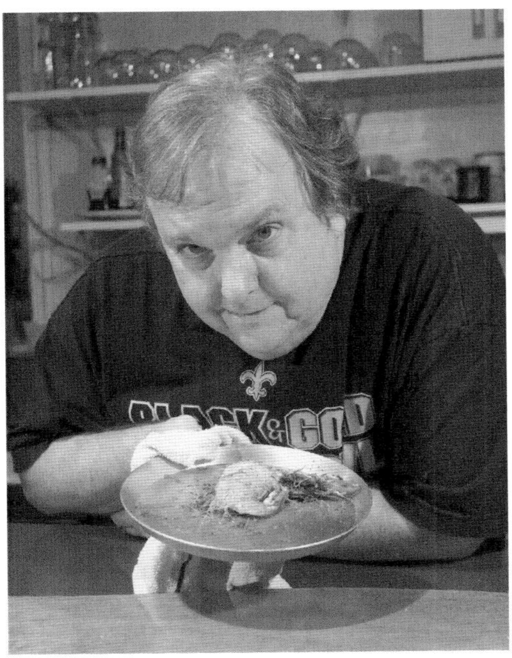

G-Man
Chris DeBarr, (1961) chef and blogger extraordinaire, was the creative genius at Delachaise on St. Charles Avenue, then his own place, Green Goddess, in Exchange Alley. DeBarr (@ChefCDB on Twitter) apprenticed at Commander's Palace under the late Jamie Shannon. DeBarr left Green Goddess in the spring of 2012 to open Serendipity, a 100-seat restaurant in the American Can Company building in Mid City. (Courtesy Louisiana Seafood Board.)

Bananas Foster

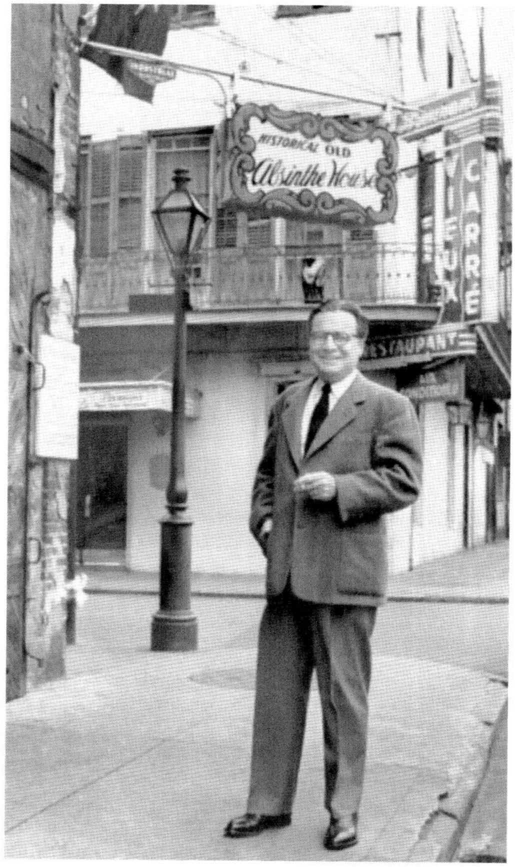

Owen Edward Brennan (1910–1955) bought the Old Absinthe House, the legendary hangout of Jean Lafitte, in 1943. He became a successful tavern keeper, but he could not resist the challenge from "Count" Arnaud Cazenave, proprietor of Arnaud's Restaurant around the corner. Arnaud got fed up one day with Brennan's regular relaying of complaints from the restaurant's customers and told him that if he could run a restaurant better, he should try. Brennan did more than just try, leasing the Bourbon Street location across from the Absinthe House and opening the Vieux Carre Restaurant. The restaurant became a success, as the house dessert, Bananas Foster, grew in popularity. In 1954, Brennan was ready to grow the restaurant and leased the Morphy family house at 417 Royal Street, across from the courthouse building. He opened Brennan's on November 1, 1955, continuing to promote the notion of "Breakfast at Brennan's." Owen's untimely death at age 45 forced his sister, Ella, into the role of manager. Ella masterfully ran the restaurant, growing the family's interests in the business at a dramatic rate. (Right, courtesy Brennan's Restaurant; below, courtesy Derek Bridges.)

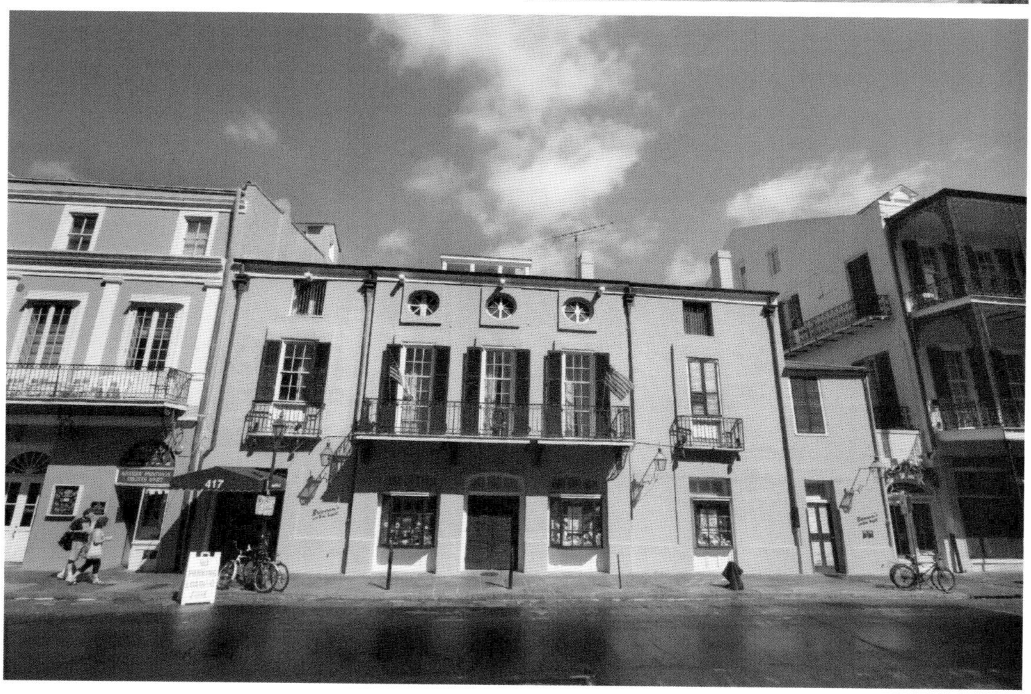

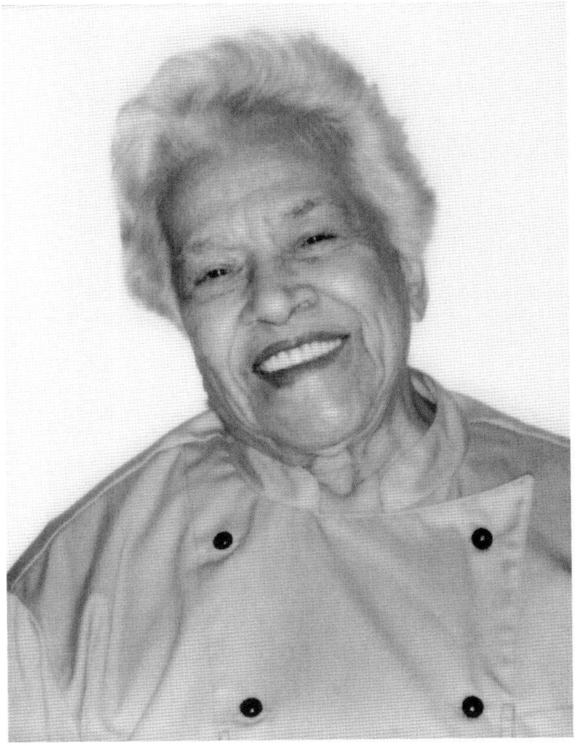

Creole Queen
Leah Chase (born 1923) began her cooking career like many New Orleanians, working part-time while in high school. She graduated from St. Mary's Academy, then married Edgar "Dooky" Chase II in 1945. Dooky's family owned the Dooky Chase restaurant on Orleans Avenue, in Faubourg Treme. Ms. Leah settled in at Dooky Chase's in the 1950s, shaping the restaurant in her own style, cooking the Creole dishes she grew up with. The restaurant was hit hard by Hurricane Katrina, but the community came to Ms. Leah's aid. Dooky Chase's reopened in 2007, and both Ms. Leah and Dooky Chase's are going strong. (Courtesy Blake Nelson Boyd.)

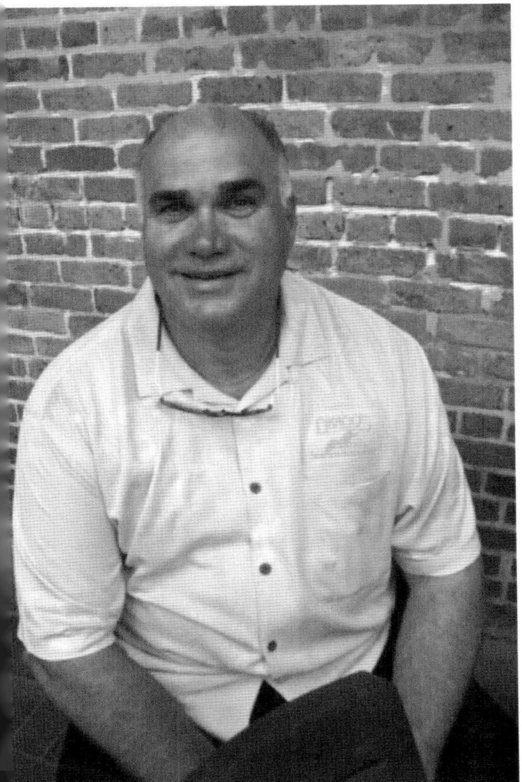

Oysters!
Tommy Cvitanovich (born 1959) was relatively lucky, as far as Hurricane Katrina went. His family's restaurant, Drago's (named for his father), is located in Metairie and did not fall victim to the devastation many neighborhoods in the city did. Cvitanovich did not stay idle after the storm hit, however. Since Drago's had gasoline and generators, they quickly reopened, giving out free meals in those difficult weeks of September 2005. He also dispatched one of his mobile catering units that usually made the restaurant's signature char-grilled oysters at fairs and festivals in the metro area, to flood-ravaged Lakeview. All told, Drago's fed over 80,000 people. The National Restaurant Association recognized Cvitanovich with an award that included a cash prize; he turned around and donated the money to Grace King High School, which is down the street from Drago's. Cvitanovich expanded restaurant operations, taking over the restaurant space in the Hilton Hotel downtown, opening a second Drago's location there. In 2011, Cvitanovich was awarded the *Times-Picayune* Loving Cup Award, which the paper has given since 1901 to those who do exceptional work for the community. (Courtesy Tommy Cvitanovich.)

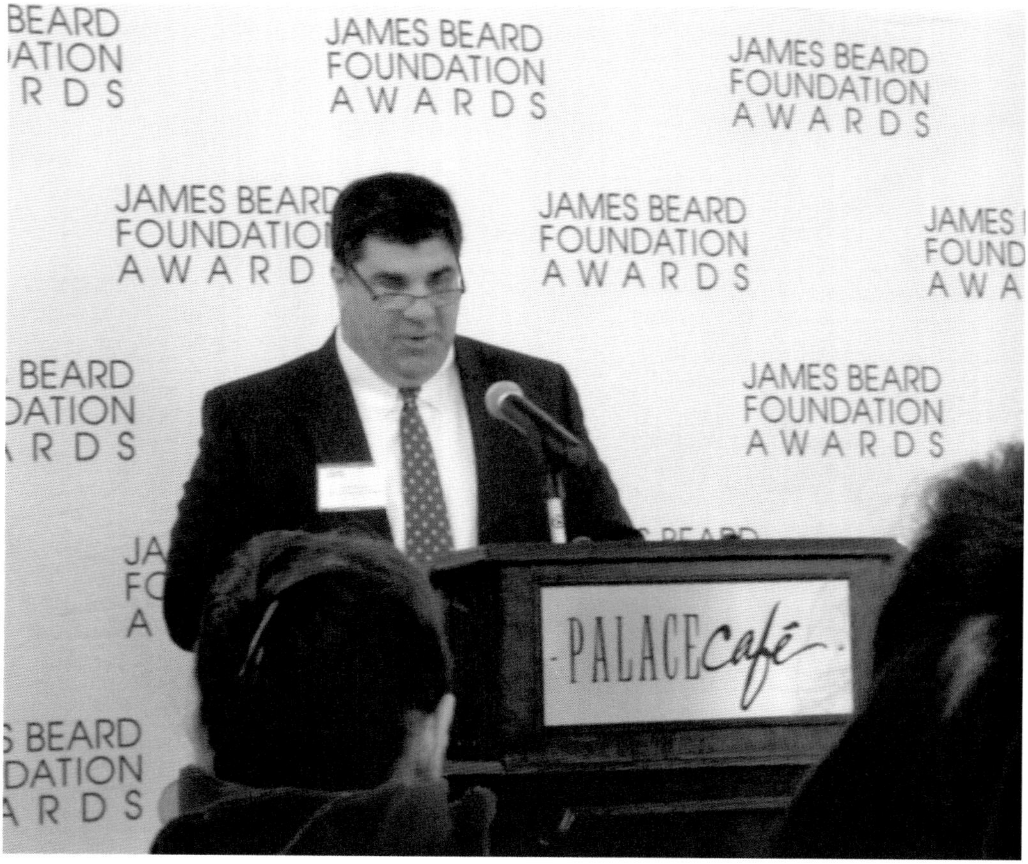

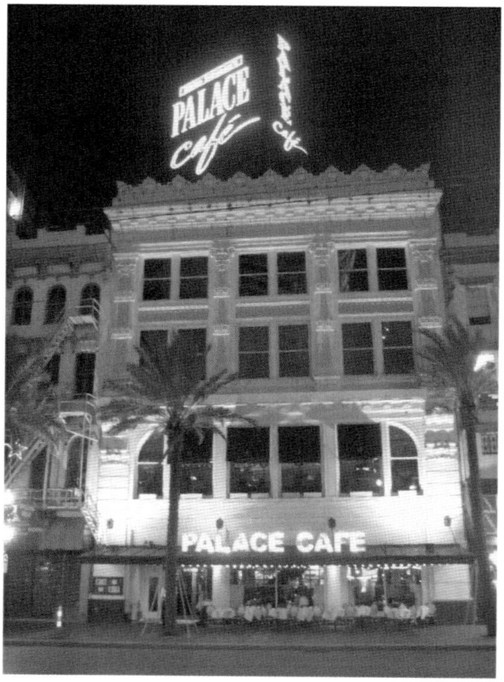

Palace

Richard J. "Dickie" Brennan Jr. is the nephew of the late Owen Brennan. Growing up in one of New Orleans's prominent restaurant families, it was natural for Dickie to go into the business, working at Commander's Palace under then-executive chef Paul Prudhomme. Dickie took his skills to Paris for a time and then supervised the opening of the family's Canal Street restaurant, Palace Café, in 1991. In 1996, Brennan partnered with his sister Laura Brennan Brower and Palace Café general manager Steve Pettus to open Dickie Brennan's Steakhouse on Bienville Street in the French Quarter. The partners acquired Palace Café from the family, then opened a third French Quarter restaurant, Bourbon House Seafood and Oyster Bar. (Above, courtesy Robert Peyton; right, courtesy Carlos "Froggy" May.)

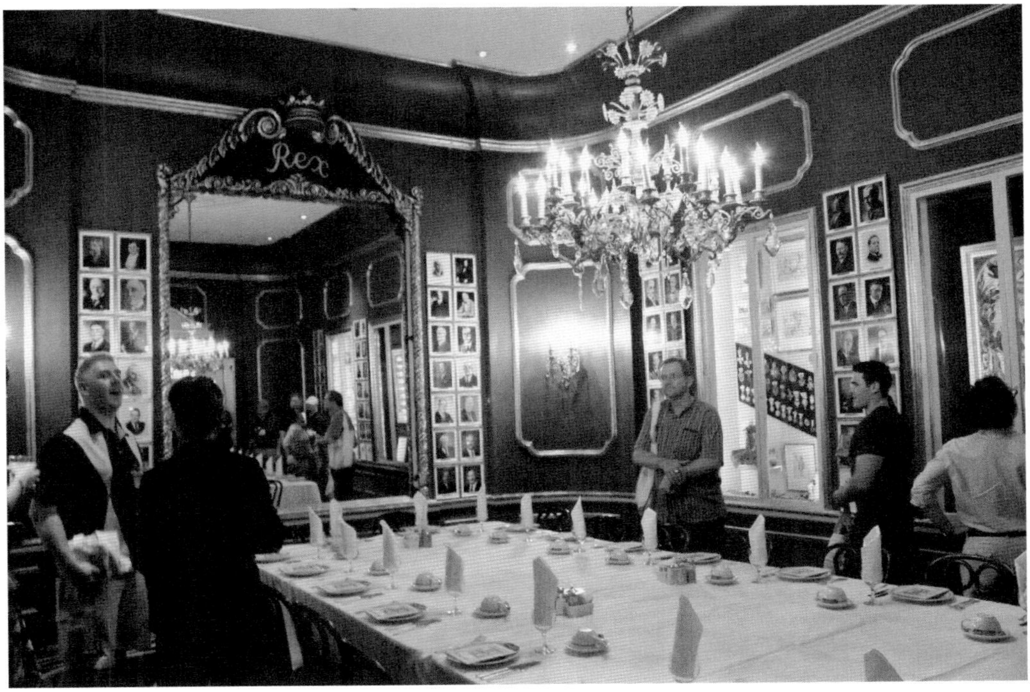

La Cuisine Provencal

Antoine Alciatore (1825–1877) came to New Orleans from Marseilles, France, opening a pension and small restaurant on Rue St. Louis. His reputation grew, and Antoine moved his restaurant to Rue St. Peter. By 1868, Restaurant Antoine had outgrown that second location, moving to the Rue St. Louis location where New Orleans's oldest continuously operating restaurant still serves some of the best food in town. Today, under the direction of chief executive officer Rick Blount, Antoine's is entering into what local critic Tom Fitzmorris calls "a new golden age." (Above, courtesy Antoine's Restaurant; below, Carlos "Froggy" May.)

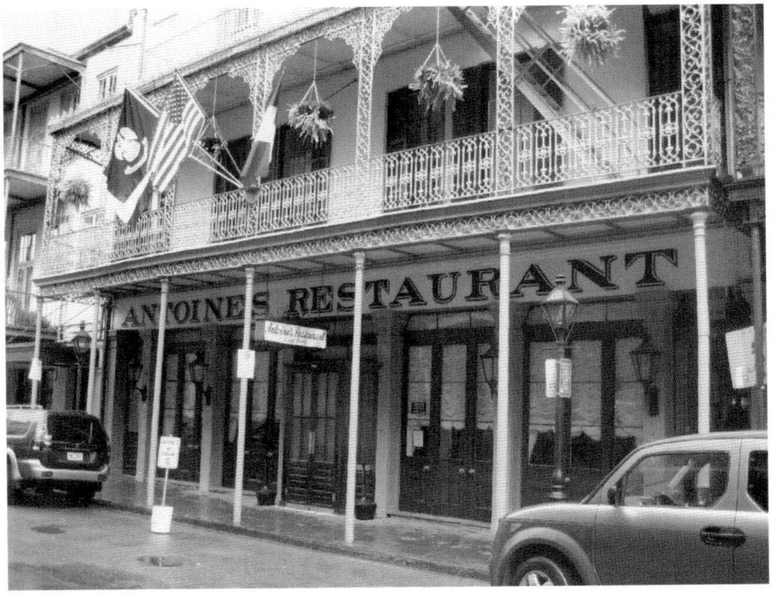

K-Paul's

Paul Prudhomme (born 1940) grew up in Southwest Louisiana (Opelousas) and traveled the country while in his 20s, settling in New Orleans. He rose to the position of executive chef at Commander's Palace. In 1979, Prudhomme and his wife, K, opened K-Paul's Restaurant in the French Quarter. K-Paul's was an instant success, boosting Prudhomme's profile. He released his first of 11 cookbooks in 1984 and has starred on several cooking shows. (Courtesy Brett Rosenbach.)

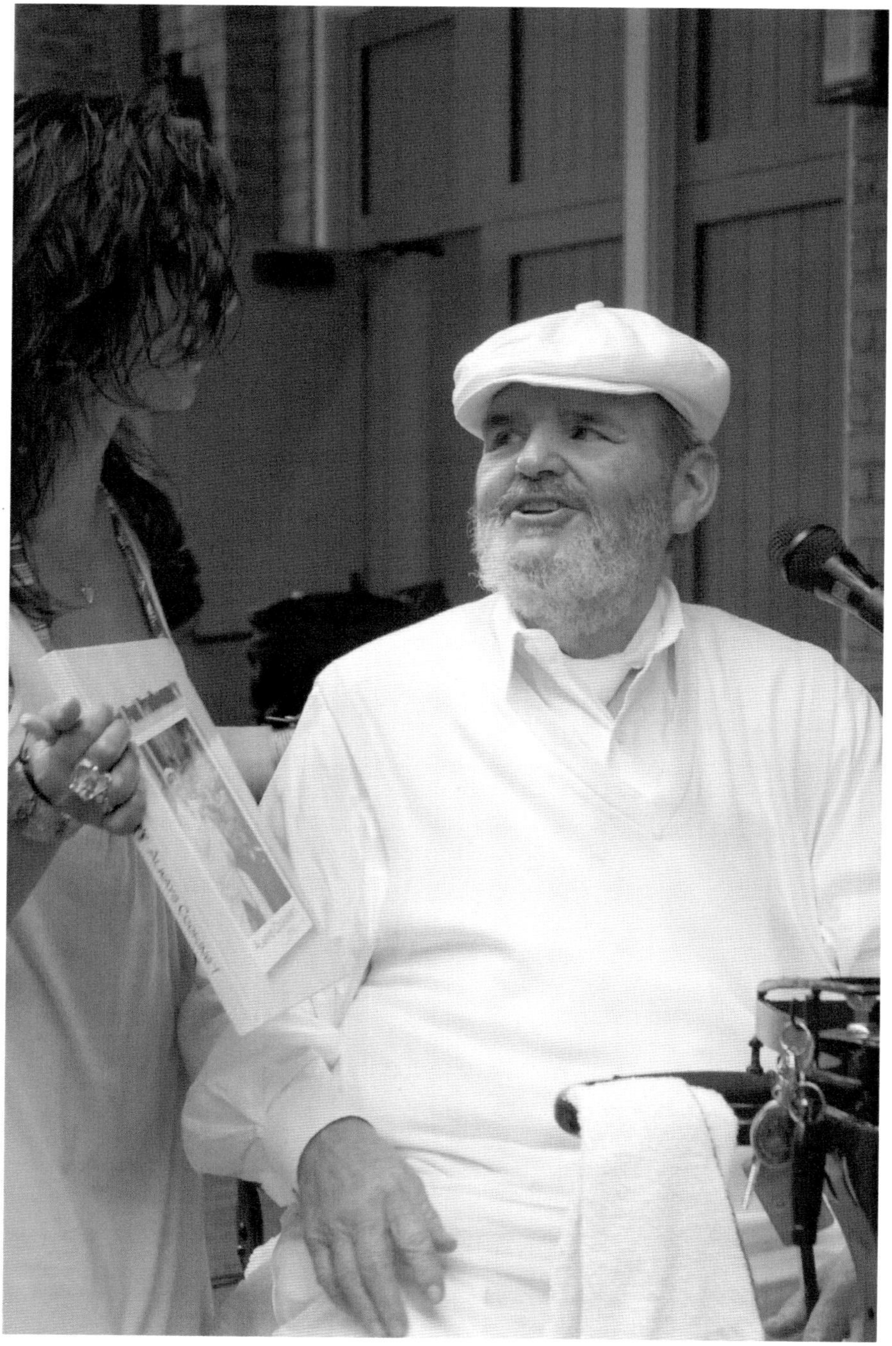

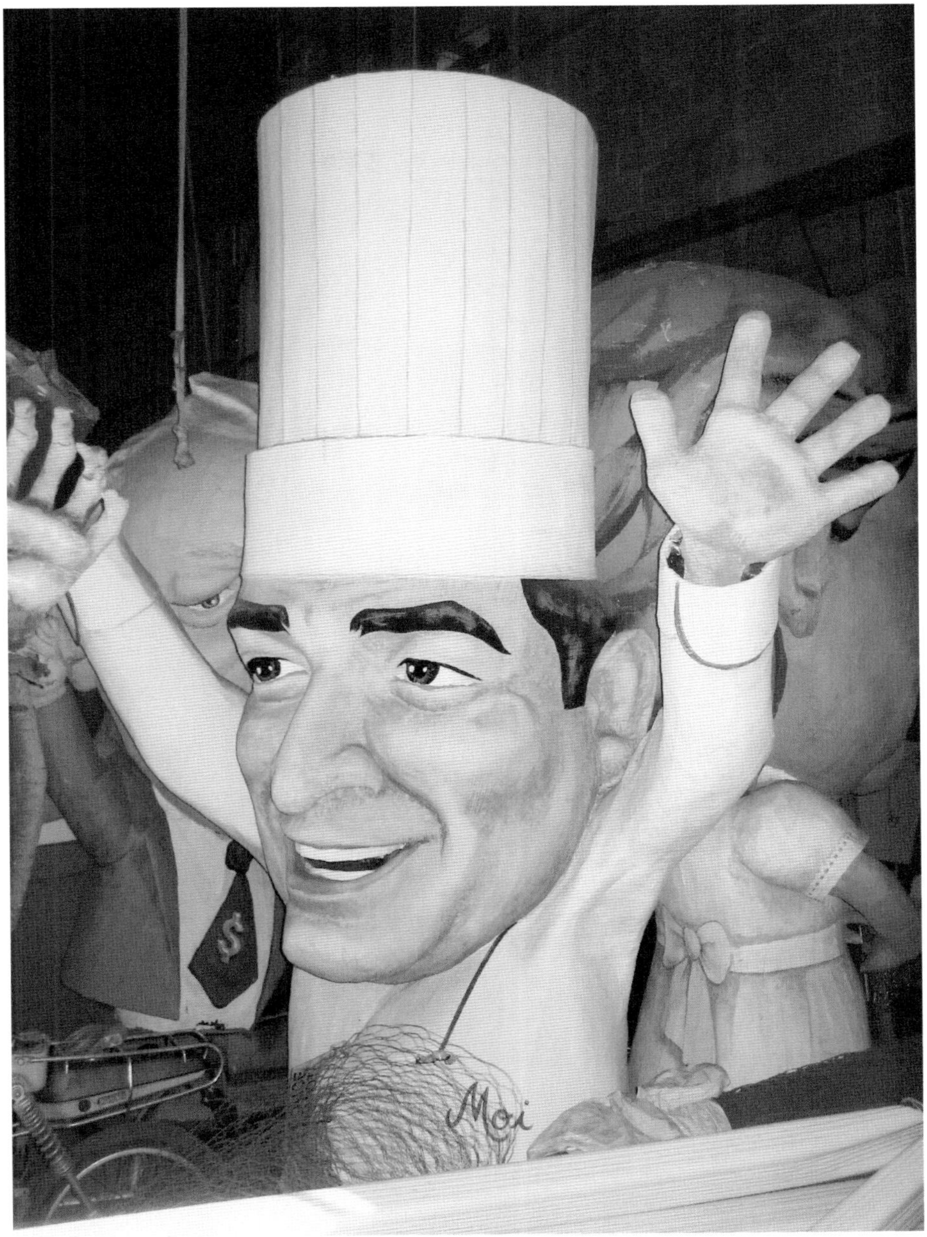

Bam!

It is hard to think of Emeril Lagasse (born 1959) being anyone's sous chef, but that's exactly what he was in the early 1980s. Lagasse took over the reins at Commander's Palace from Paul Prudhomme in 1982, leaving the Brennan family's Uptown restaurant in 1990. It was that year he opened his own place, Emeril's, located on Tchoupitoulas Street, in the Warehouse District. In its first year, Emeril's received the accolade of Best Restaurant of the Year by *Esquire*. Lagasse now operates three restaurants in New Orleans: Emeril's (the flagship), NOLA (in the French Quarter), and Emeril's Delmonico (on St. Charles Avenue), as well as 10 in other cities. His success as star on the Food Network made his trademark exclamations ("Bam!" and "Kick it up a notch!") household terms nationally. Emeril is such a part of New Orleans, he is even featured on Carnival parade floats. (Courtesy Carlos "Froggy" May.)

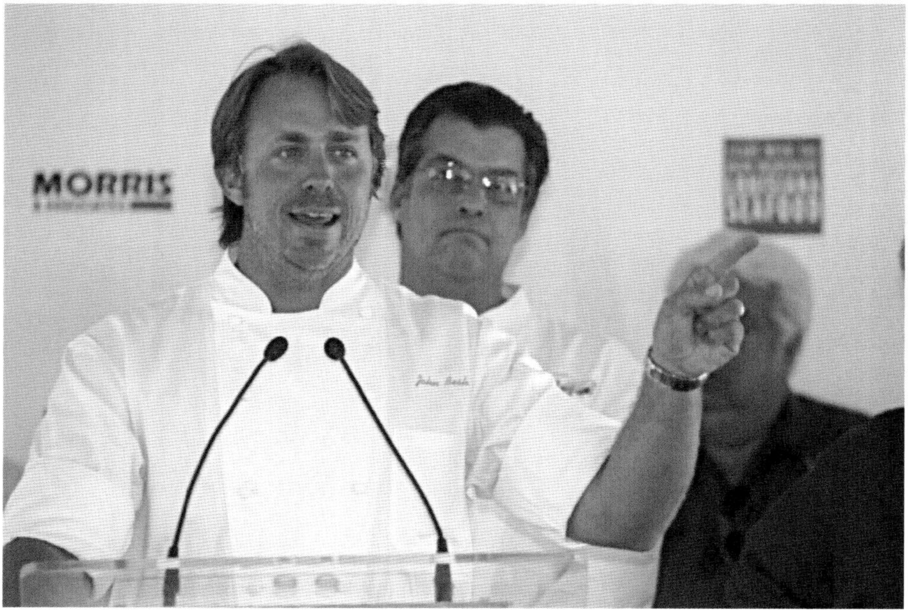

August

John Besh (born 1968) was a Marine Corps reservist after graduating from St. Stanislaus College in Bay St. Louis, Louisiana. Upon returning from serving in Operation Desert Storm, he attended the Culinary Institute of America. Besh began receiving recognition and awards, leading to the opening of his own place in August 2001. Chef Besh's restaurant group now includes eight more restaurants: seven in New Orleans and one in San Antonio. When Besh's mentor Chef Chris Kerageorgiou passed away in 2006, Besh acquired Chef Kerageorgiou's La Provence restaurant, on the north shore of Lake Pontchartrain. Besh's restaurants all feature differing styles of cuisine, reflecting both his personality and those of the executive chefs who supervise day-to-day operations, such as "Canard Roti" from Luke. (Above, courtesy Louisiana State University; below, courtesy Chef John Besh.)

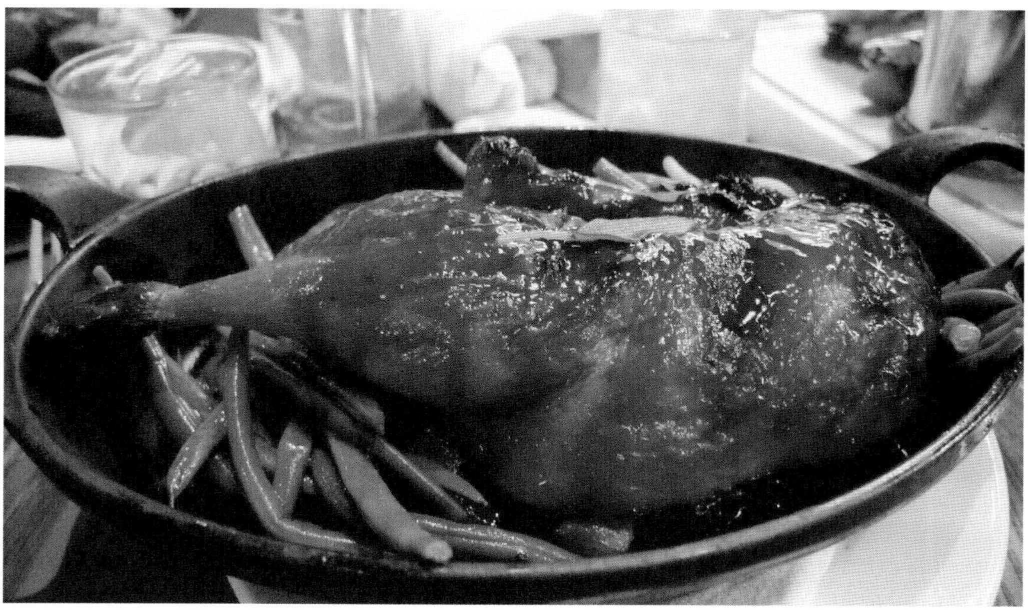

CHAPTER FOUR

Public Service, Politics, and Military

New Orleans has had many people from all walks of life commit to making the city a better place. Some earn enough money in their chosen careers to finance public service projects; others give their careers in direct service to the city. Sometimes those careers are cut tragically short when public servants and military men and women make the ultimate sacrifice. While New Orleans did not nurture a culture of war, the city still produced some brilliant military strategists and many hard-working men and women wearing the uniform of the US armed forces. The dynamics of the Civil War complicated the roles of military men and women. A woman everyone firmly believed to be a Confederate loyalist turned out to be a Union spy. After the war, officers and generals who desired to get involved in business ventures in the North found themselves sandbagged by criticism of fellow officers.

Politics is one of the few constants throughout New Orleans; it has been crazy since the Spanish came here. Some of those Civil War dynamics return a century later, as African Americans pressed forward in their struggle for equal rights and equal opportunity. What began with a train ride by Homer Plessy during Reconstruction continued on with the hard work of men like A.P. Tureaud and became reality when black politicians like Dutch Morial took to the inauguration podiums and got down to working on the problems of the city.

In addition to those in uniform who protect the city, men of the cloth also dedicated their lives to public service. The heavy Catholic influence on the population of the city means that priests, nuns, and bishops all have an impact on New Orleans's future. Men like Joseph Rummel backed up the Supreme Court by excommunicating those who wanted to continue segregation. Rabbis care for the needs of the area's Jewish population, and the nuns just take care of anybody on the social ladder in need of their help.

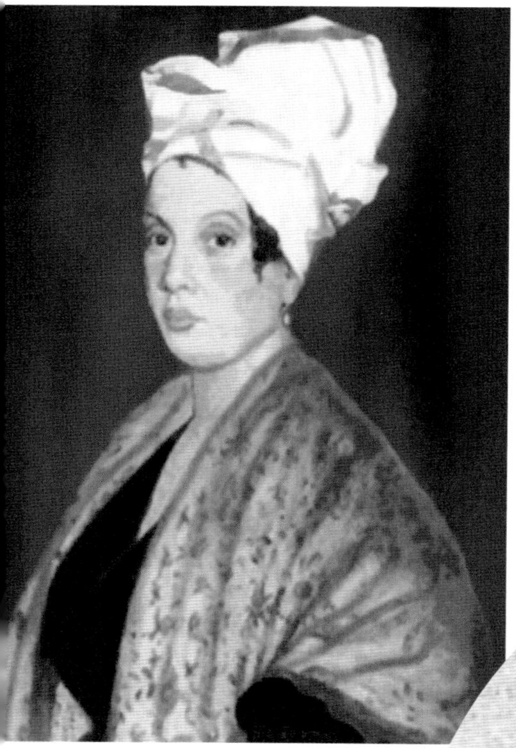

Voudon

Marie Laveau (1794–1881) was the daughter of a white planter from New Orleans whose mistress was a free woman of color. Marie married a Haitian émigré named Jacques Paris, who died in 1820. Marie then began a career as a hairdresser, catering to many of the wealthy white women of the city. She took a lover, Louis Christophe Dumesnil de Glapion, with whom she is believed to have had as many as 15 children. Marie was reputed to be a voodoo priestess, mixing her fervent Catholicism with worship of African gods, goddesses, and spirits. When Marie died in 1881, she was interred in the Glapion family tomb in St. Louis Cemetery No. 1N. To this day, visitors to the cemetery will leave three Xs on the tomb as well as offerings of food and rum to court the favor of Marie's spirit. (Courtesy NOPL.)

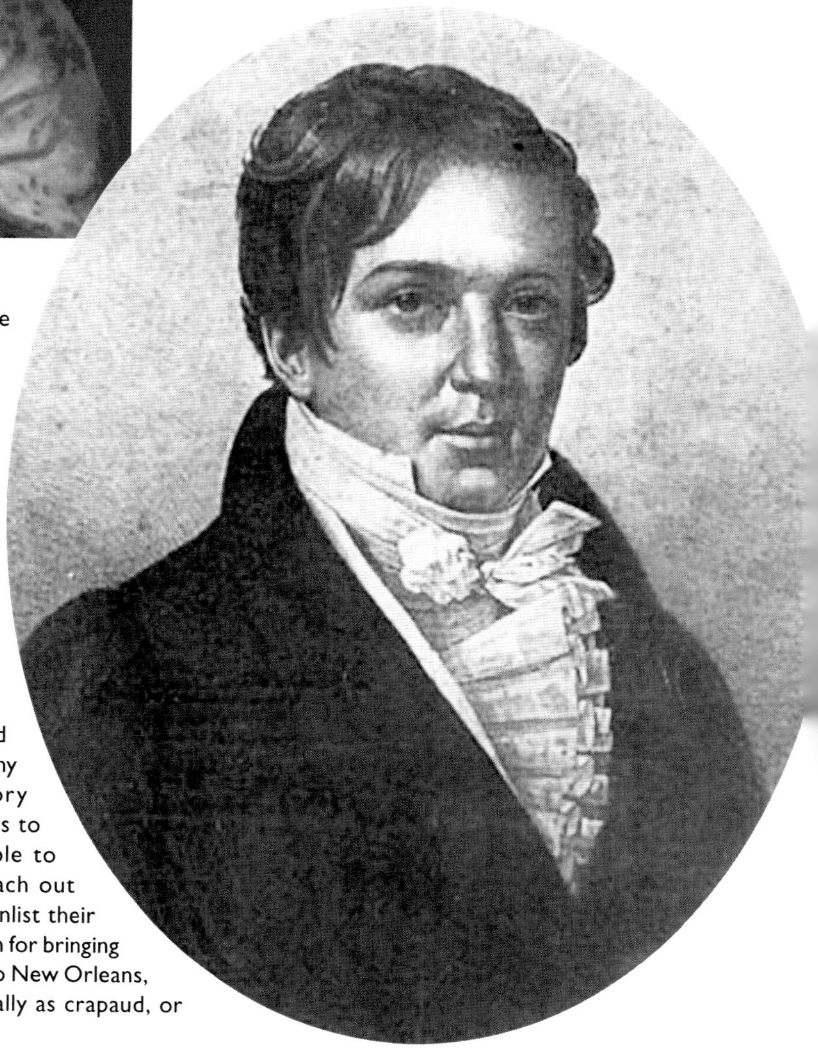

Playboy

Bernard Xavier Philippe de Marigny de Mandeville (1785–1868) was New Orleans's first major real estate developer. In 1806, when he reached his majority, Bernard subdivided the family plantation, selling lots to Creole families and free men of color. The neighborhood resulting from these sales became known as Faubourg Marigny. During the British military campaign of December 1814, Andrew Jackson established his headquarters at the Marigny plantation home on Victory Street. Even with such access to Jackson, Bernard was unable to convince the general to reach out to the Lafitte brothers and enlist their support. Marigny is also known for bringing the British dice game hazard to New Orleans, where it became known locally as crapaud, or craps. (Courtesy NOPL.)

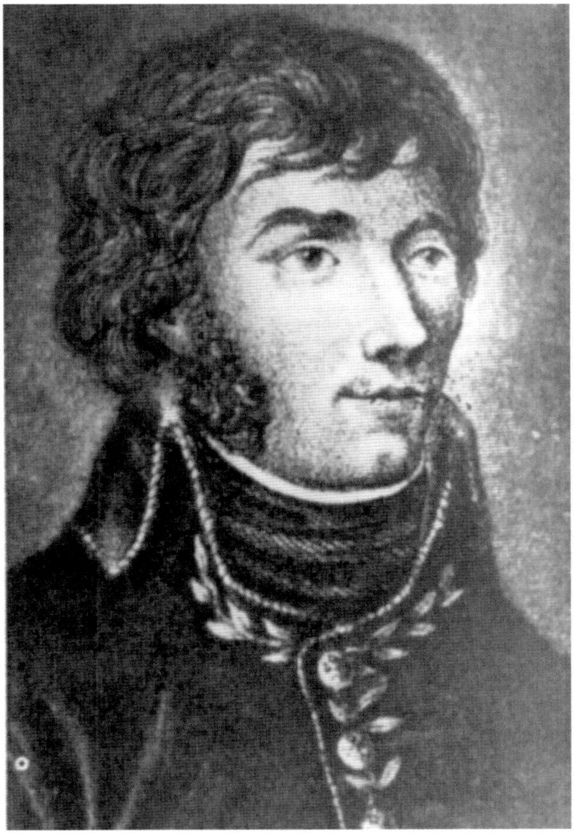

Indiscreet

Jean Joseph Amable Humbert (1755–1823) rose to the rank of brigadier general in the army of the French Republic. He was appointed governor of Saint-Domingue after participating in the suppression of the slave rebellion there, but indiscreet affairs with a general's wife and Bonaparte's sister landed Humbert in exile by 1808. Escaping France, he made his way to New Orleans. When the British moved on New Orleans in late 1814, Humbert offered his services to Andrew Jackson. In spite of being a skilled soldier and good leader, Humbert did not speak English well enough for Jackson's backwoods riflemen, making him ineffective as a leader, despite his personal courage. Humbert became a minor celebrity after the battle, appearing in his French uniform. (Courtesy NOPL.)

Muses

Barthelemy Lafon (1769–1820) was an architect, engineer, and surveyor. At the direction of planters living north of the French Quarter, he subdivided land upriver from the French Quarter so it could be sold and developed as housing for many of the Americans that were migrating to the city. Lafon's most detailed work was in the Lower Garden District, where he laid out a grid of streets named after the nine muses of Greek mythology. Those street names—Calliope, Clio, Erato, Thalia, Melpomene, Terpsichore, Euterpe, Polymnia, and Urania—have provided Americans outside of New Orleans with amusement as they listen to New Orleanians butcher their pronunciation. Lafon's role in the Battle of New Orleans is unclear, but after the battle, he gave up architecture and engineering to join with the Lafitte brothers as a smuggler and a pirate. (Courtesy LSM.)

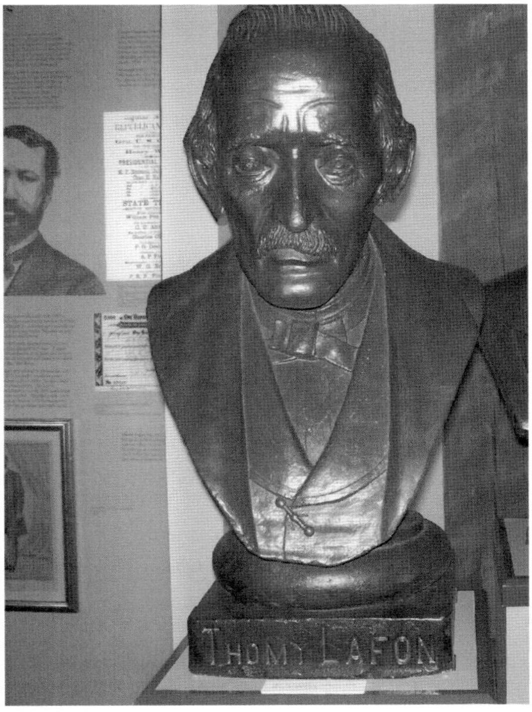

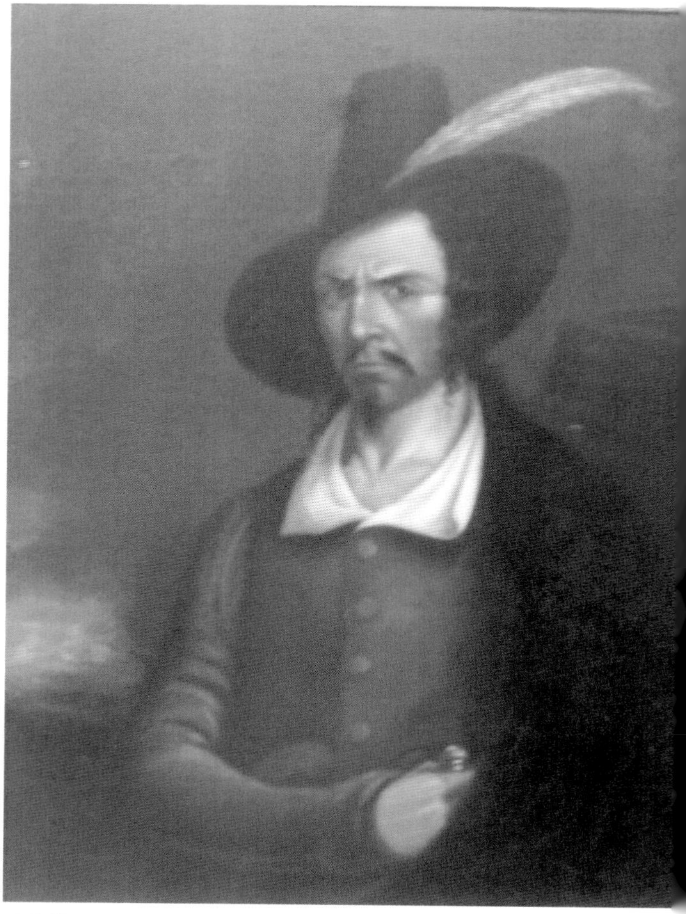

Privateer

Jean Lafitte was born somewhere between 1776 and 1780, but where exactly is still a subject of debate. Jean and his older brother Pierre gave a number of differing accounts of their origins. By the early 1800s, the Lafitte brothers had reconnected, and they began a smuggling operation running from Barataria Bay up to the city itself. Jean Lafitte was already a cult hero in New Orleans by the time Andrew Jackson took over the defense of the city in late 1814. The Embargo Act and subsequent actions by the US Navy had created such a rift between the government and the sailors who regularly worked the ships based in New Orleans that none of the Barataria men were interested in fighting for the United States, even to defend New Orleans. Although he initially did not trust dealing with Lafitte, Jackson gave in, offering the brothers and their men a full pardon if they assisted him. Assist they did, taking a major role in the defense of New Orleans in December 1814 and January 1815. (Courtesy NOPL.)

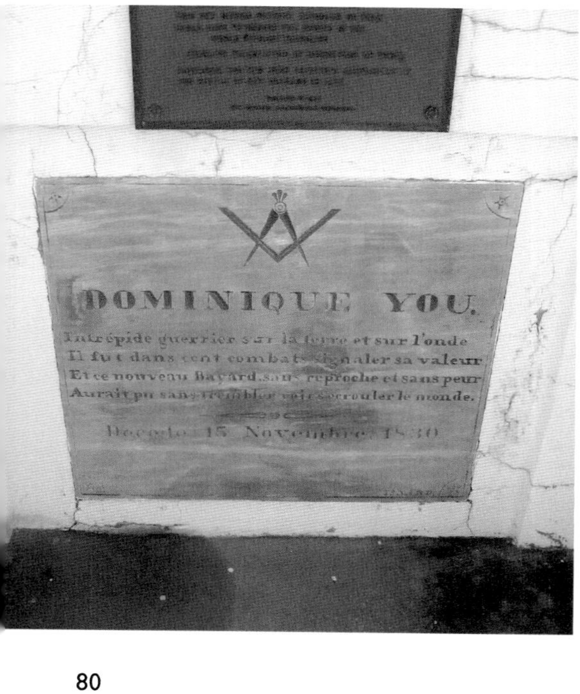

Gunner

Dominique Youx (1775–1830) was born in Santo Domingo (Haiti). He was a stowaway on a ship heading to France. When he was discovered, he was taken on as a cabin boy, learning the seaman's trade. Still in France at the time of the French Revolution, the then-teenaged Youx joined an artillery company of the French army. He honed his skills in the Haitian revolution and was an experienced gunner by the time of the Battle of New Orleans in 1815. General Jackson sent Youx to Fort St. John to defend the Lake Pontchartrain entrance to the city but quickly recalled him when it was clear the British were invading from the East. Youx fought with distinction in Chalmette, receiving a full pardon from President Madison. Youx lived in Faubourg Marigny in the 1820s, and was given a hero's funeral when he died in 1830. He was buried in St. Louis Cemetery No. 2. (Courtesy Mark Ghstol.)

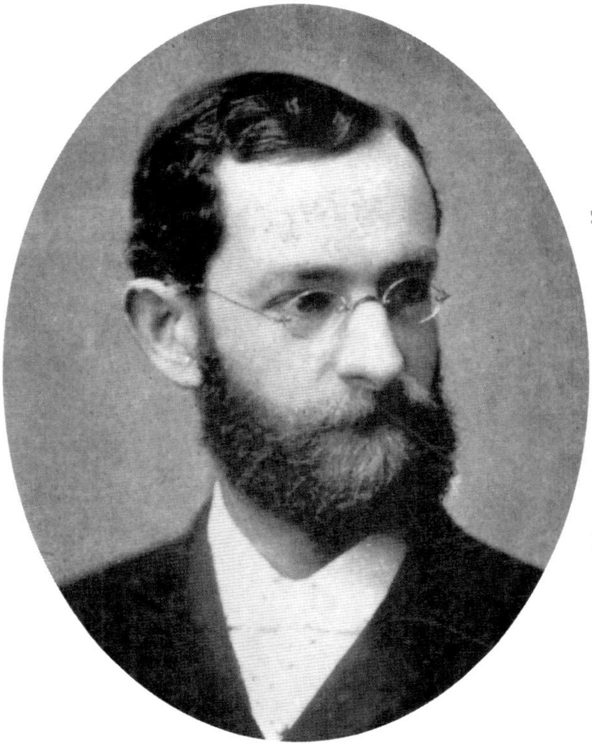

Scholar

Maximillian Heller (1860–1929) was a distinguished Jewish scholar, rabbi, and ardent zionist. A native of Prague, Heller came to the United States at an early age. He was educated at McMicken University and at the Hebrew Union College. After living in Cincinnati for some years, he was named rabbi of Temple Sinai in New Orleans and became a professor of Hebrew and Hebrew Literature at Tulane University in 1912. (Courtesy NOPL.)

Civil Rights

Homer Plessy (1862–1925) was persuaded by a local citizens group to sit in a "whites-only" railroad car in 1892. The Citizens' Committee notified the railroad of Plessy's intentions, and he was arrested. Plessy's arrest led to the court battle resulting in a decision against Plessy and the establishment of the "separate but equal" clause. Plessy was considered "7/8ths white," but that was enough to bar him legally from the "whites" train car. (Courtesy Carlos "Froggy" May.)

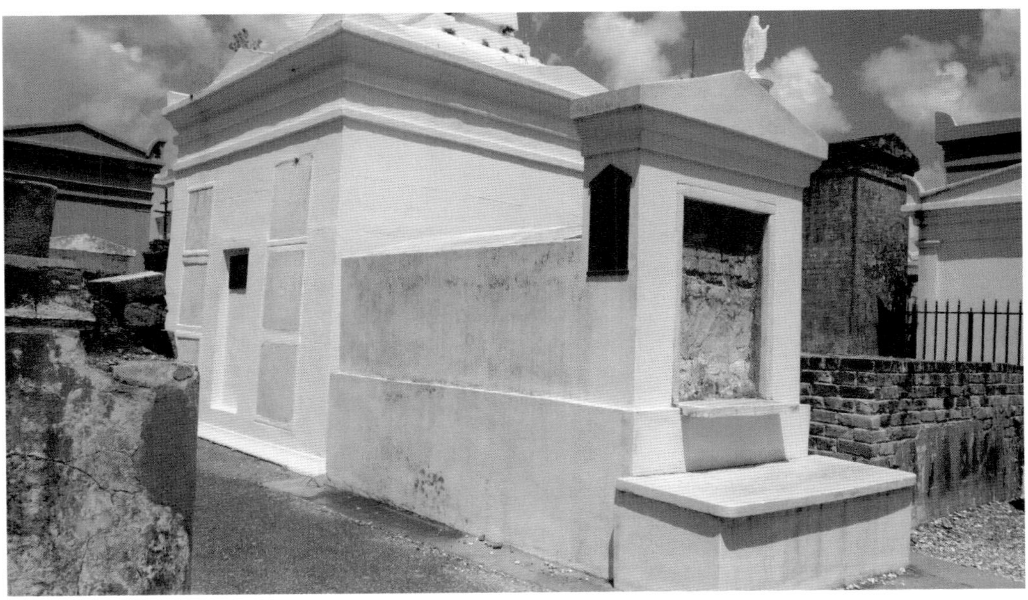

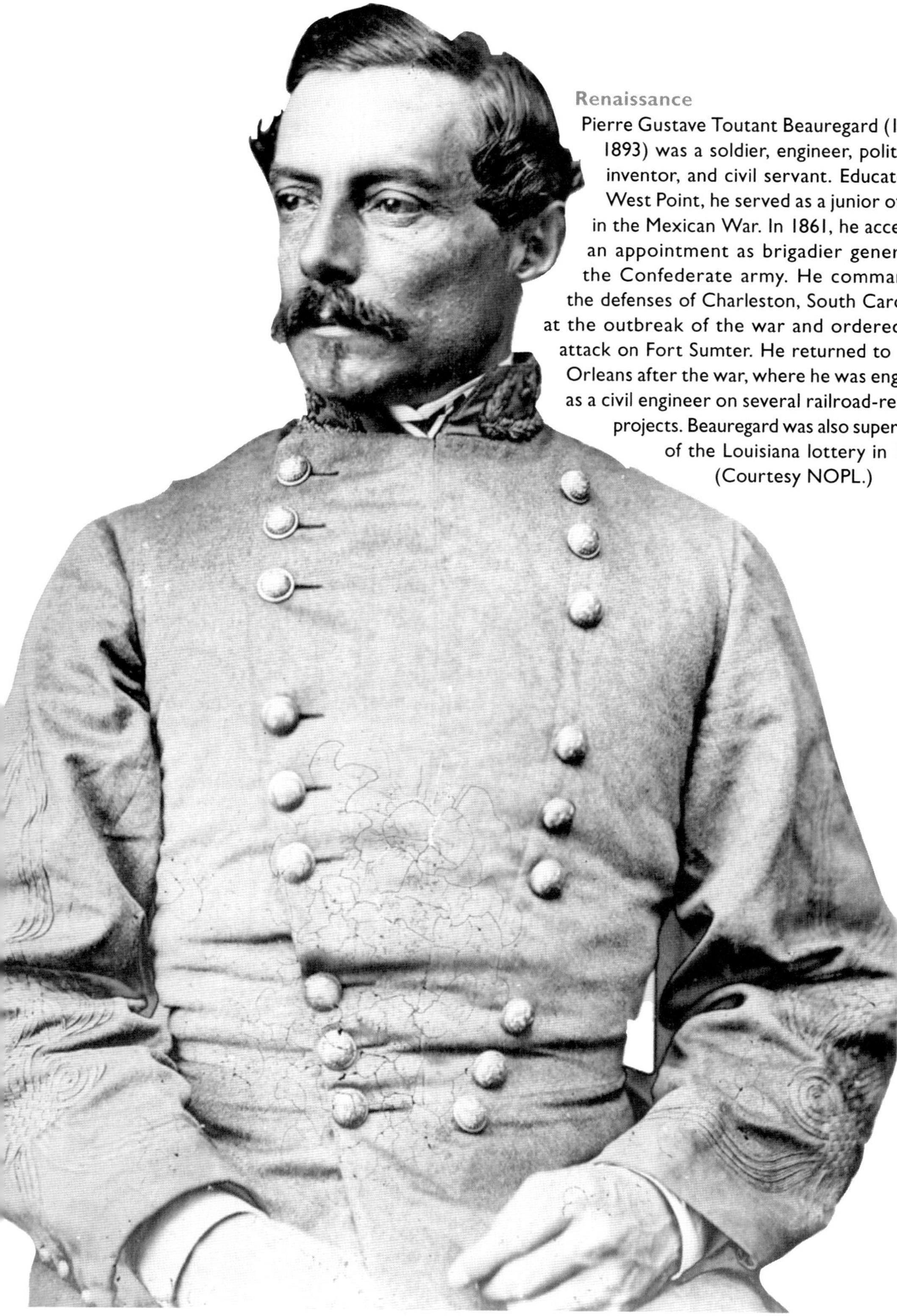

Renaissance

Pierre Gustave Toutant Beauregard (1818–1893) was a soldier, engineer, politician, inventor, and civil servant. Educated at West Point, he served as a junior officer in the Mexican War. In 1861, he accepted an appointment as brigadier general in the Confederate army. He commanded the defenses of Charleston, South Carolina, at the outbreak of the war and ordered the attack on Fort Sumter. He returned to New Orleans after the war, where he was engaged as a civil engineer on several railroad-related projects. Beauregard was also supervisor of the Louisiana lottery in 1877. (Courtesy NOPL.)

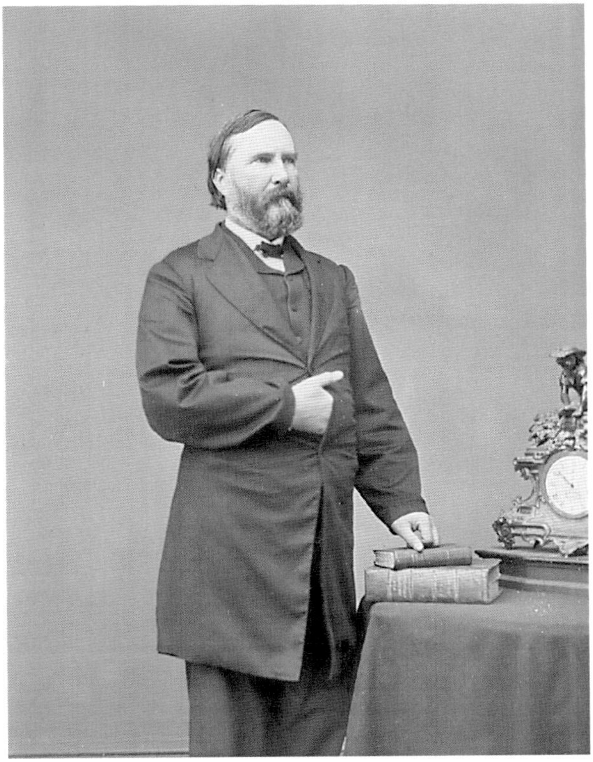

Gettysburg

Lt. Gen. James Longstreet (1821–1904) was Gen. Robert E. Lee's right-hand man throughout the Civil War. He was a major force in numerous Confederate victories in the early stages of the war. His conduct of the Battle of Gettysburg has been the subject of debate and controversy for over 100 years. After the war, Longstreet settled in New Orleans, working for the railroad industry, and serving as an officer of the Mobile and Ohio Railroad. (Courtesy NARA.)

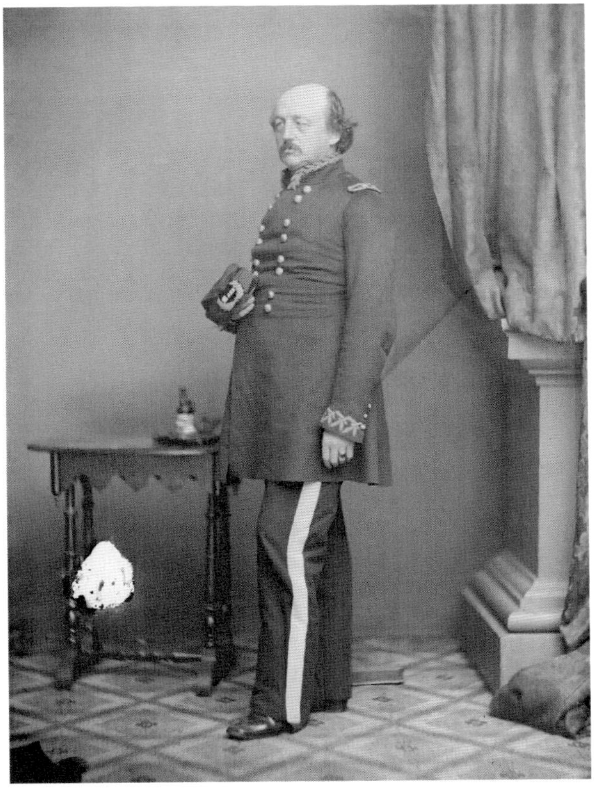

"Beast"

Benjamin Franklin Butler (1818–1893) was the military governor of New Orleans during the Civil War. The New Hampshire native is best known in New Orleans for his General Order No. 28, which declared that any woman insulting an officer or soldier of the United States could be treated as if she was a prostitute. Butler also ordered the execution of William B. Mumford for desecrating the US flag. Butler was nicknamed "Beast," or "Spoons," the latter originating from his proclivity to pocket dinner spoons from various households where he dined. While he was ruthless when dealing with opposition, Butler was a charitable man, giving thousands of dollars to widows of men who were lost in battle. (Courtesy NARA.)

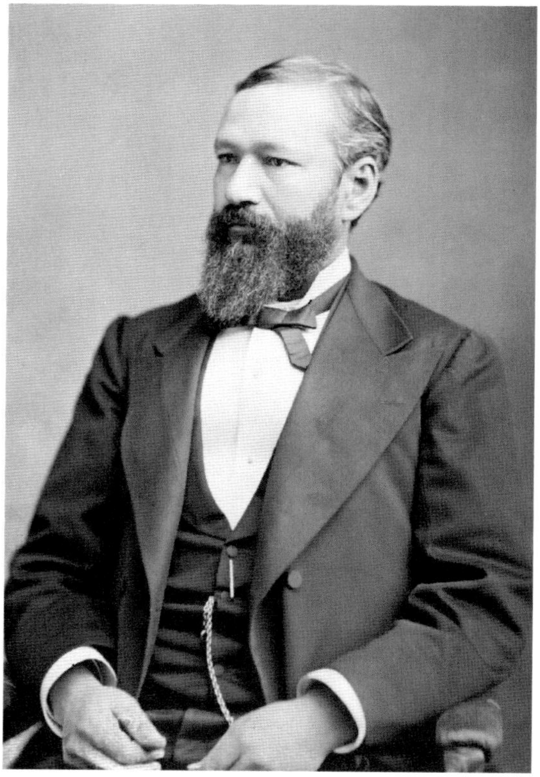

Governor

Pinckney Benton Stewart Pinchback (1837–1921) was the 24th governor of Louisiana and the first person of African American descent to hold the position in Louisiana or any state. After the start of the Civil War, Pinchback made his way to New Orleans and assisted with the growth of the Union's 1st Native Guards Regiment. He resigned from the Army in 1863. Living now in New Orleans with his family, Pinchback became active in the Republican/Reconstruction government. (Courtesy NARA.)

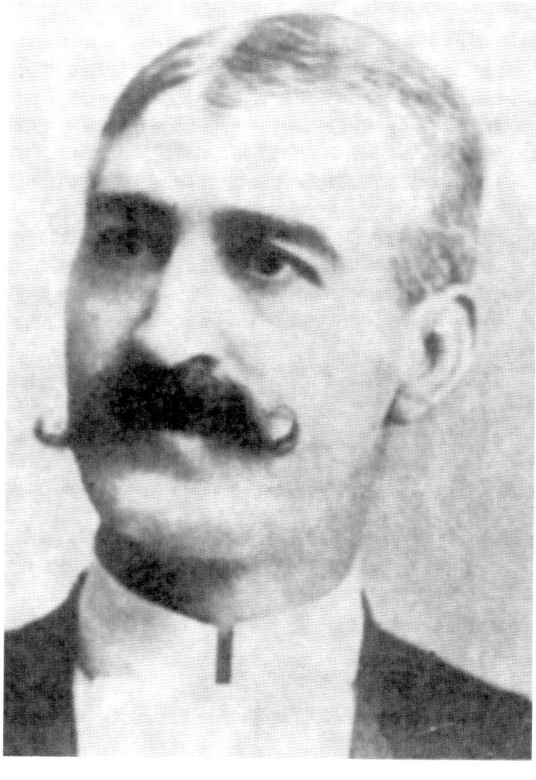

Cop

David Hennessy (1858–1890) was a native New Orleanian who joined the New Orleans Police Department as a bicycle messenger. An opponent of organized crime, he was assassinated in 1890. Sicilian newcomers to the city were suspected, leading to an ugly incident where several Italians were lynched in retaliation for Hennessy's killing. (Courtesy NOPL.)

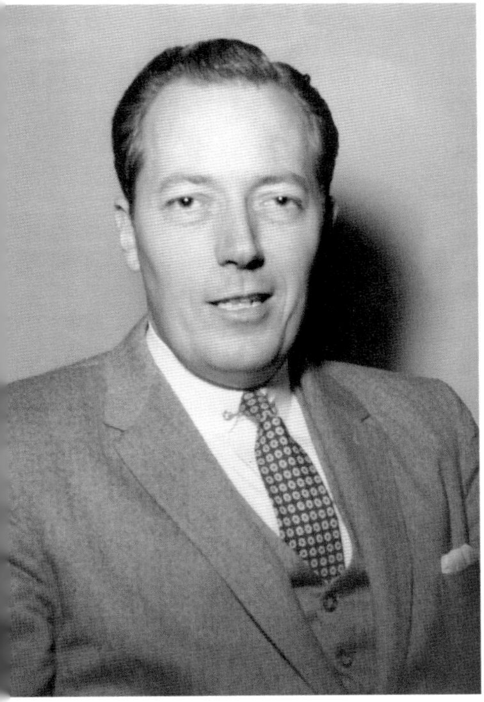

Conspiracy

Jim Garrison (1921–1992) was Orleans Parish district attorney from 1961 to 1978. He is best known for his 1966 investigation into the Kennedy assassination, during which Garrison subpoenaed the Zapruder film, enabling the public to see the amateur film of Kennedy's death for the first time. Garrison indicted businessman Clay Shaw. The case against Shaw was so lacking in evidence that a jury acquitted him in less than two hours. Garrison was defeated in 1978 by Harry Connick Sr., ran for a seat on the appeals court bench, and won. He held that job until the time of his death. Garrison's investigation and Shaw's trial were the focal points in Oliver Stone's film *JFK*. (Courtesy NOPL.)

Judge

Israel Augustine Jr. (1924–1994) was the first African American district judge in Louisiana. Judge Augustine graduated from McDonogh 35 High School, then Southern University, receiving his law degree from Lincoln University in St. Louis. In 1970, Augustine was elected to Criminal District Court, where he oversaw the Black Panther Trial that year. (Courtesy NOPL.)

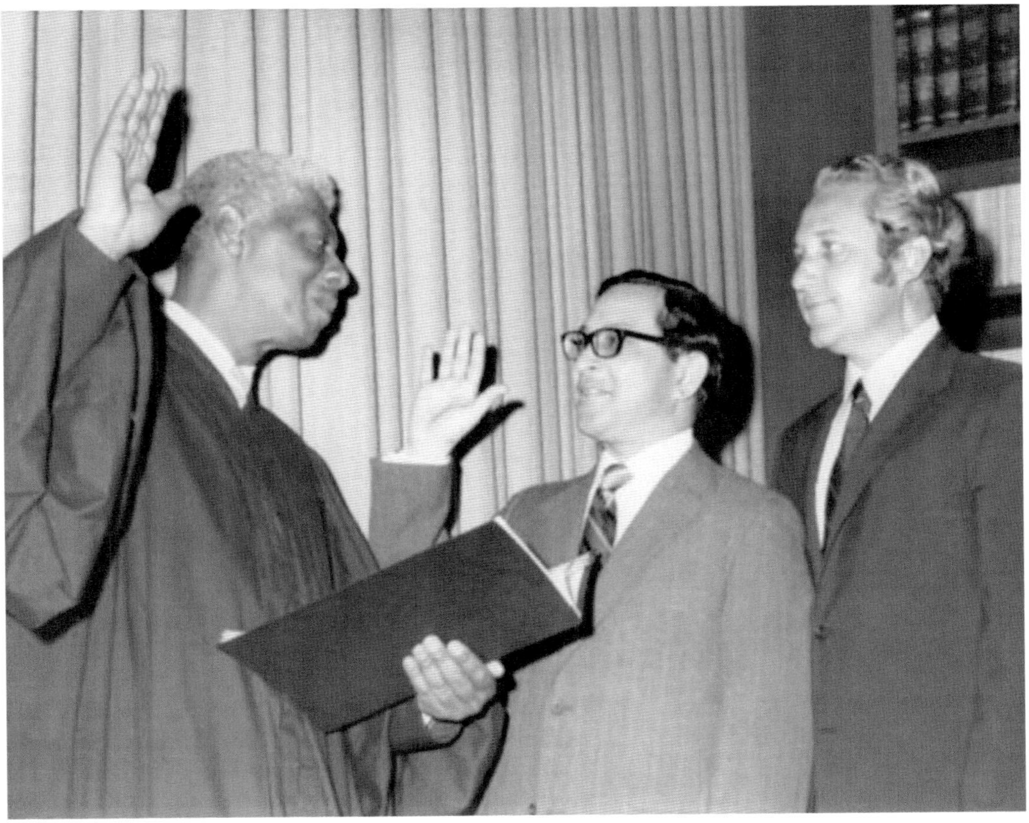

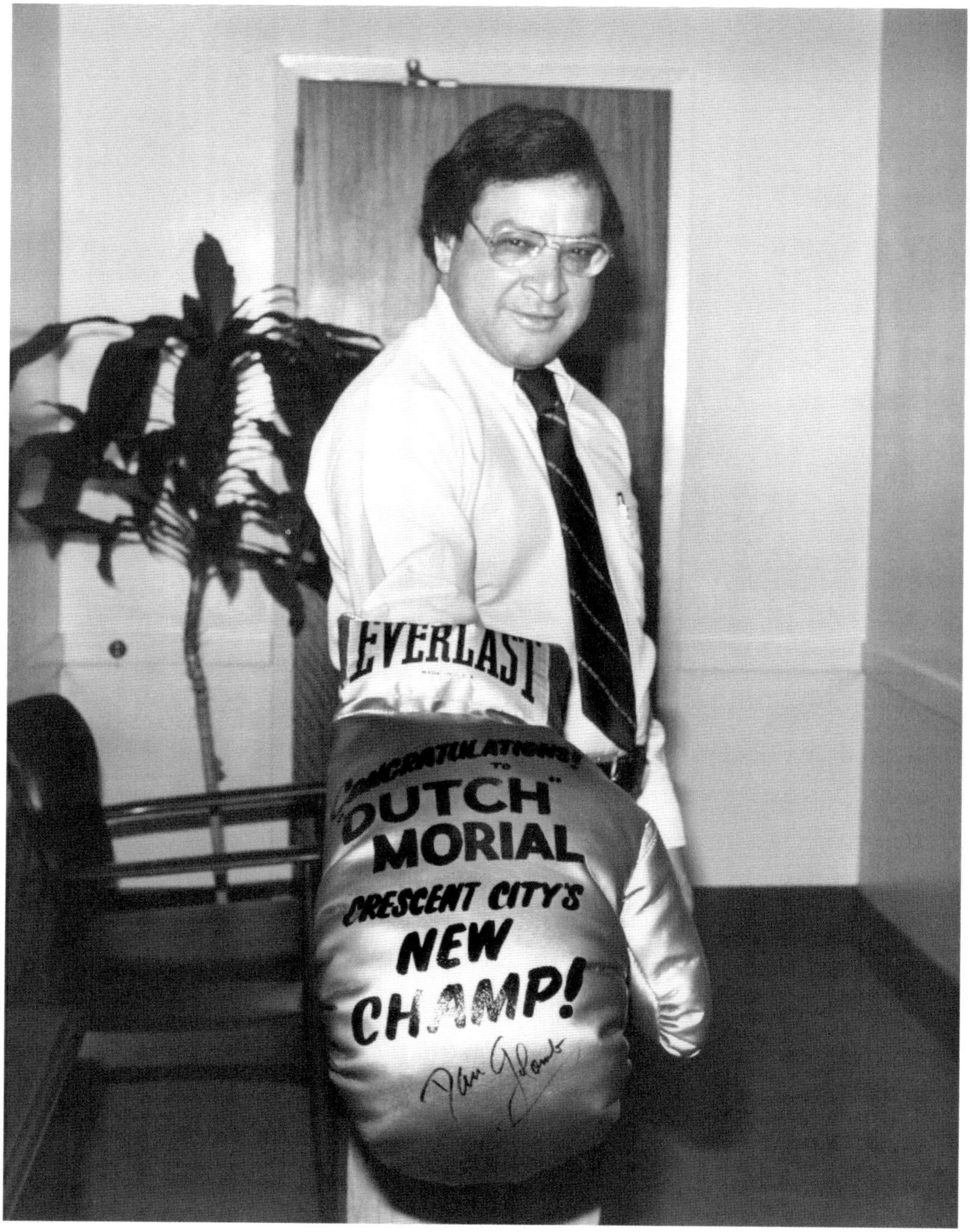

Dutch

Ernest N. "Dutch" Morial (1929–1989) was New Orleans's first black mayor. Dutch received his bachelor of science degree in 1951 from Xavier University and was the first African American to receive a law degree from Louisiana State University. As a lawyer, Morial worked extensively with A.P. Tureaud, his mentor, on a number of desegregation lawsuits. Morial became mayor in 1977 and was faced with a labor dispute with the police department that led to a strike. Morial canceled all of the Carnival parades for that season, a bold move backed by most of Carnival's leaders. (Courtesy NOPL.)

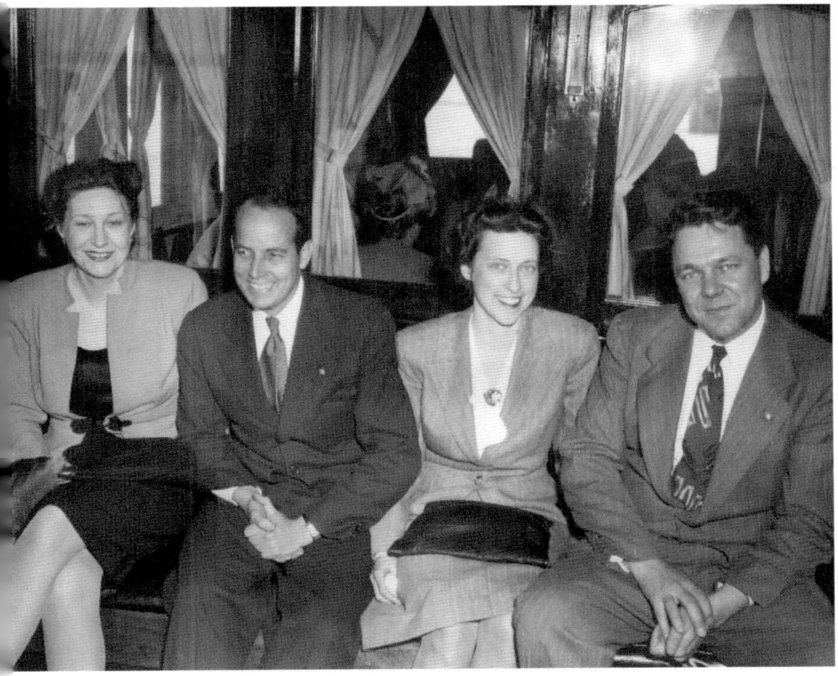

Whip

Hale Boggs, (1914–1972) became a political leader in the movement against Huey P. Long. He was first elected to Congress in 1941, but failed to win reelection. Boggs joined the US Navy and served for the remainder of the war. He returned to Congress in 1946, rising to the post of majority whip for the Democratic Party. He helped get such important legislation as the Civil Rights Act of 1964 and the Voting Rights Act of 1965 through for President Johnson. Boggs (far right, seated next to his wife, Lindy, and Mayor and Mrs. "Chep" Morrison) was traveling in Alaska in 1971 when the twin-engine plane carrying him and several others disappeared. He was declared dead in 1973. (Courtesy NOPL.)

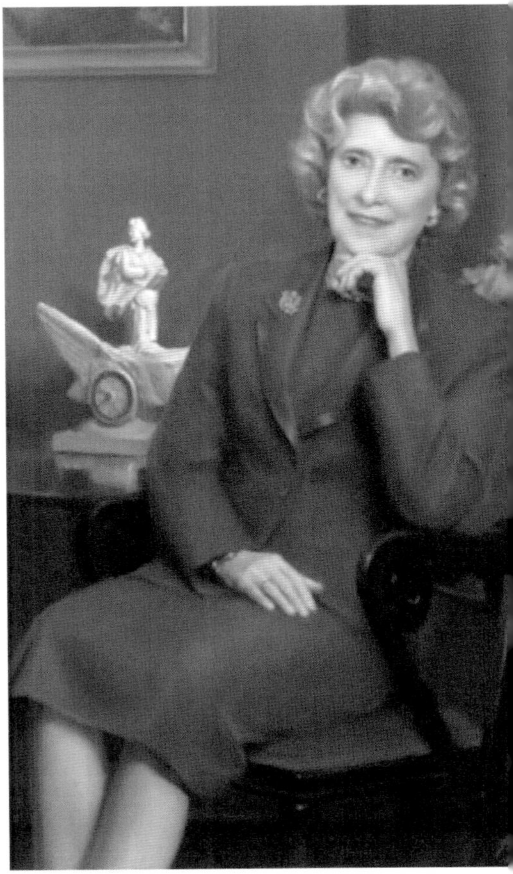

Ambassador

Lindy Boggs (born 1916) was appointed to fill the unexpired term of her husband, T. Hale Boggs, in 1973. She stood for election later that year and won a full term in another election in 1974. Lindy held until 1991, at which time she was appointed by President Clinton to be ambassador to the Holy See in 1991. (Courtesy US House of Representatives.)

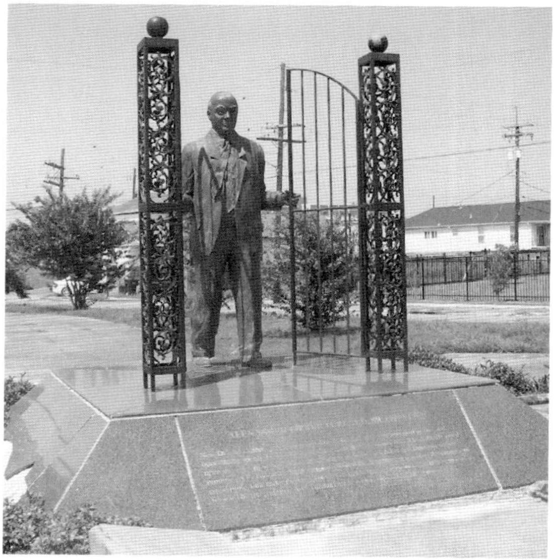

Advocate

A.P. Tureaud Sr. (1899–1972) was a civil rights leader and attorney. Tureaud opened his law office in 1926. He joined the NAACP's legal team in 1927 and fought discrimination with that organization for over 50 years. The only black lawyer in the state for years, Tureaud is listed on almost every significant antidiscrimination legal action in Louisiana. (Author's collection.)

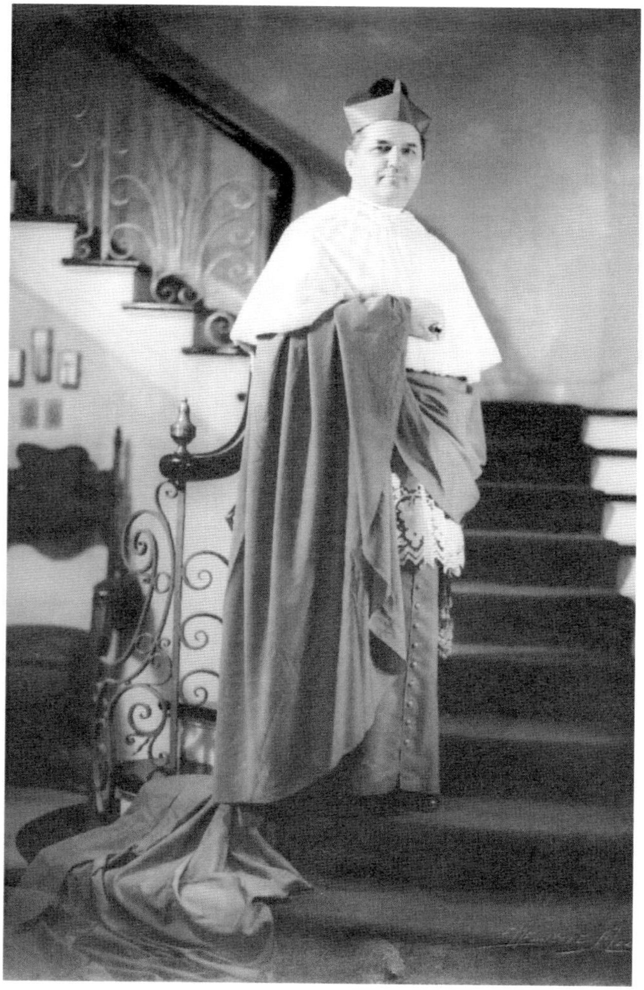

Progressive

Joseph Rummel (1876–1964) was born in Germany and came to the United States with his family when he was six. Answering the call to his vocation as a priest, Rummel was ordained in Rome in 1902. He returned to America and was assigned to the Archdiocese of New York. Rummel was named Bishop of Omaha in 1928, then archbishop of New Orleans in 1935. He presided over the desegregation of the archdiocese, admitting black men into Notre Dame Seminary in 1948. He then ordered segregated seating in Catholic churches abolished in 1951. He opened St. Augustine High School, a college-prep school for black boys, later that same year. In 1962, Rummel excommunicated Leander Perez of St. Bernard Parish, a judge and de facto "boss" of the parish. Perez and two others were excommunicated for defying Rummel's authority on the issue of segregation. He died in 1964, and Archbishop Rummel High School in suburban Metairie is named in his honor. (Courtesy NOPL.)

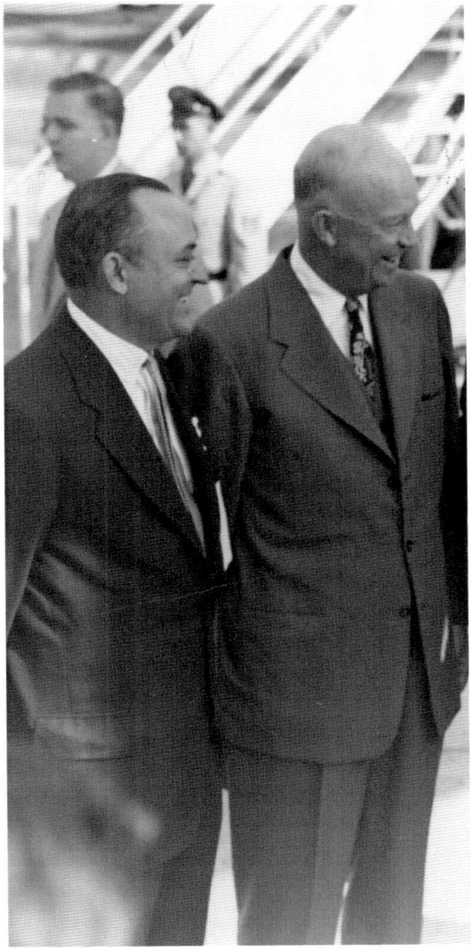

Liberal

John Minor Wisdom (1905–1999) was born in New Orleans, attended Isidore Newman School, and received his law degree from Tulane University. Active in politics as an attorney from 1938 to 1957, Wisdom played a significant role in the election of President Eisenhower. Ike (standing to the right of Judge Wisdom in the photograph at left) nominated Wisdom as judge, US Court of Appeals for the Fifth Circuit, in 1957. He was one of the "Fifth Circuit Four" responsible for many decisions relating to civil rights of African Americans. President Clinton awarded Judge Wisdom the Presidential Medal of Freedom. (Courtesy NARA.)

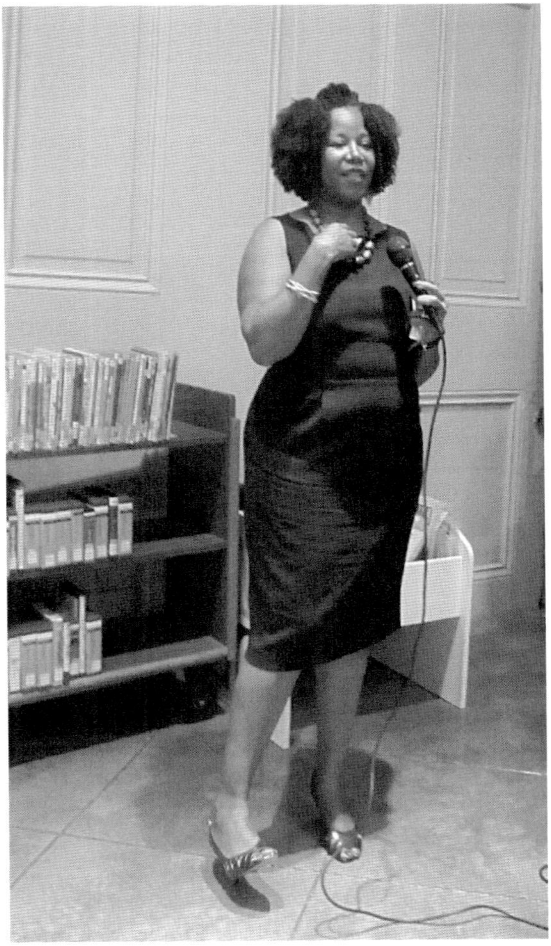

Courage

Ruby Nell Bridges Hall (born 1954) was the first African American child to attend an all-white elementary school in the south. Her first day of school at William Frantz Elementary in New Orleans was November 14, 1960, and was commemorated by Norman Rockwell. In Rockwell's painting "The Problem We All Live With," Ruby is shown being escorted to class by US marshals sent to New Orleans by President Eisenhower. Bridges married Malcolm Hall, and the couple has four sons, and still lives in New Orleans. (Courtesy Carlos "Froggy" May.)

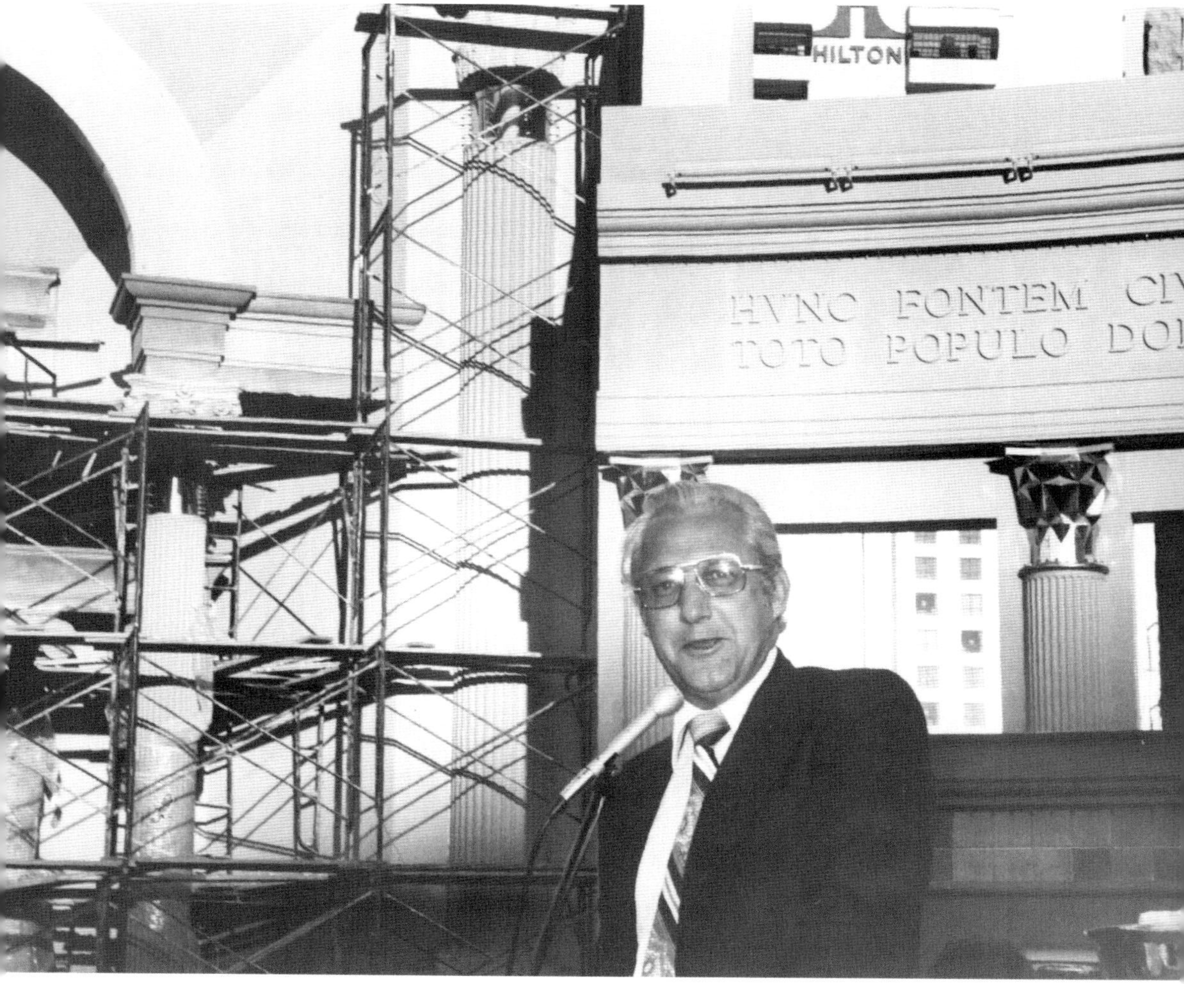

Current Leadership

Along with the Morials, the other single most influential family in New Orleans politics has been the Landrieus. Maurice "Moon" Landrieu (born 1930) served in the Louisiana House of Representatives for six years, from 1960 to 1966, on the New Orleans City Council from 1966 to 1970. He defeated Lt. Gov. Jimmy Fitzmorris in 1970 to become mayor. He served for two terms and was appointed by Pres. Jimmy Carter as secretary of housing and urban development. Moon (above, posing in Piazza d'Italia in 1975) was elected to the Louisiana Fourth Circuit Court of Appeals in 1992 and served as a judge until his retirement in 2000. After attending LSU and working as a real estate agent, Moon's daughter Mary Landrieu (born 1955) served in the state legislature from 1980 to 1988, then as state treasurer from 1988 to 1996. After losing in the 2005 race for governor, Mary (opposite page, top, speaking to a reporter in 2011) was elected to the US Senate in 1996, winning reelection in 2002 and 2006. Mary's brother Mitch Landrieu (born 1960) also began his political career in legislature, winning election to the Louisiana House of Representatives in 1987. He held the same seat as his sister and father for 16 years. While a legislator, he ran for mayor in 1994, losing to Marc Morial, the son of Ernest "Dutch" Morial, the city's first black mayor. Mitch (opposite page, bottom, speaking in 2011) ran for lieutenant governor of Louisiana in 2003. He ran again for mayor in 2006, losing to incumbent C. Ray Nagin. With Nagin out of the race in 2010 because of term limits, Mitch made one more attempt at running for mayor and was elected with 67 percent of the vote, a huge mandate. (All, courtesy NOPL.)

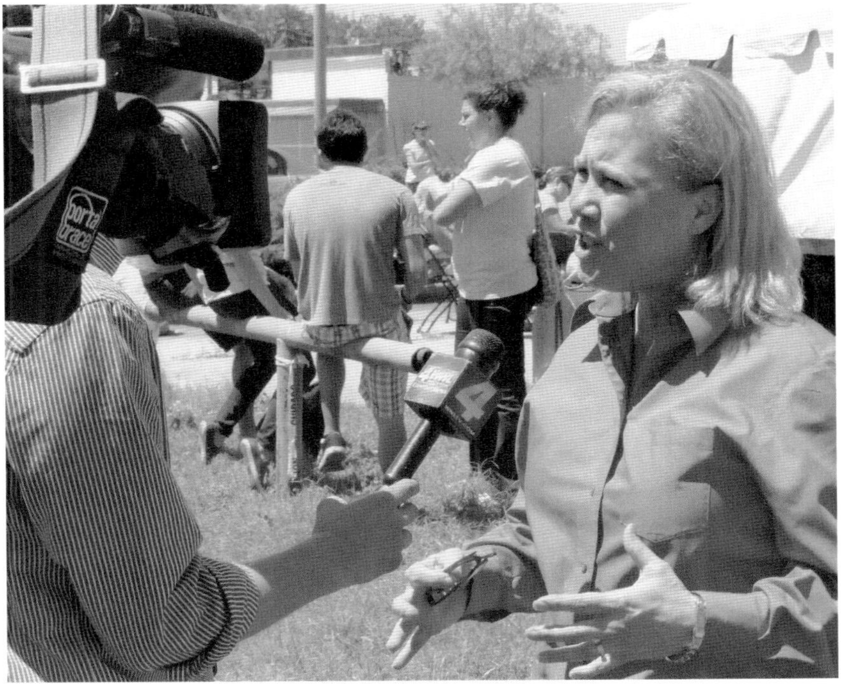

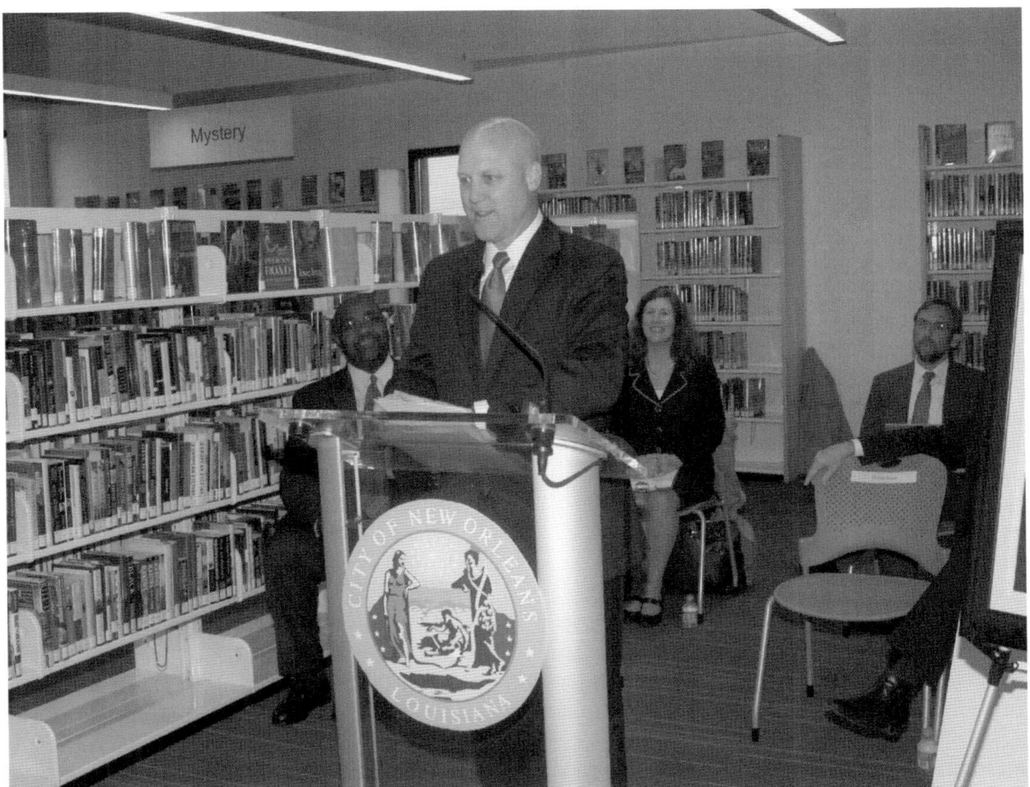
Mystery
CITY OF NEW ORLEANS
LOUISIANA

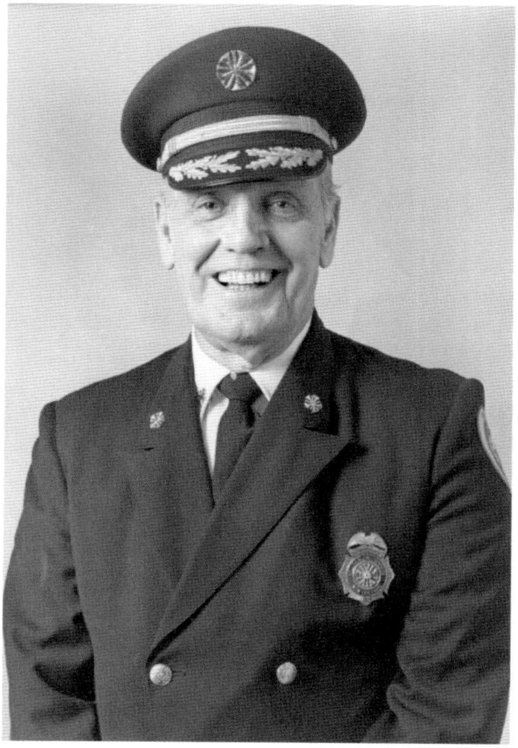

Chief
William McCrossen (1914–2004) served 51 years with the New Orleans Fire Department. McCrossen was three years old when his father died. Living in the Irish Channel in New Orleans, he had to drop out of eighth grade to get a job as an errand runner to help support the family. Working as a laborer, McCrossen developed the political connections to get a job with the fire department. He joined the department in 1942, at the age of 28. With the exception of two tours as a Navy Seabee in World War II, McCrossen served NOFD for 51 years, almost 20 of which as the department's superintendent. (Courtesy NOPL.)

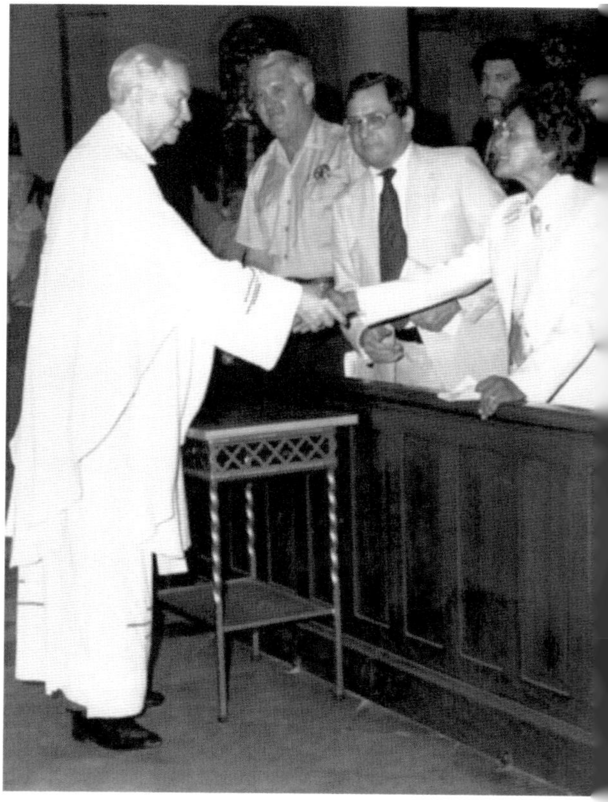

Airborne
Phillip Matthew Hannan (1913–2011) succeeded John Patrick Cody as archbishop of New Orleans, upon Cody's 1965 appointment as archbishop of Chicago. Hannan was ordained in 1939 in Rome, making him a witness to the rise of fascism and developments in Germany. He returned to the United States in 1940. Father Hannan was commissioned in the US Army and assigned as a chaplain in the 82nd Airborne Division. He dropped with the 82nd on D-Day and was with them during the Battle of the Bulge. After the war, Hannan was assigned as a parish priest in Washington, DC, being named a monsignor by Pope Pius XII in 1952, then as auxiliary bishop of Washington in 1956. Hannan was appointed archbishop of New Orleans in 1965, serving until his 75th birthday in 1988. (Courtesy NOPL.)

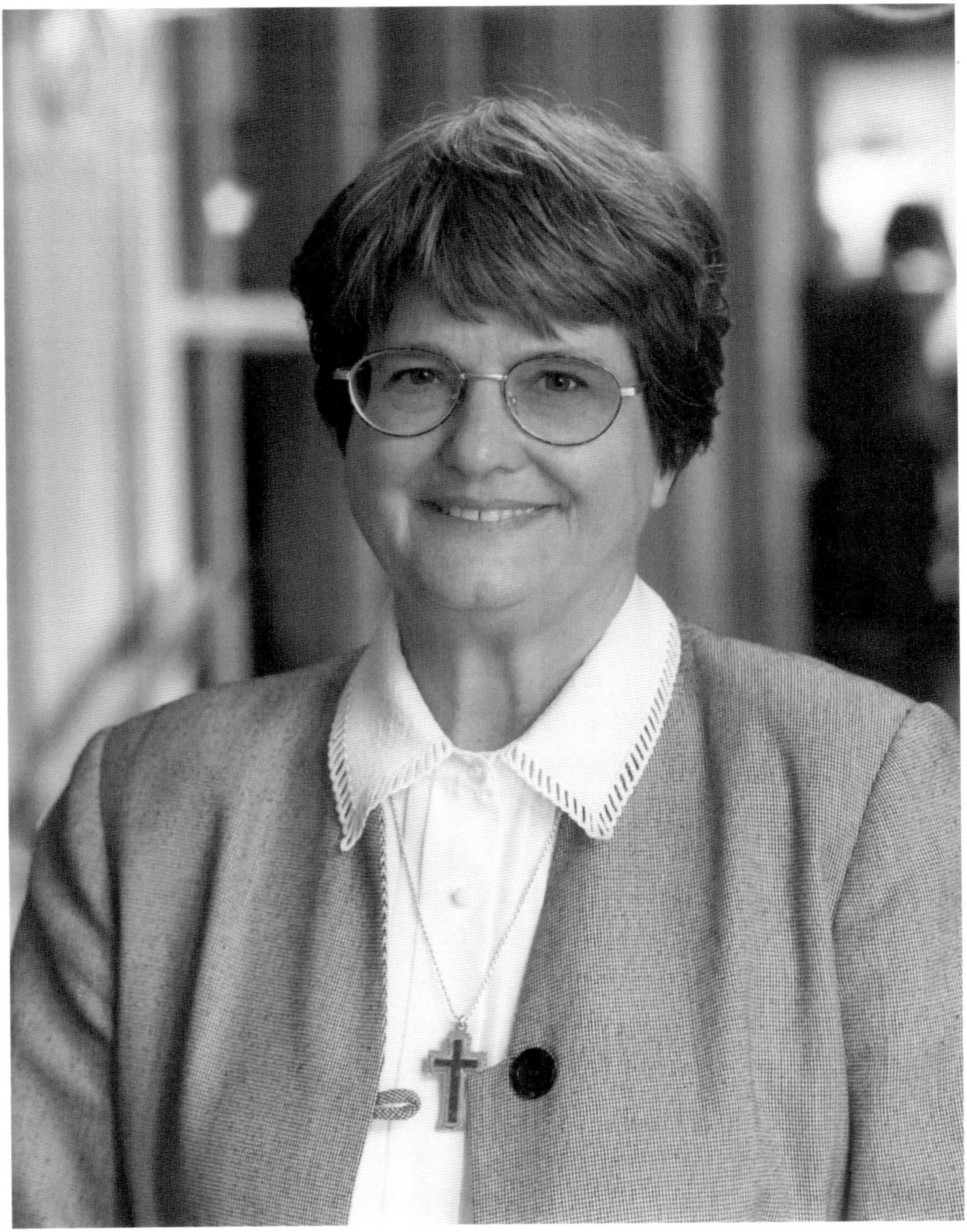

Compassion
Sr. Helen Prejean, CSJ (born 1939), is a Catholic nun and member of the Congregation of St. Joseph. After engaging in postal correspondence in 1982 with condemned murderer Elmo Patrick Sonnier, Sister Prejean agreed to be Sonnier's spiritual advisor. Since then, she has been a tireless advocate for those on death row, and for the abolition of capital punishment. She continues to write and speak as part of the Death Penalty Discourse Network, based in New Orleans. (Courtesy Sister Helen Prejean.)

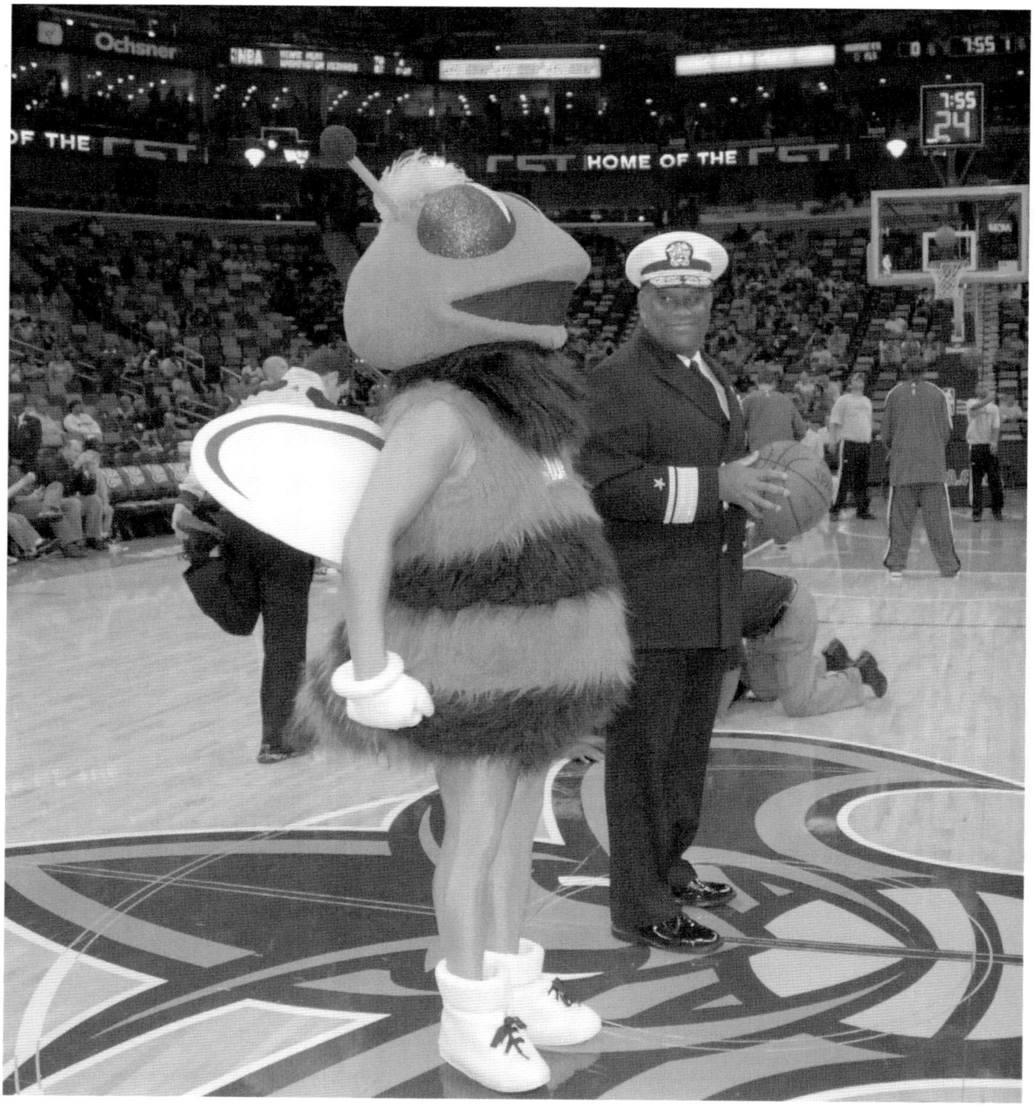

Sailor

Victor Guillory (born 1956) graduated from the US Naval Academy in 1978. After several junior-officer and department-head tours, Guillory was the commissioning executive officer of USS *Gettysburg* (CG64). He was skipper of the frigate USS *Underwood* and the cruiser USS *Lake Champlain*. He became a flag officer in 2004 and was in command of US Naval Forces Southern Command/US Fourth Fleet when the earthquake hit the island of Haiti in January 2010. Fourth Fleet provided approximately 15,000 sailors and Marines, led by Rear Adm. Guillory. Guillory (above, standing next to the mascot of the New Orleans Hornets at a game in 2009) retired from the Navy in 2011. (Courtesy Department of the Navy.)

Prelate

Gregory Michael Aymond was born in Gentilly, attended Cor Jesu High School, and was ordained to the priesthood in 1975. He served as a teacher and later as rector of St. John Vianney Preparatory Seminary in New Orleans. In 1981, he was named to the faculty of Notre Dame Seminary, serving as president-rector from 1986 to 2000. He was named bishop of Austin in 2000, then archbishop of New Orleans in 2009. Aymond continues the archdiocese's work to rebuild and recover in the wake of Hurricane Katrina, while at the same time working to reestablish the credibility of the archdiocese (and the Church as a whole) in the wake of clergy sex-abuse scandals. (Courtesy Brother Martin High School.)

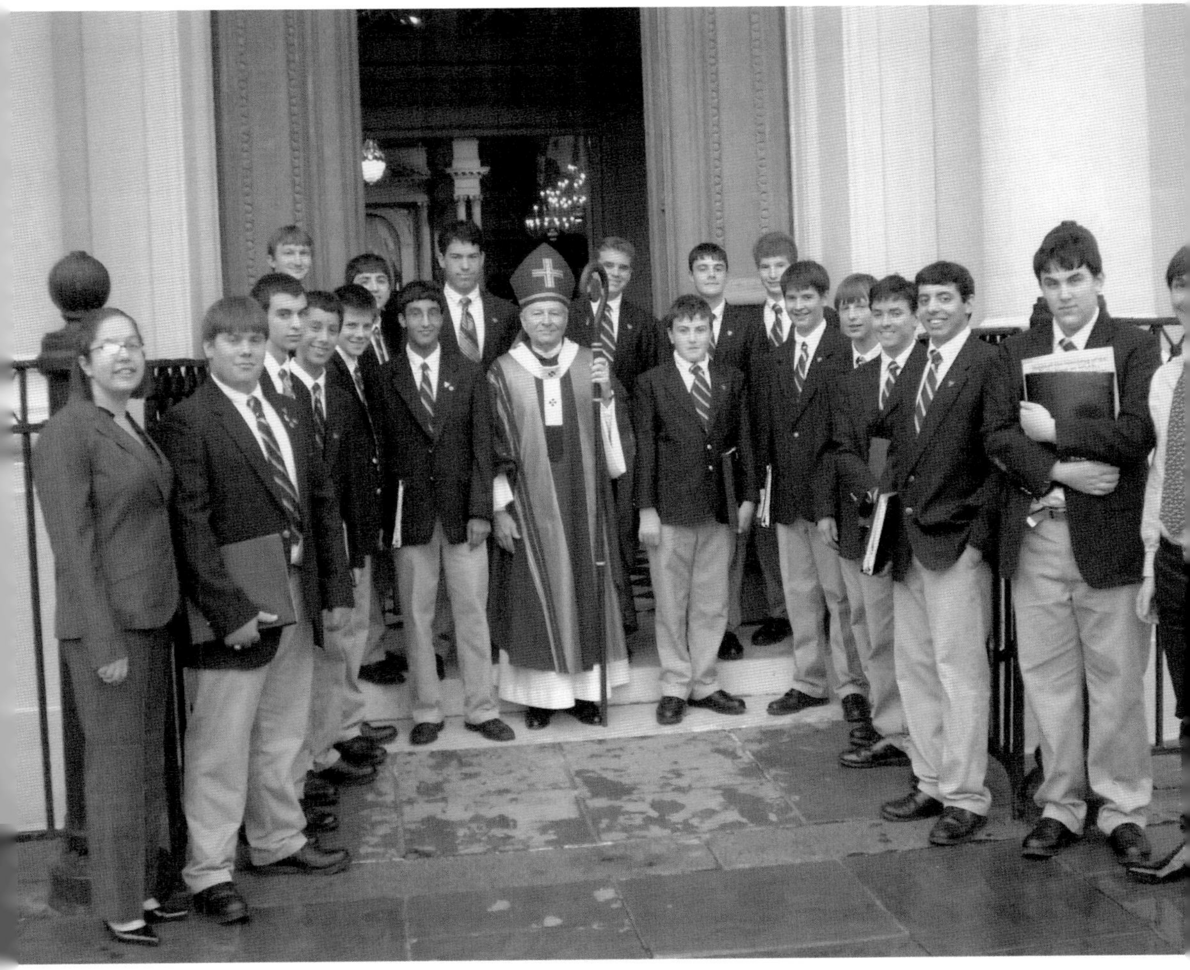

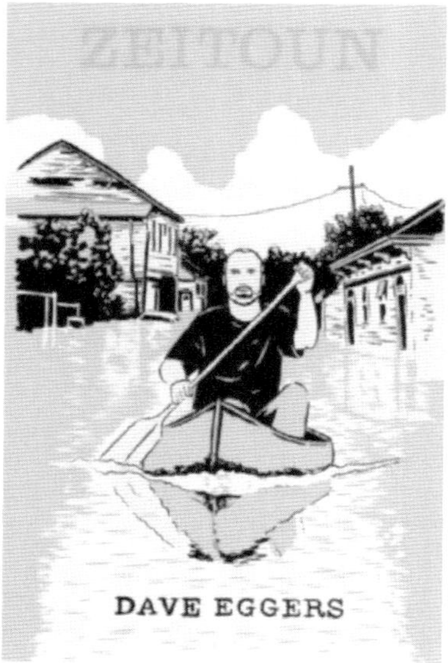

Rescuer

Abdulrahman Zeitoun (born 1957) stayed behind as he sent his wife and four children to Baton Rouge to ride out Hurricane Katrina. After the storm passed, Zeitoun ventured out into the flooded streets of the city in a canoe. He brought supplies with him, helping out where he could. Zeitoun was arrested by members of the New Orleans Police Department on September 14, 2005, and was held for over three weeks in prison. His story is told by Dave Eggers in the book *Zeitoun*, which is being made into a movie, set for release in 2014. Zeitoun's story is one of a local hero and a cautionary tale of police abuse. (Courtesy Dave Eggers.)

Guardsmen

In September 2005, in the aftermath of Hurricane Katrina, members of the Army National Guard descended upon New Orleans, offering aid and assistance to the flooded city. Providing medical aid (shown here), rescue assistance, and security patrols to prevent looting, this group of brave men and women kept it together, helping locals pull the city back up as the waters drained from the streets. Most of those soldiers and rescue workers left New Orleans once their immediate jobs were done, but the city's recovery would not have been as successful as it has been without them. (Courtesy US Navy.)

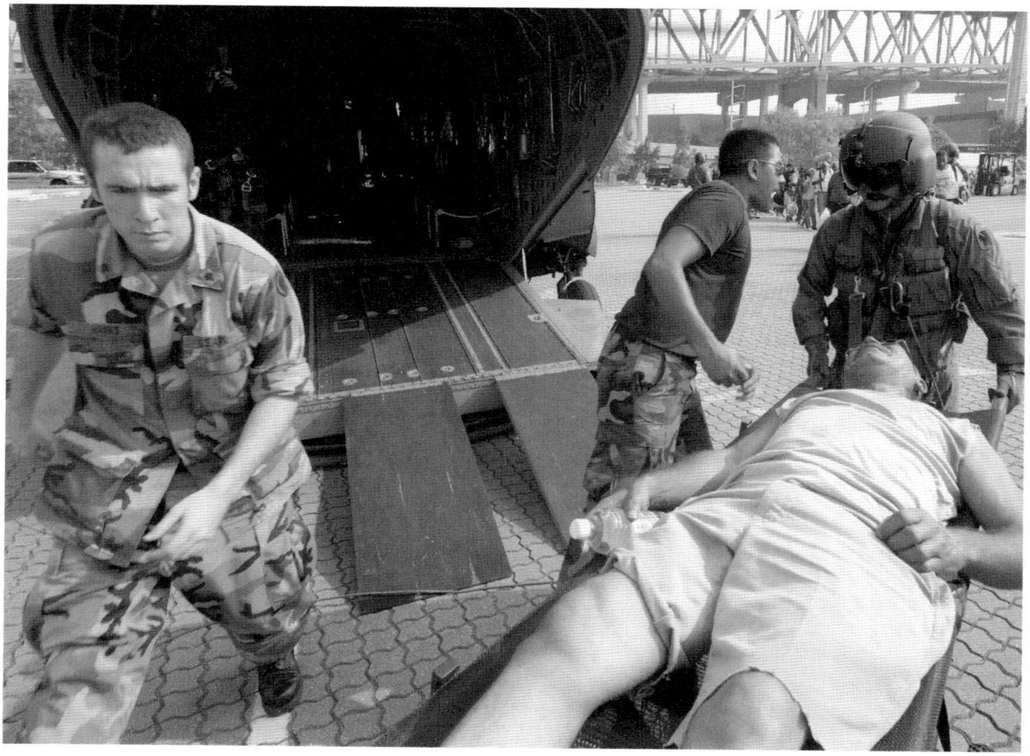

CHAPTER FIVE

Academia, Media, Arts, and Literature

New Orleans has long been a college town. The city's Catholic roots are strong here, with orders of priests, nuns, and brothers ministering to the educational needs of the city since the Ursulines arrived in the early days of the colony: the Jesuits, the Holy Cross Fathers, School Sisters of Notre Dame, Dominicans, Brothers of the Sacred Heart, and the list goes on. In addition to the Catholic commitment to education, others took up the academic torch at Tulane, the University of New Orleans, and the many elementary and secondary schools across the metro area.

New Orleans has always been linguistically diverse and full of unique accents, from the mixture of French, Spanish, and African that make up the city's Creole population to the Yats of the turn of the century. Chroniclers of the city over time include its newspaper writers, television and radio reporters, and the social media community of today.

Southern Louisiana has offered much to the visual artist, from birds in their natural habitat, to women in brothels, to still-life settings. Action in and around the city and the port feeds the imagination of the painter and sculptor alike, and some of the end products of those bursts of imagination have become priceless masterpieces. There are those who will argue that a plate of Chicken Rochambeau is just as artistic as an oil-based painting on canvas, but the chicken is gone in an hour. The blending of thoughts and words with food and images offers opportunities for so many kinds of works. The novel leads to a sculpture of the main character, which leads to a dramatization based on what the author did not say in his book. Speculation and spirituality come together in ways impossible to duplicate in other parts of the country.

Historian
Charles Etienne Arthur Gayarre (1805–1895) was the grandson of Étienne de Boré, the first mayor of New Orleans and a sugar planter. Gayarre studied law and held political office, but he is best known for *The History of Louisiana*, published in 1846. (Courtesy NOPL.)

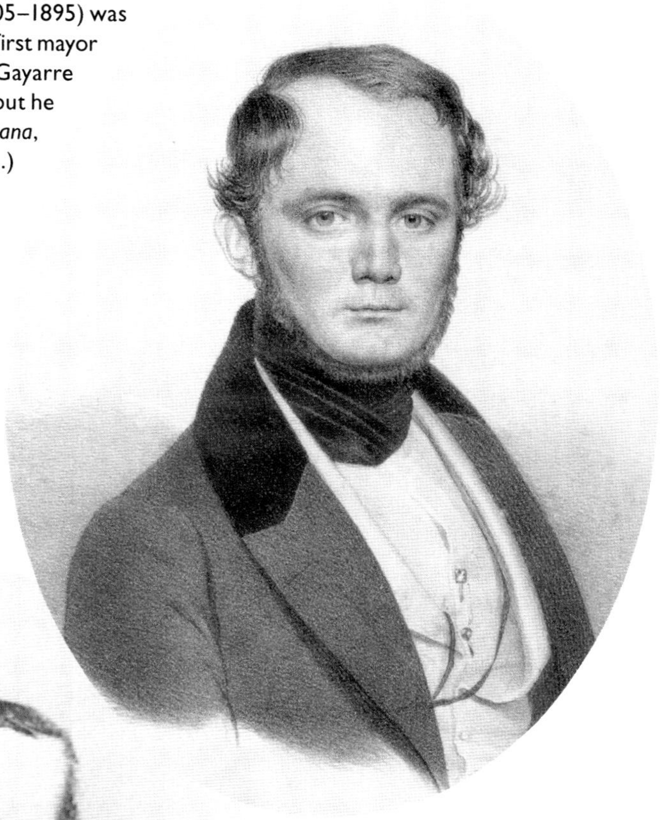

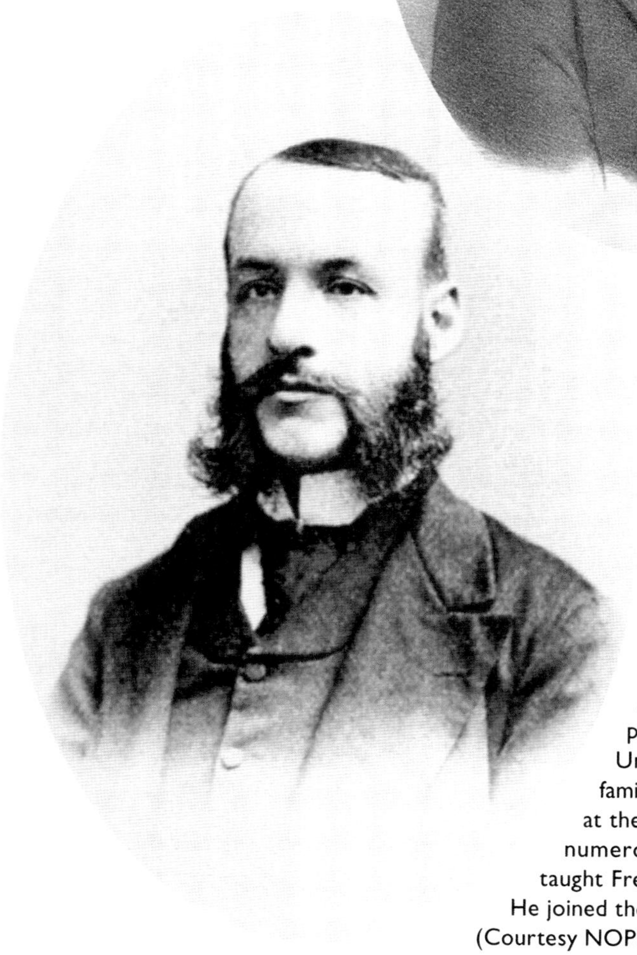

Linguist
Alcee Fortier (1856–1914) was a professor of languages at Tulane University. A descendant of the Aimé family of sugar cane planters, Fortier studied at the University of Virginia. Fortier wrote numerous books on French literature and taught French in the public schools of the city. He joined the faculty of Tulane University in 1880. (Courtesy NOPL.)

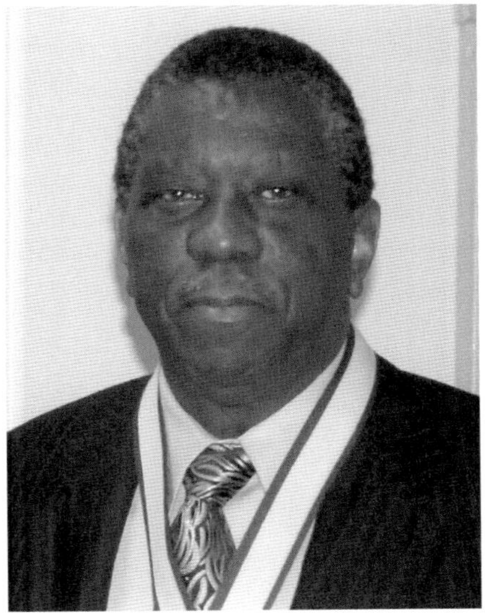

True Teacher
Raphael Cassimere Jr. (born 1942) graduated from Joseph S. Clark Senior High then attended LSUNO (now the University of New Orleans), receiving bachelor of arts and master of arts degrees in history. He earned a doctorate in history from Lehigh University in 1971 and joined the faculty at LSUNO that same year. The Seraphia D. Leyda University Teaching Professor Emeritus, he was named one of the university's all-time most popular teachers in 2005. He has worked with the NAACP in various capacities since 1971 and, in 1982, received the A.P. Tureaud Black Citizenship Medal, the highest award conferred by the NAACP in Louisiana. (Courtesy NOPL.)

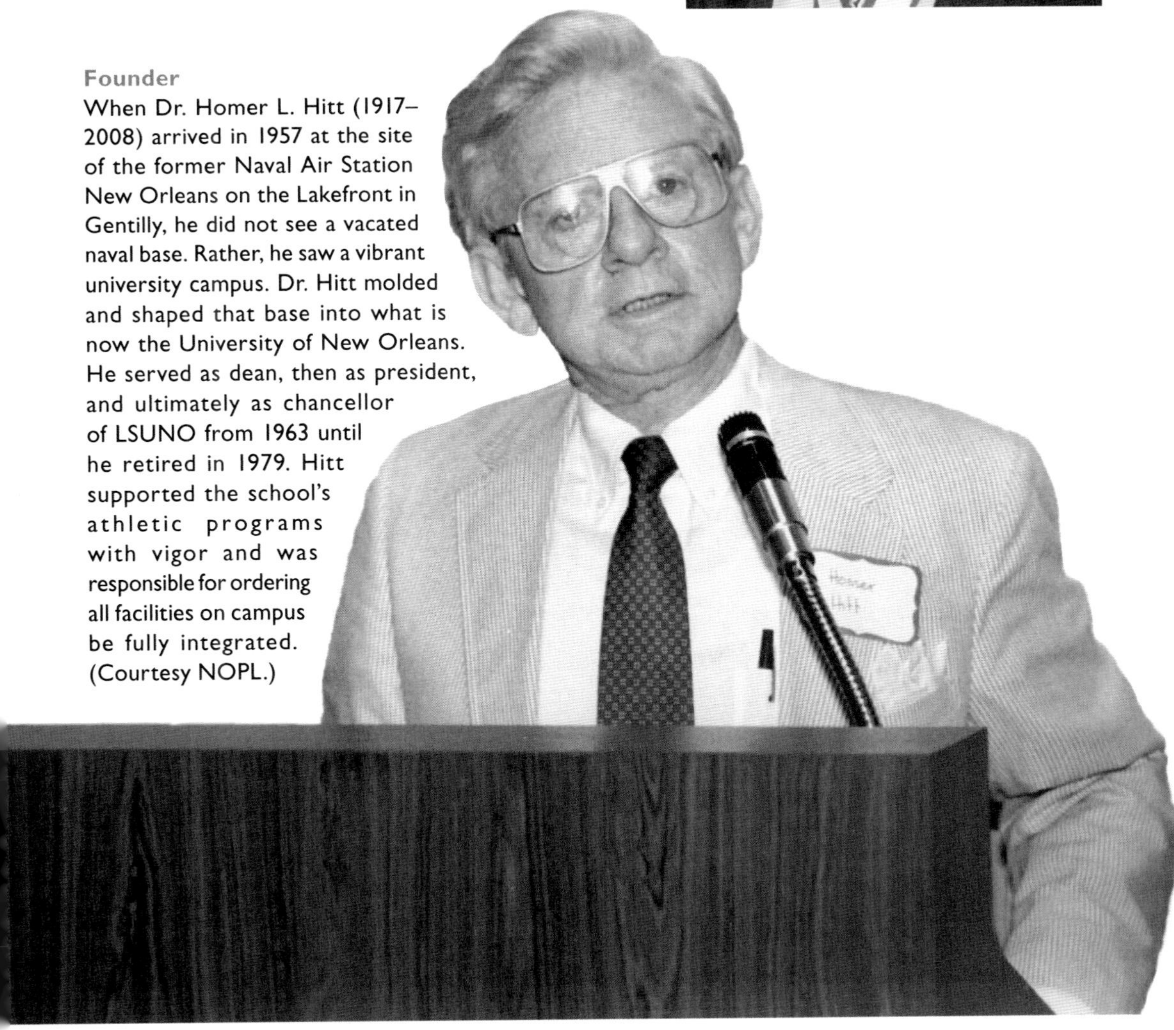

Founder
When Dr. Homer L. Hitt (1917–2008) arrived in 1957 at the site of the former Naval Air Station New Orleans on the Lakefront in Gentilly, he did not see a vacated naval base. Rather, he saw a vibrant university campus. Dr. Hitt molded and shaped that base into what is now the University of New Orleans. He served as dean, then as president, and ultimately as chancellor of LSUNO from 1963 until he retired in 1979. Hitt supported the school's athletic programs with vigor and was responsible for ordering all facilities on campus be fully integrated. (Courtesy NOPL.)

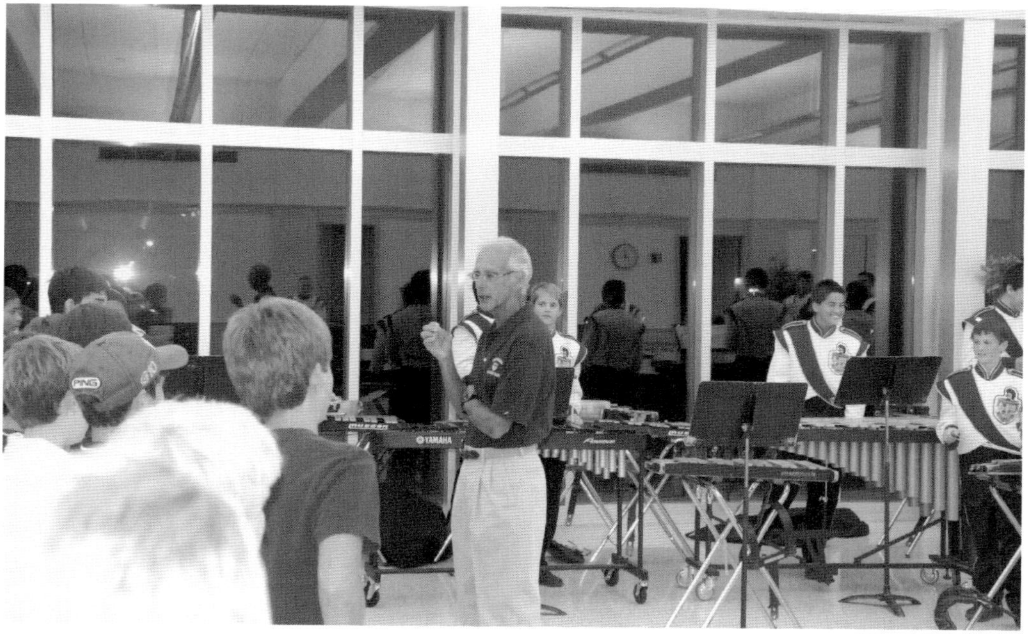

Phantom

Marty Hurley (1946–2011) joined the faculty of Brother Martin High School in 1974, as codirector (with Arthur Hardy) of the school's band program. Hurley took sole control of the school's band when Hardy left in 1989 to pursue his *Mardi Gras Guide*. A percussionist and arranger, he was widely regarded as an expert on marching band skills and techniques. A veteran of the US Air Force, Hurley was originally from New Jersey, but being stationed at Keesler Air Force Base in Biloxi, Mississippi, put him close enough to New Orleans to fall in love with the city. Hurley's drum cadences are used by dozens of high school and college bands across the country. (Courtesy Brother Martin High School.)

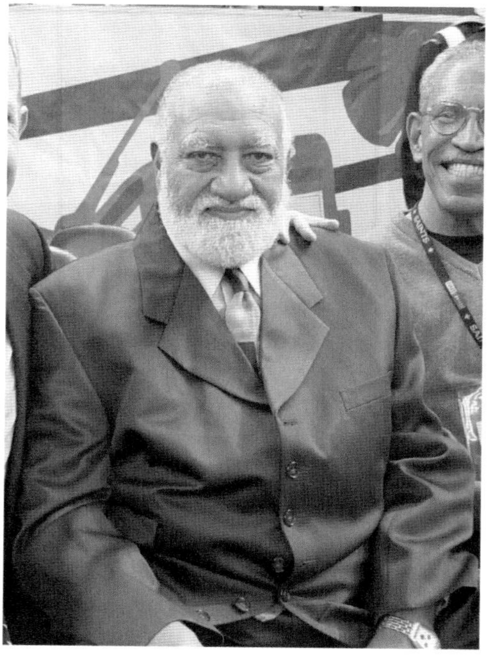

Mentor

Edwin Hampton (1928–2009) joined the faculty of St. Augustine High School, a Catholic school for African American males, in 1952. He formed the band shortly after getting settled at the school. The band program grew, and became known as the "Marching 100." The band's color guard carries banners proclaiming their performances in both the Tournament of Roses and Macy's Thanksgiving Day parades. The high-stepping style of the Purple Knights makes them one of the most popular bands during both football and Carnival seasons. (Courtesy People's Health Network.)

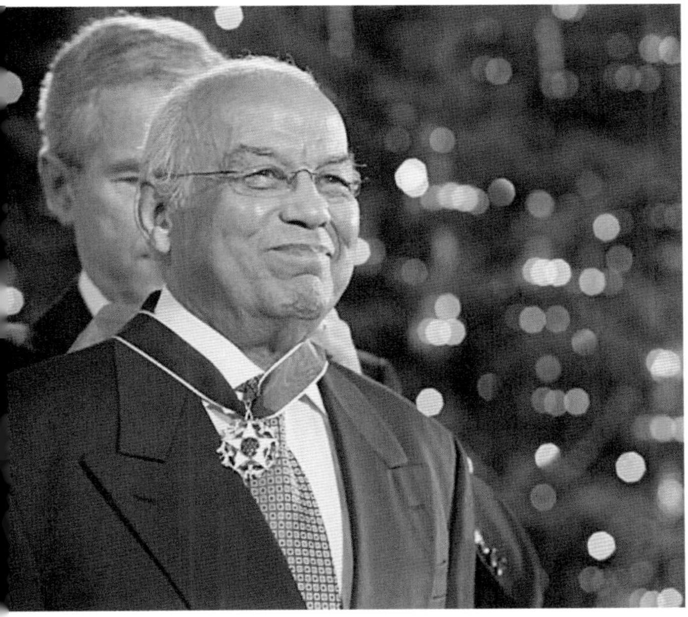

Role Model
Norman Francis (born 1931) was one of the first African Americans to integrate Loyola Law School in New Orleans. A graduate of Xavier University of New Orleans, Francis joined the Army after receiving his law degree, then returned to Xavier as dean of men in 1957. Active in the civil rights movement, Dr. Francis was appointed to several administrative posts at Xavier, eventually becoming president in 1968. He was awarded the Presidential Medal of Freedom. (Courtesy The White House.)

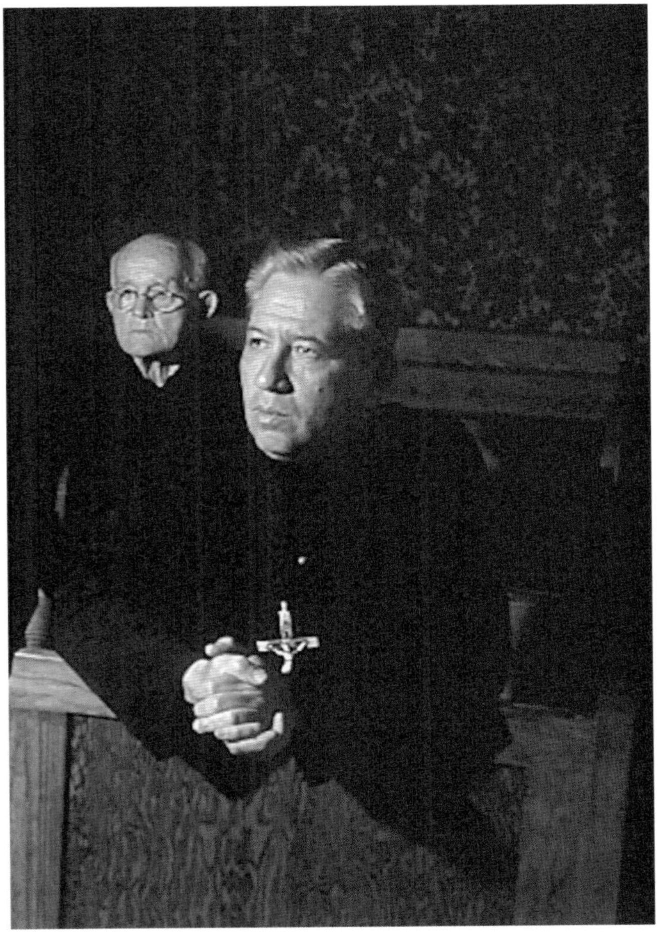

Principal/Provincial
Brother Martin Hernandez, S.C., was assigned by the Brothers of the Sacred Heart as a teacher at St. Aloysius College in 1935. Brother Martin became principal in 1939, guiding the school through World War II. He took over as provincial for the United States in 1949, overseeing the expansion of the institute's educational mission with the addition of three high schools: one in New Orleans, one in New York, and Catholic High in Baton Rouge. In 1968, when it was clear that the St. Aloysius High campus was no longer a viable site, Brother Martin helped guide the process and smooth over the closure of the century-old school while transferring its traditions to the Gentilly campus of Cor Jesu High. The brothers recognized Brother Martin's role in the formation of the new school and named the combined school in his honor. (Courtesy Brother Martin High School.)

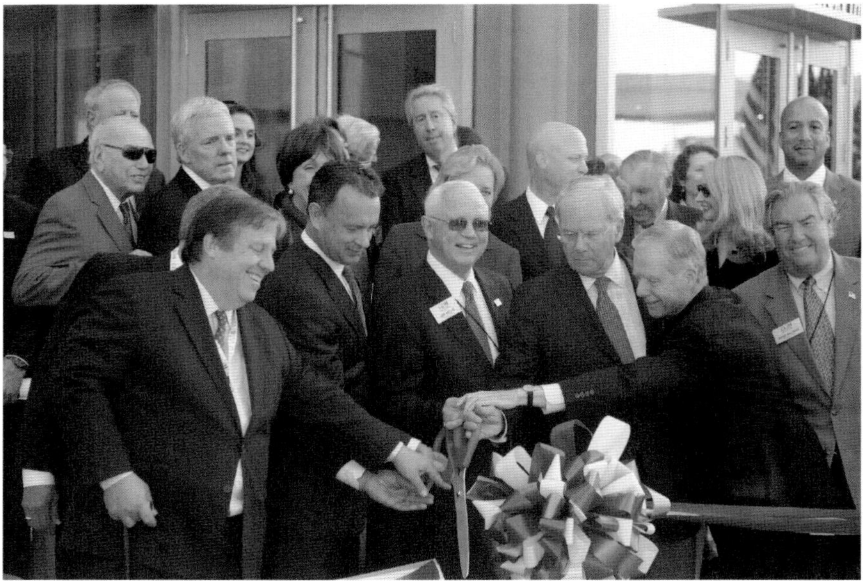

Victory

Gordon H. "Nick" Mueller (center, seen with other dignitaries at the opening of the Solomon Victory Theater) retired in 2002 from the University of New Orleans, where he enjoyed a 34-year career as professor of European diplomatic history, dean, vice chancellor of extension, and president of the UNO Research and Technology Park. He is currently president and chief executive officer of the National World War II Museum. He has overseen the growth of the museum from its origins as the D-Day Museum to its current configuration. (Above, courtesy US Navy; below, courtesy Carlos "Froggy" May.)

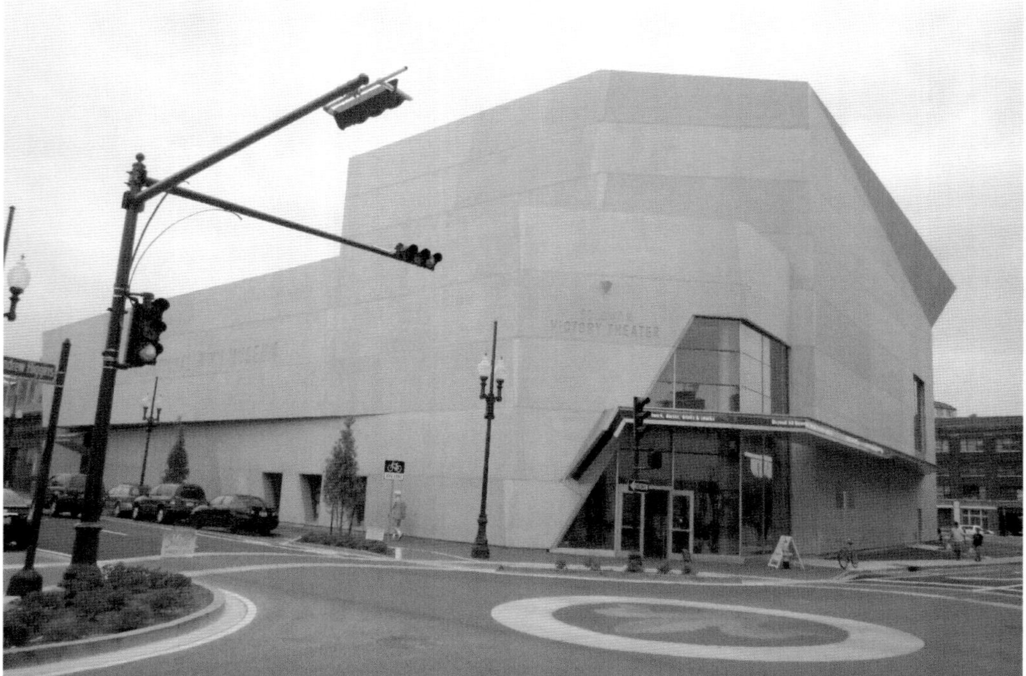

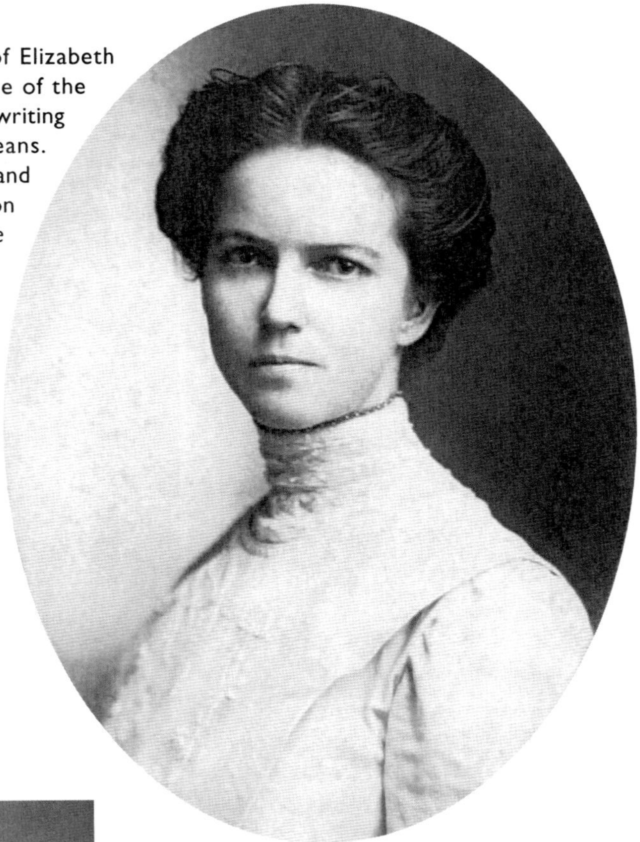

Advice

Dorothy Dix was the pseudonym of Elizabeth Meriwether Gilmer (1861–1951), one of the country's original advice columnists, writing for the *Daily Picayune* in New Orleans. She received nationwide recognition and popularity when she signed a syndication deal with the *Public Ledger Syndicate* (Philadelphia) in 1923. At the peak of her popularity, Dix had a readership of over 60 million people and received 100,000 letters a year. (Courtesy LOC.)

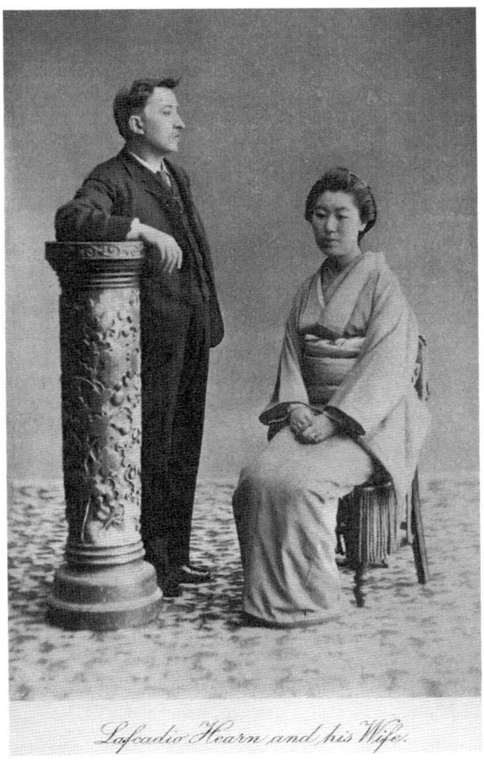

Ohio

Lafcadio Hearn (1850–1904) lived in New Orleans for 10 years, from 1877 to 1887, writing on a wide range of topics, including history, lifestyle, cooking, and family anecdotes. Hearn, who was an international writer for magazines such as *Harper's*, was once quoted as saying about New Orleans, "Times are not good here. The city is crumbling into ashes. It has been buried under taxes and frauds and maladministrations so that it has become a study for archaeologists . . . but it is better to live here in sackcloth and ashes than to own the whole state of Ohio." (Courtesy LOC.)

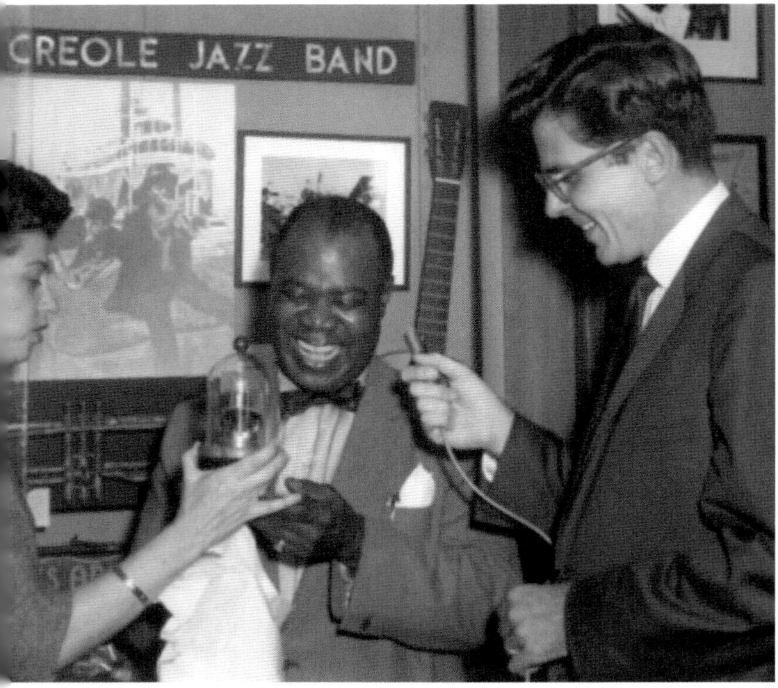

Broadcaster

Mel Leavitt was born in St. Louis, Missouri, where he wrote for the *St. Louis Globe-Democrat*. He entered broadcasting after a stint in the US Army, calling games for the AAA baseball team the Newark Bears. In 1949, Leavitt came to New Orleans to work for WDSU-TV. He became a fixture on local television, spending most of his career at WDSU but also working for WGNO and public stations WYES and WLAE. Leavitt (right, with Louis Armstrong, center, and a WDSU producer) also wrote three books on New Orleans from 1982 to 1990. (Courtesy NOPL.)

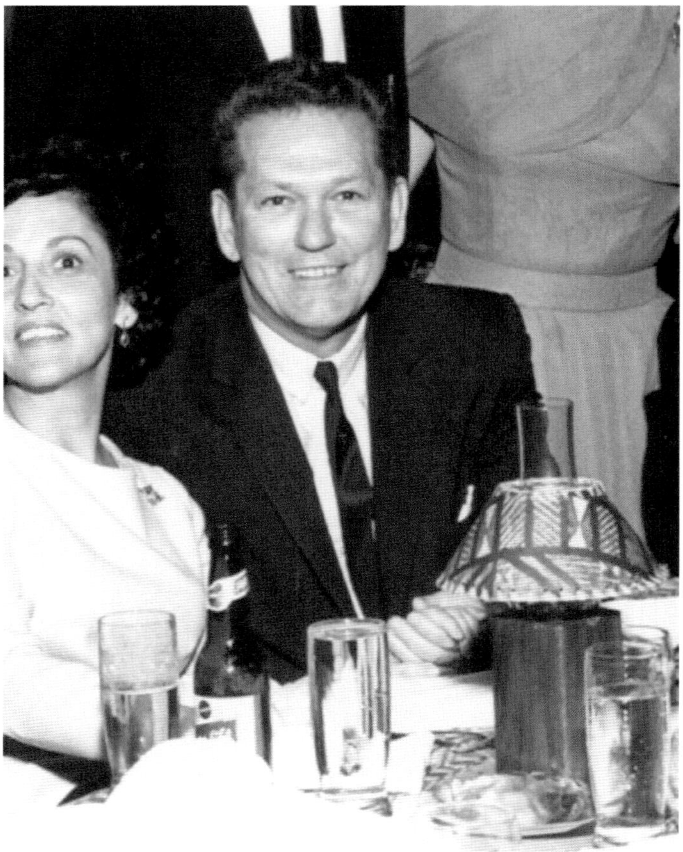

"Point After"

Lloyd A. "Hap" Glaudi (1912–1989) was a graduate of Jesuit High School and attended Loyola University. He began his journalism career at the *New Orleans Item* and wrote for the paper for 25 years. Glaudi transitioned to television in 1964, becoming sports director for WWL-TV. He left WWL-TV for WWL-AM radio in 1978, doing call-in shows weeknights and on Sundays for Saints games. (Courtesy NOPL.)

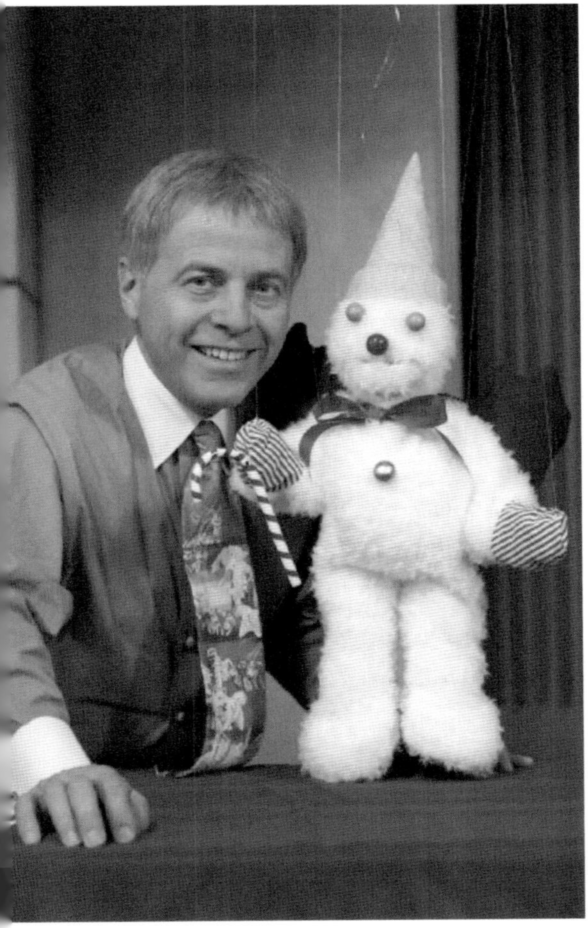

"Bubbly"
Bob Breck (born 1948) is chief meteorologist at WVUE-TV, the local Fox affiliate station. Breck has been with the station for 33 years, after stints in Tampa and Dayton. Known for his outgoing, bubbly style, he signed a long-term contract with WVUE in the 1980s and settled in for a long career. He is seen here, with one of the original Mr. Bingle puppets that was restored after being extensively damaged during Hurricane Katrina. (Courtesy Jefferey Kent.)

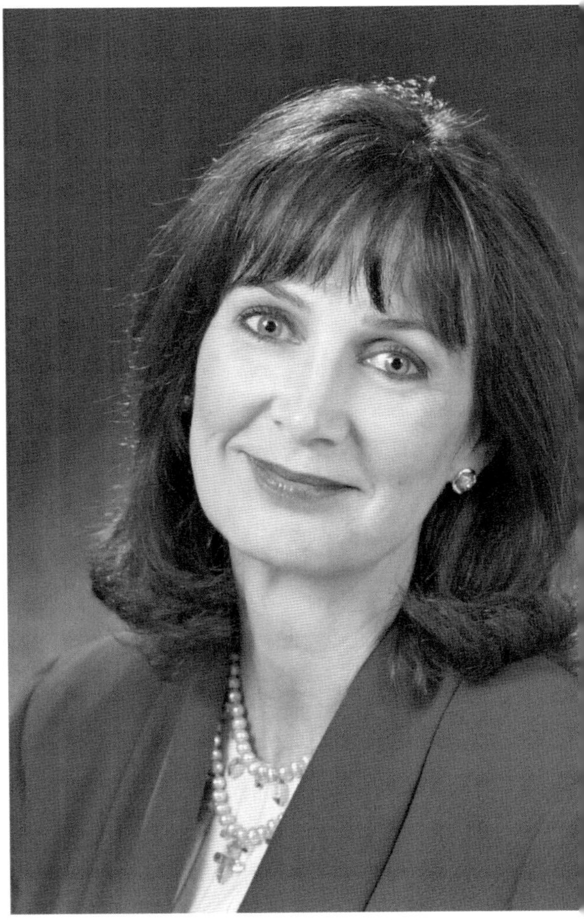

Hurricane Tracker
Margaret Orr (born 1954) is chief meteorologist at WDSU-TV. Orr got her start in television in Charleston, South Carolina, when an opening as weathercaster came up. Returning to New Orleans, she joined the WDSU team as a general assignment reporter, eventually cohosting the station's morning show. Now in her 33rd year with the station, she has been the station's top weathercaster since the retirement of Dan Milham in 2008. Margaret has embraced social media, particularly Twitter, to connect with viewers on the Internet and get their feedback. (Courtesy Margaret Orr/WDSU.)

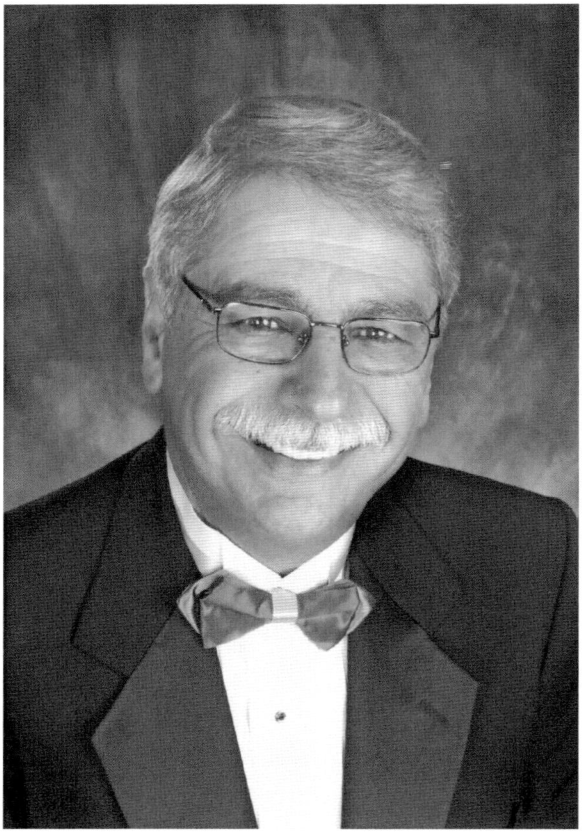

Mardi Hardy

Arthur Hardy (born 1947), a graduate of Warren Easton High School on Canal Street, currently serves on the school's board of directors. Hardy was director of the Brother Martin High School band when he decided to publish his first *Mardi Gras Guide* in 1977. The guide is now in its 36th year, and Arthur is regarded internationally as an expert on Mardi Gras in New Orleans. (Courtesy Arthur Hardy Publications.)

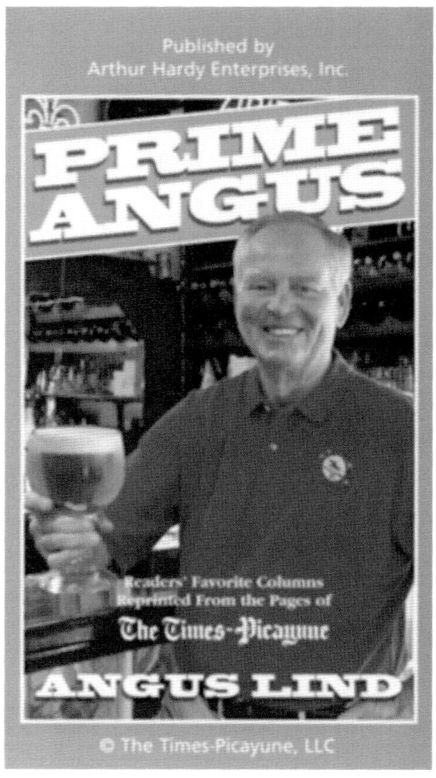

Prime

Angus Lind (born 1944) retired in July 2009 after 39 years as a columnist with the *Times-Picayune* and the now-defunct afternoon *States-Item* newspaper. He began as a general assignment reporter for the *States-Item* in 1970 and covered the biggest local news stories of that decade, including the plane crash of US representative Hale Boggs in Alaska, the downtown Howard Johnson sniper incident, the Rault Center fire in which five women leaped to their deaths, the Upstairs Lounge fire, and the construction of the Louisiana Superdome. His memoir, Prime Angus, was released in 2008. (Courtesy Arthur Hardy Publications.)

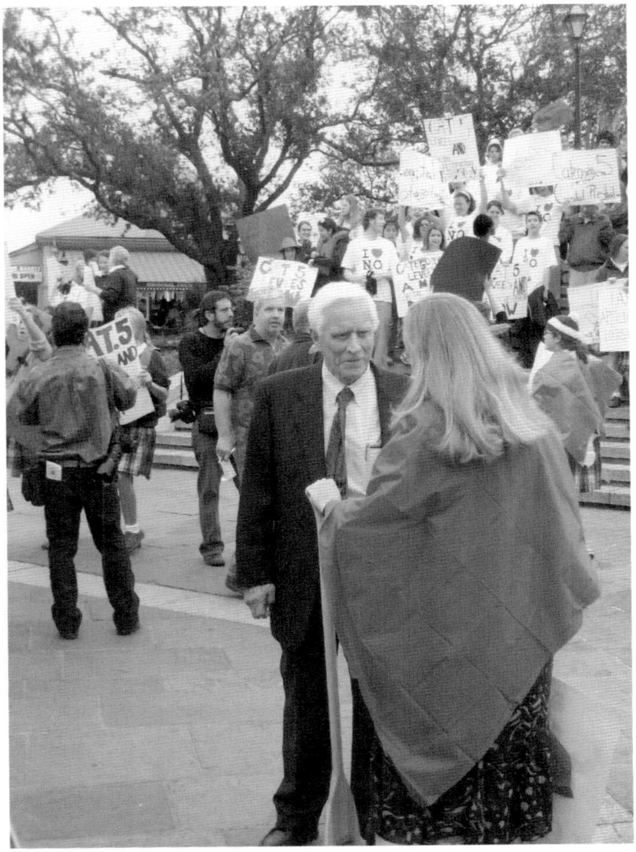

Veteran
Alec Gifford began his run at WDSU-TV in 1955. Until his retirement in 2006, Gifford covered almost every major story in that five-decade span, including the three big hurricanes (Betsy, Camille, and Katrina), as well as interviewing President Kennedy during the 1960 campaign. (Courtesy Carlos "Froggy" May.)

Murrow
Angela Hill (left) joined the WWL-TV news team in 1975, and has been a fixture on the station's anchor desk ever sense. She has been the recipient of numerous awards, including an Edward R. Murrow Award in 2010. Always active within the community, Hill is seen here with Lucille McDonnell in 2004. (Courtesy Peoples Health Network.)

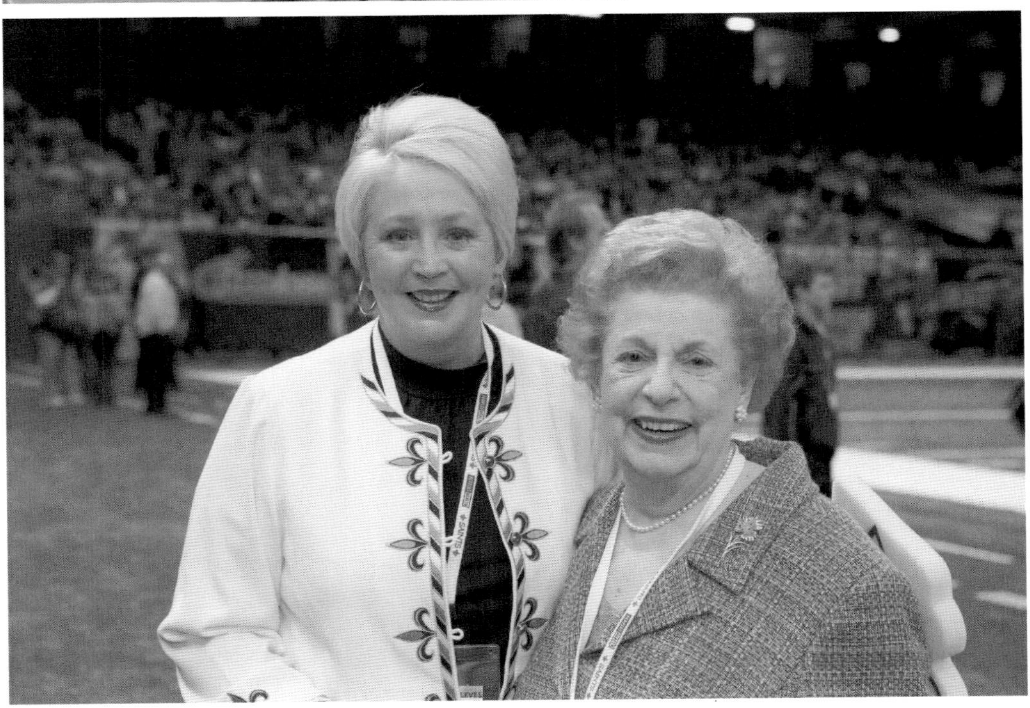

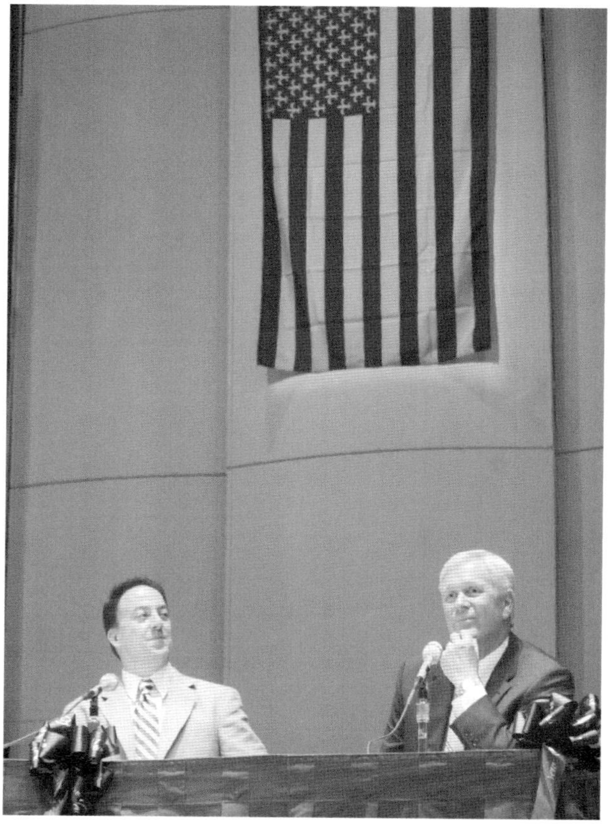

Voice of the Saints

Jim Henderson (born 1947) began his career calling Little League games on the radio in his home town of Rochester, New York. He graduated from State University of New York and joined WWL-TV in New Orleans in 1978. He retired from the station on January 31, 2012, but continues to be the radio voice of the New Orleans Saints. (Courtesy Loyola University.)

War Room

James Carville (born 1944) is a political consultant, most noted for his success with business partner Paul Begala on the 1992 Clinton presidential campaign. He was cohost of the popular CNN show *Crossfire* until its final broadcast in 2005. Carville worked on Hillary Clinton's unsuccessful presidential run in 2008. He currently lives in New Orleans and teaches political science at Tulane University. (Courtesy Tulane University.)

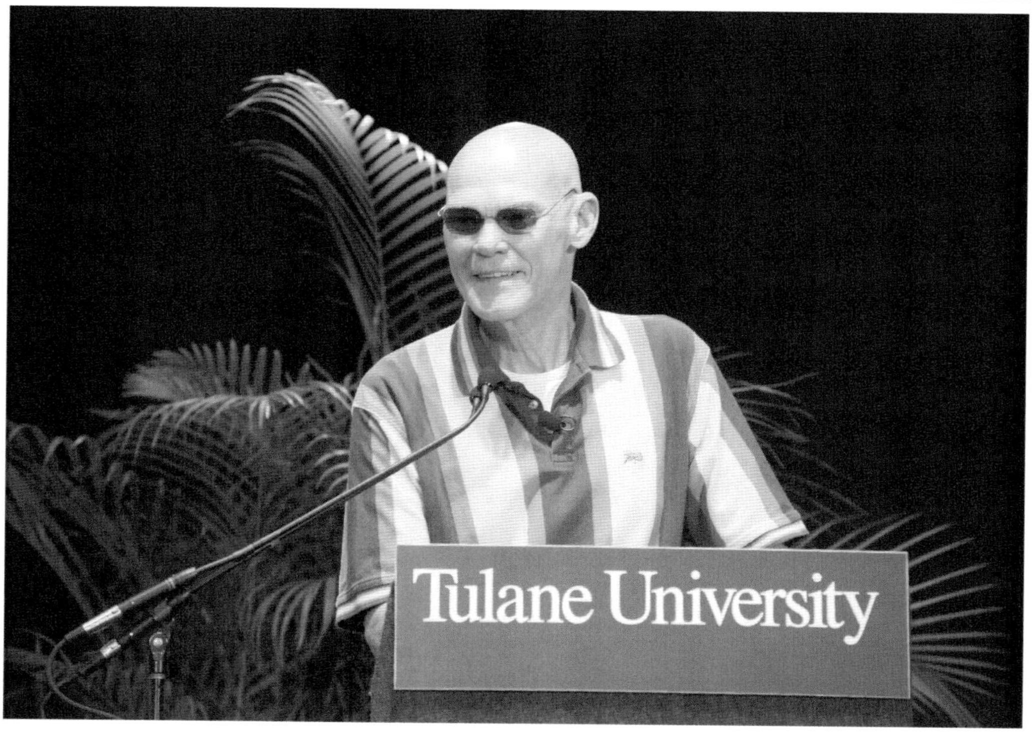

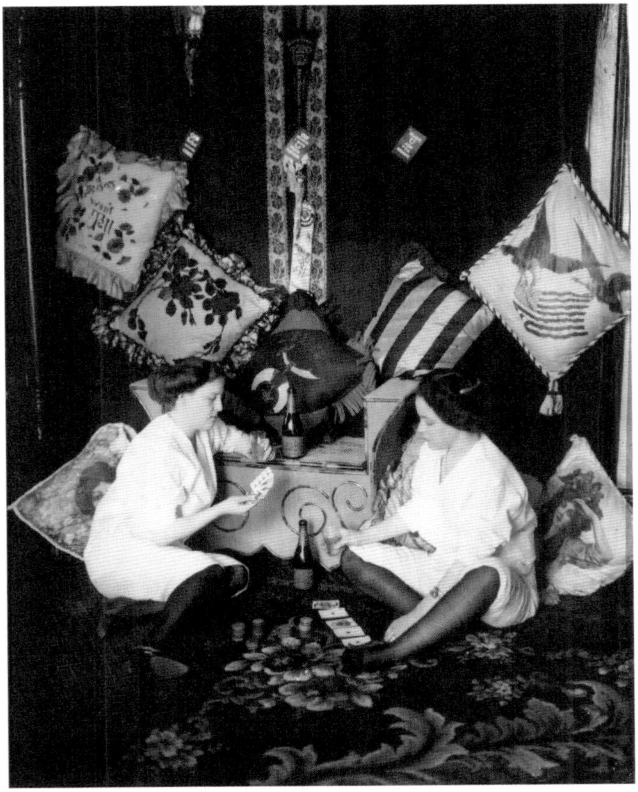

Storyville
E.J. Bellocq (1873–1949) was a professional photographer most noted for his "Storyville" photographs. As in "Girls Playing Cards," shown here, Bellocq's images documented the lives of the workers in the brothels of New Orleans's red-light district. (Courtesy NOPL.)

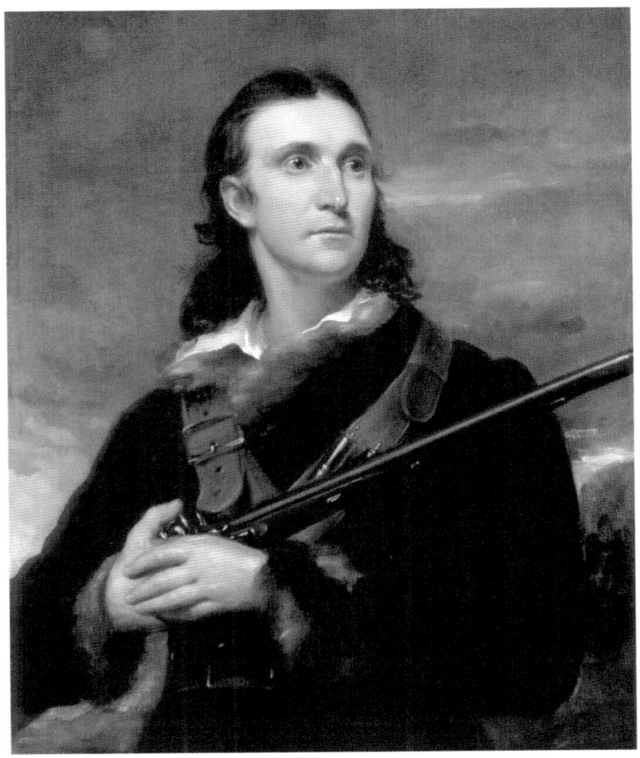

Ornithologist
John James Audubon (1785–1851) was a naturalist, ornithologist, and painter. His extensive illustrations of birds in their natural habitats offer a fascinating look into birds and wildlife of the period. Born in Haiti, Audubon emigrated to the United States via New York. His business ventures brought him to New Orleans, where he attempted to set up a headquarters. The War of 1812 complicated his plans to move to the city, but he regularly traveled up and down the Mississippi for his illustrations. (Courtesy White House Historical Association.)

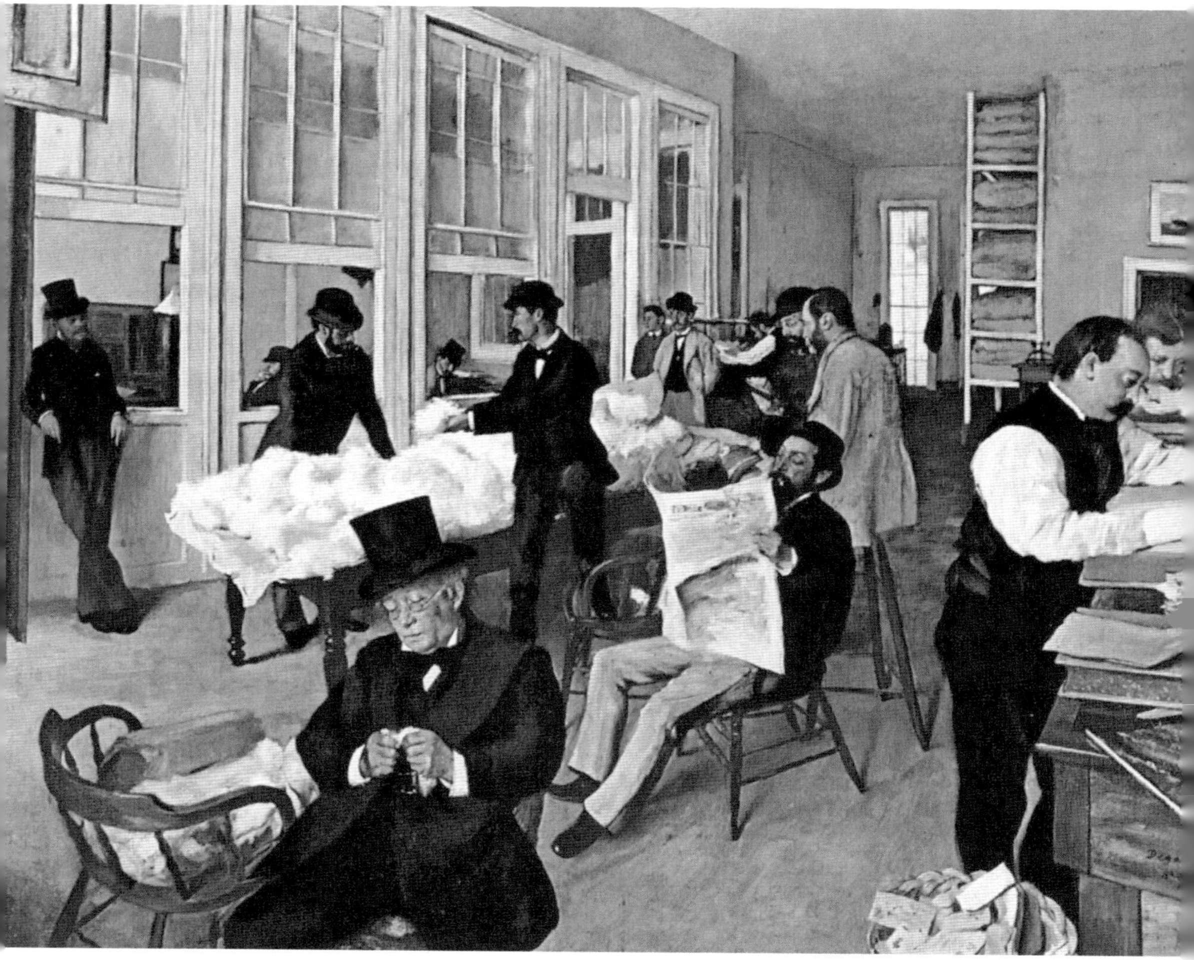

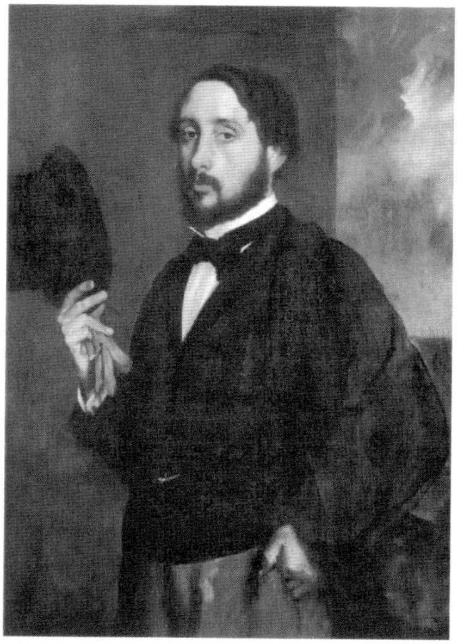

Cotton Exchange

Edgar Degas (1834–1917) was born in Paris to a Creole mother from New Orleans. After the Franco-Prussian War, in 1872 Degas embarked on an extended stay in Louisiana. Degas (right, in a self-portrait) produced many paintings (like the one above, of the New Orleans Cotton Exchange) while living with his cousin. That house, on Esplanade Avenue, is now the Degas House Museum (opposite page). (Above, courtesy the Calouste Gulbenkian Museum, the Yorck Project; right, courtesy Carlos "Froggy" May.)

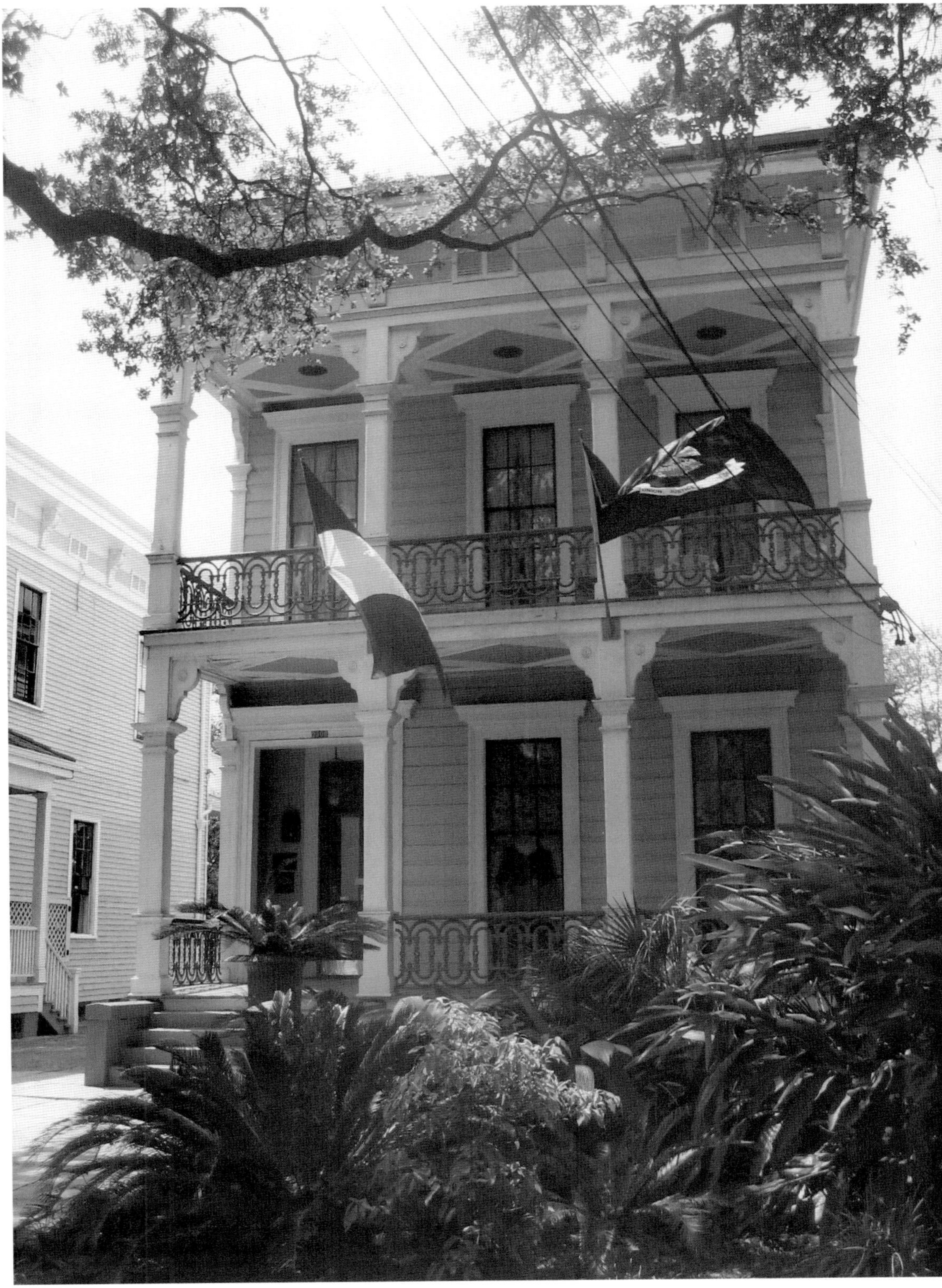

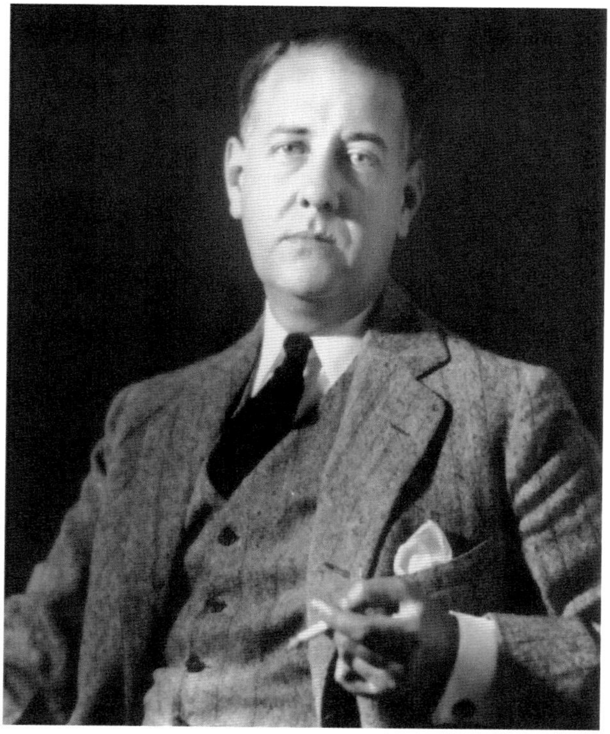

Lifestyle Guides

Lyle Saxon (1891–1946), a writer in his own right, was director of the WPA-funded Federal Writers' Project. He also wrote for the *Times-Picayune*. Saxon's detailed histories of the city are regularly referenced by contemporary historians. (Courtesy NOPL.)

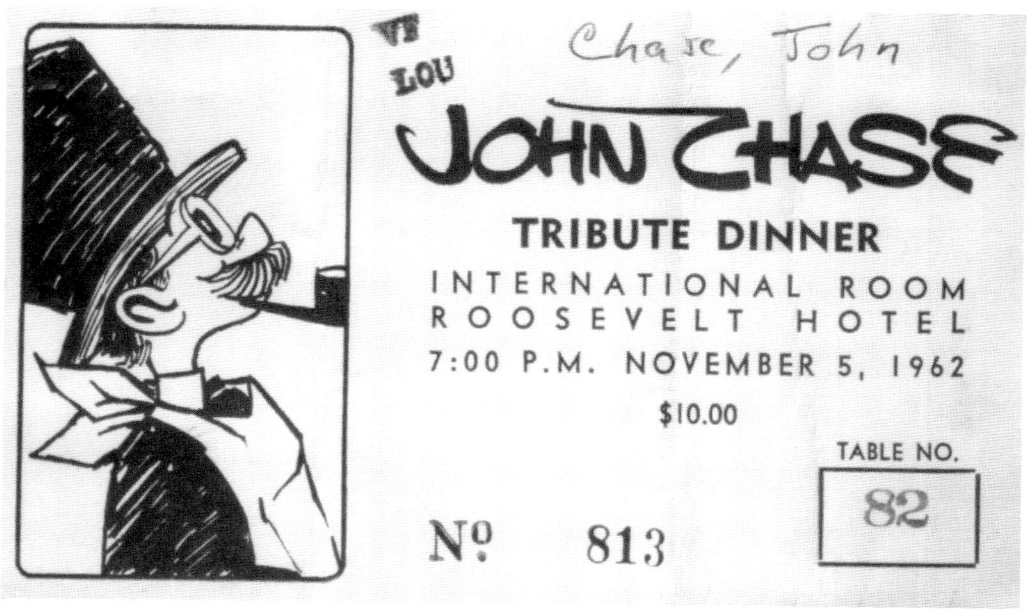

"Little Man"

John Churchill Chase (1905–1986) was a cartoonist and writer. He was the longtime editorial cartoonist for the *New Orleans Item*. In 1964, while still working at the newspaper, Chase was approached by WDSU-TV about doing editorial cartoons for the station's nightly news. He accepted and became the first editorial cartoonist on television. In addition to cartoons, Chase was a prolific author and lectured on New Orleans history at Tulane University. (Courtesy NOPL.)

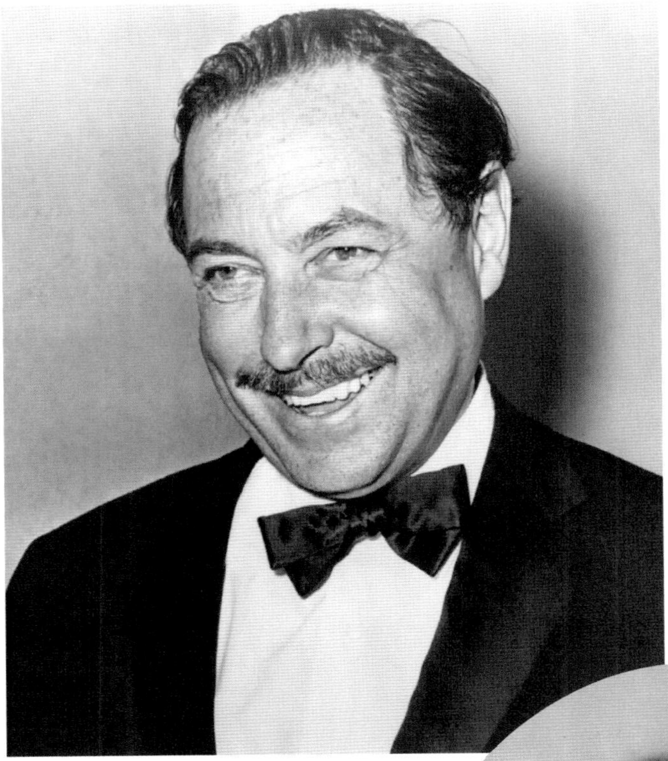

Stella!
Tennessee Williams (1911–1983) is best known in New Orleans for his play *A Streetcar Named Desire*, for which he won a Pulitzer Prize. Williams moved to New Orleans in 1939 and became part of the WPA's Federal Writers' Project. Williams moved regularly, arguing that it stimulated his writing. New Orleans was a regular stop. (Courtesy LOC.)

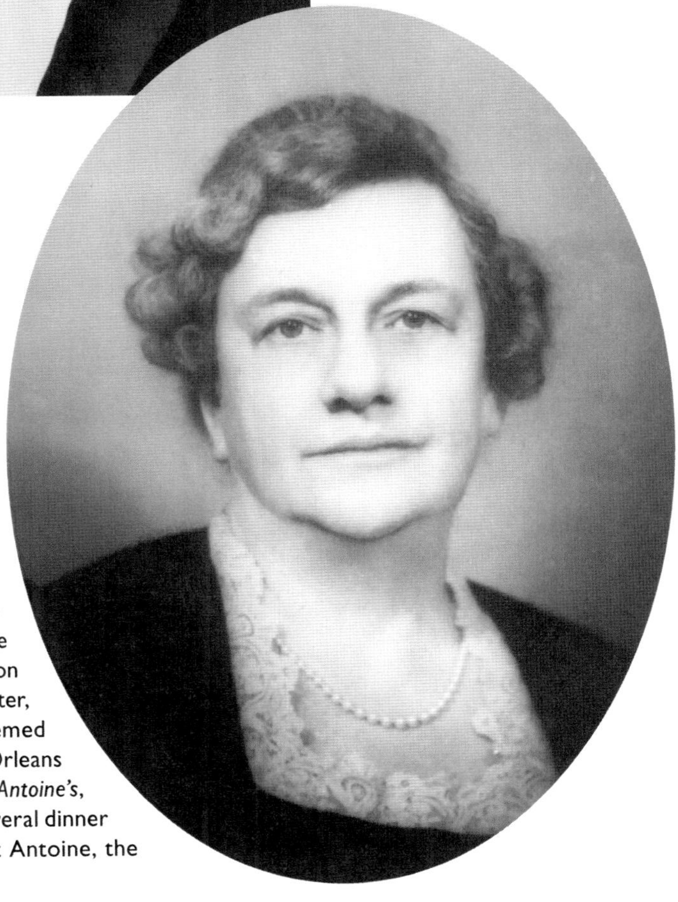

Antoine's
Frances Parkinson Keyes (1885–1970) was a prolific writer from New England. In the 1950s, she lived in the Beauregard House (one of the homes of P.G.T. Beauregard), on Chartres Street in the French Quarter, and began to write Southern-themed novels. She is known best in New Orleans for her murder mystery *Dinner at Antoine's*, set in the French Quarter, with several dinner scenes taking place at Restaurant Antoine, the city's oldest. (Courtesy NOPL.)

Dunces

John Kennedy Toole (1937–1969) was a native New Orleanian who had a career as a teacher at Columbia University in New York and St. Mary's Dominican College in Uptown New Orleans. Toole's manuscript for *A Confederacy of Dunces*, featuring the incredible character Ignatius J. Reilly, was rejected by publishers during Toole's lifetime. Claiming to be going on a journey around the country, Toole only got as far as Biloxi, where he took his own life. His mother took the *Dunces* manuscript to novelist Walker Percy, who saw merit in the novel and pushed it through the publication process. At right, a statue of Ignatius J. Reilly stands below the clock at the old D.H. Holmes Department Store (now the Hyatt Hotel French Quarter). Reilly's main job in the novel was a hot dog vendor. Toole based this career on the exploits of the real-life Lucky Dog vendors, who push carts similar to the one below, now enshrined in the Louisiana State Museum. (Right, courtesy Carlos "Froggy" May; below, courtesy LSM.)

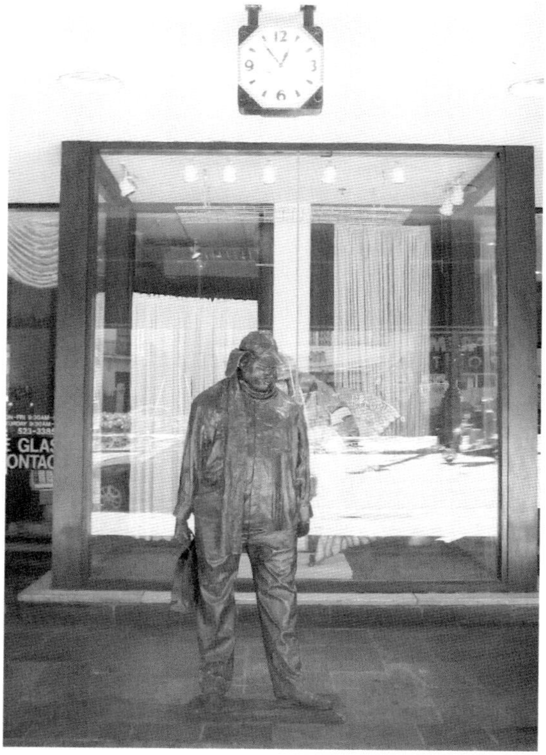

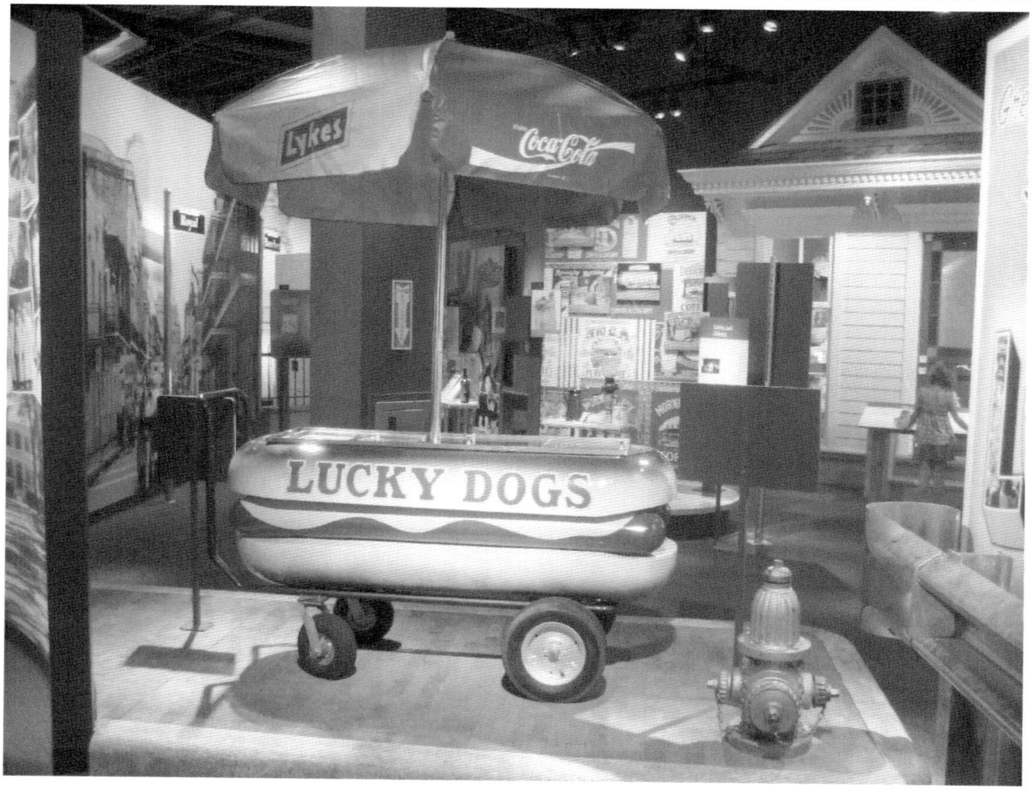

CHAPTER SIX

Business, Invention, and Science

If necessity is the mother of invention, New Orleans certainly has needs. The most significant necessity throughout the history of the city has been defending itself from the river and the lake. The men and women who master this work are true New Orleans heroes. The levees that hold back the flow, the canals that drain off the water, and the pumps that send it out into the swamps combine to keep New Orleans's homes dry. When these protective measures fail, residents' confidence and faith in the world is shaken to its core. Restoring that confidence requires a great deal of time and patience.

Along with the inventors and scientists whose breakthroughs make living easier, the businesspeople and entrepreneurs who finance many of those projects must also be recognized. Putting money back starts at basic levels, such as a successful planter or baker who sees the value in good public schools and is willing to finance them, or the financial tycoon who identifies the need for vocational training and builds a school for that. Those willing to support higher education by funding faculty positions in various disciplines are important.

There's a corollary to donating money to finance such worthy causes—one has to make the money in the first place. That requires the aggressive businessperson, who is willing to risk what he or she has to better the business, farm, or other venture. Money that passes into a second or third generation is "safe," but it often does not grow or allow the city to grow. The combination of agriculture with a solid delivery method like the river is an excellent foundation. The desire to get imports into the rest of the country faster than riverboats prompted the expansion of the railroads. The logistics of laying rails for commuters within a city or freight between cities requires a disciplined mind, perhaps the sort that attended a military academy. Businesspeople spot the innovation and run with it. In New Orleans, one can run a long way with that sort of combination.

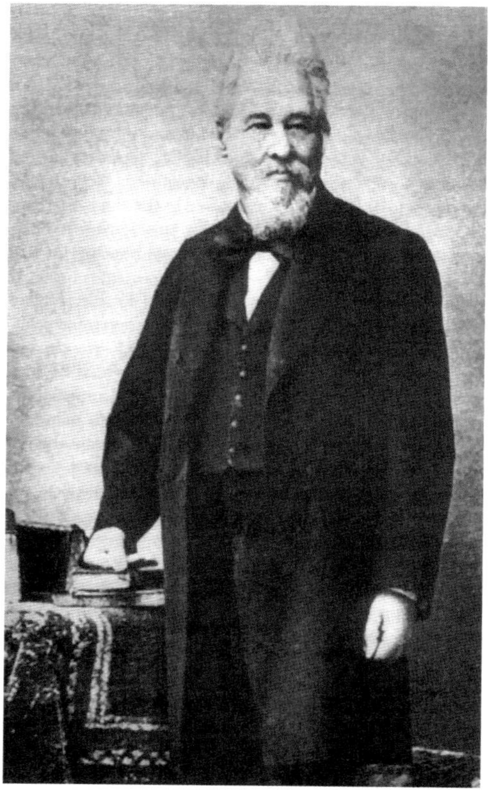

Sweetness
Norbert Rillieux (1806–1894) was a cousin of the artist Edgar Degas, but his technical skills made him a legend. Born into a Creole family, Rillieux was educated alongside the sons of wealthy white families, then he was able to travel to Europe to expand his learning. Displaying an aptitude for mechanics at an early age, he became the youngest teacher at École Centrale. Rillieux made good use of his time in Paris, focusing on techniques to improve the family's business: sugar cane. He developed and patented a method of evaporating water that sped up sugar refining and lowered the cost dramatically. (Both, courtesy NOPL.)

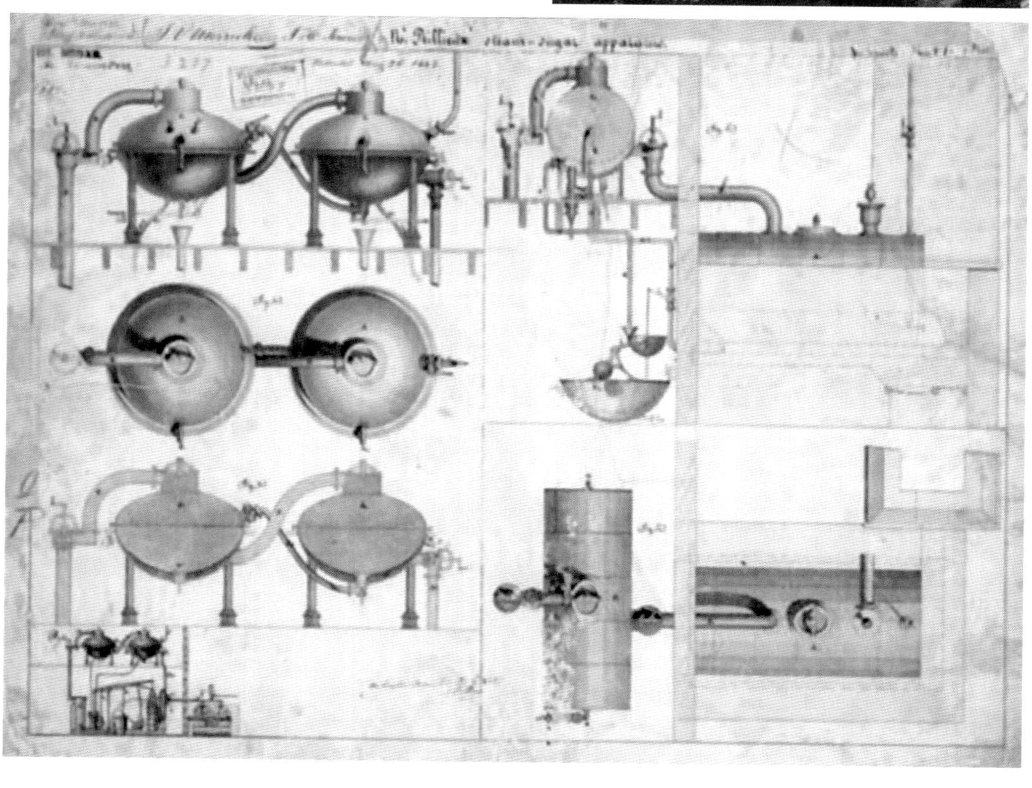

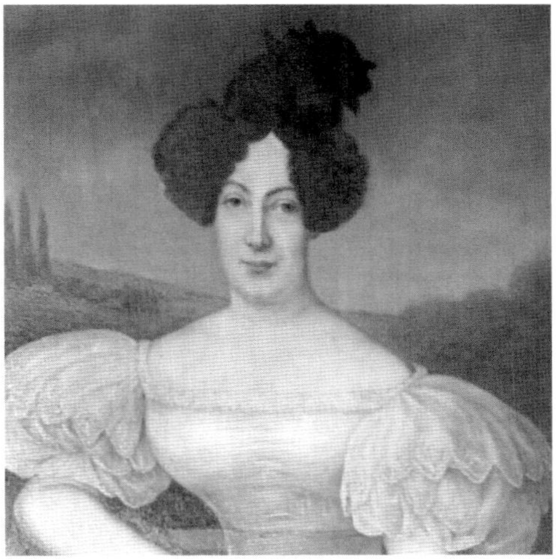

Developer

Micaela Almonester, the baroness de Pontalba (1795–1874), was the daughter of Don Andres Almonester y Rojas, the Spanish bureaucrat, later noble and philanthropist. Don Andres was an older man when he married Micaela's mother, but the union created an alliance and an heir. Even though Andres died when Micaela was three, her mother and her family were there to manage the Almonester money. Following the custom of the time, Micaela married her cousin Xavier Célestin Delfau de Pontalba in New Orleans but then immediately moved to France. She remained in France, sometimes visiting New Orleans, until 1834, when her father-in-law, the Baron Pontalba, attacked her and shot her with a set of dueling pistols. Micaela survived, but the baron took his own life the same evening. When she recovered from the attack, Micaela returned to New Orleans. She took possession of her father's land and money, building two rows of townhouses on either side of the Place d'Armes, later called Jackson Square. Those "Pontalba Buildings" were subdivided into apartments over the years and now are owned by the city and the state, which rent out the apartments. (Above, courtesy LSM; below, courtesy Jan Kronsell.)

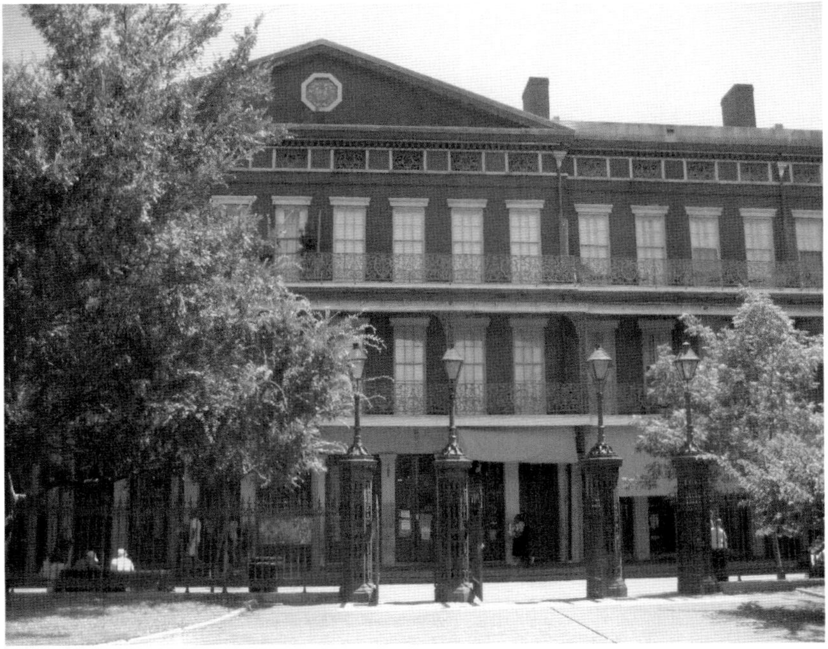

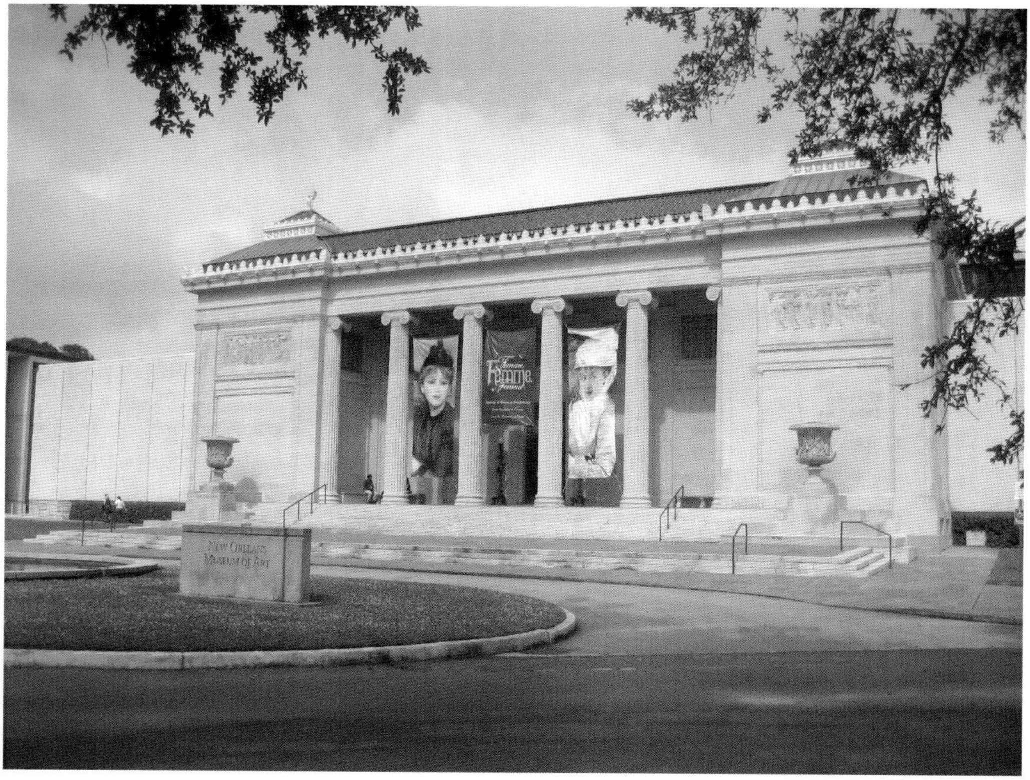

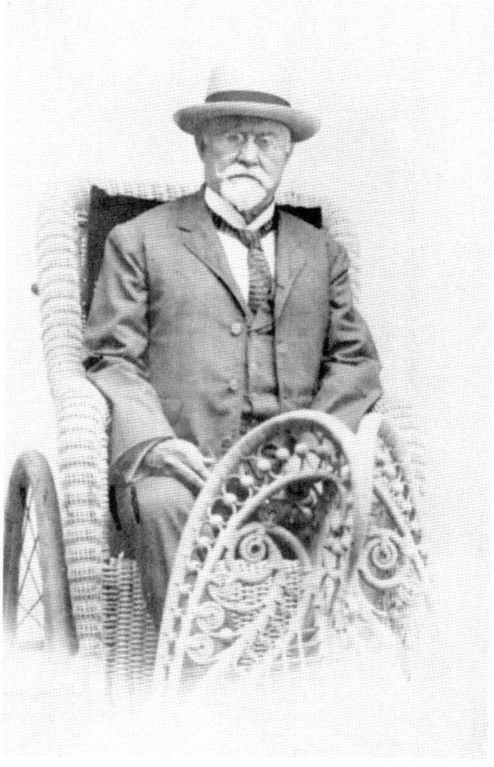

NOMA

Isaac Delgado (1839–1912) was a sugar planter. Rilleaux's evaporator and other technological developments vastly improved both sugar cane production and profits. Delgado channeled his money into philanthropic interests by founding the Delgado Art Museum (later the New Orleans Museum of Art) in City Park, as well as the Delgado Central Trades School, which evolved into the modern-day Delgado Community College. (Above, courtesy LSM; right, courtesy of NOMA.)

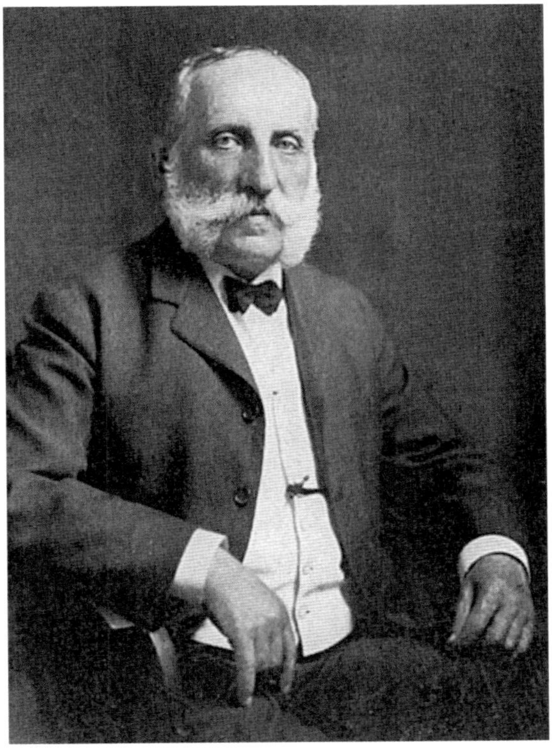

Banker, Philanthropist, Patriarch
Isidore Newman (1836–1909) left his home in Kaiserslautern, in what was then Rhenish Bavaria, at the age of 17 to come to Louisiana. By 1877, he was a successful investment banker with an office on Carondelet Street, in the heart of the city's financial district. One of Newman's best investments was in his son-in-law's career, staking S.J. Shwartz and his plan to open Maison Blanche. Newman also founded the Isidore Newman Manual Training School in Uptown New Orleans. (Courtesy NOPL.)

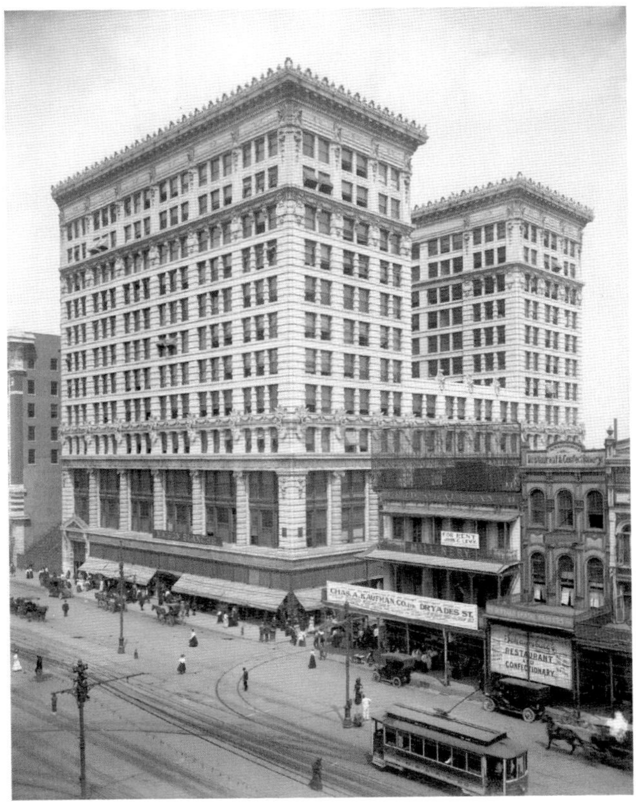

Merchant
Simon J. Shwartz, son of Abram Shwartz, worked in his father's dry goods store in the 700 block of Canal Street until 1892, when the store caught fire and burned. Rather than stay with the family business, Shwartz leased the Mercier Building at Canal and Dauphine Streets and opened the S.J. Shwartz & Co. Five years later, the concept was refined. The location was remodeled, and Maison Blanche was born. (Courtesy LOC.)

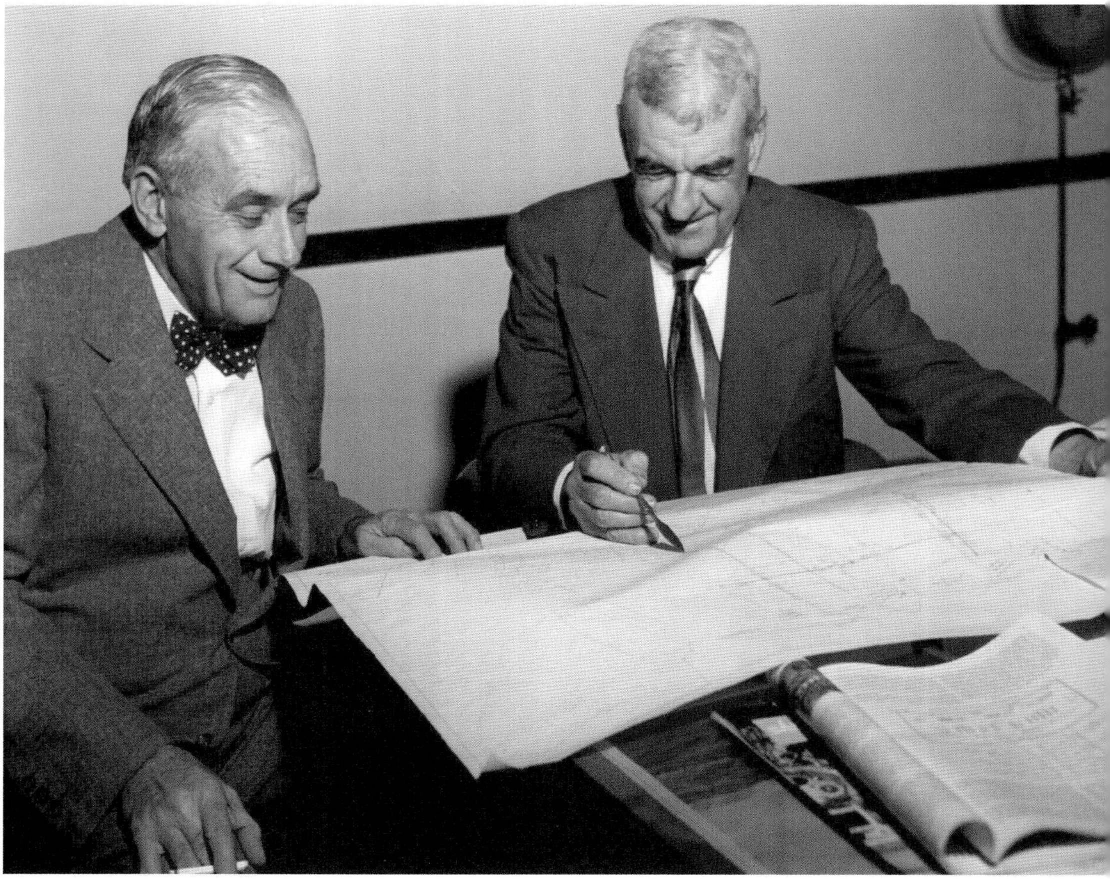

Pumps

A. Baldwin Wood (1879–1956) worked for the New Orleans Sewerage and Water Board, where he invented the wood-screw pump that revolutionized flood prevention in the city. Pumps such as the ones in the Melpomene Street Station (below) were designed by Wood (above right, reviewing plans with an unidentified sewerage and water board engineer). The pumps have been in operation in the city for over 80 years. (Above, courtesy NOPL; below, courtesy Carlos "Froggy" May.)

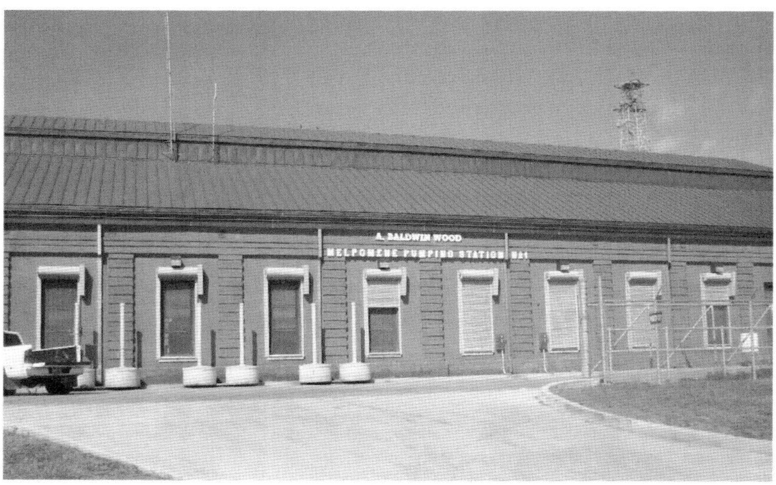

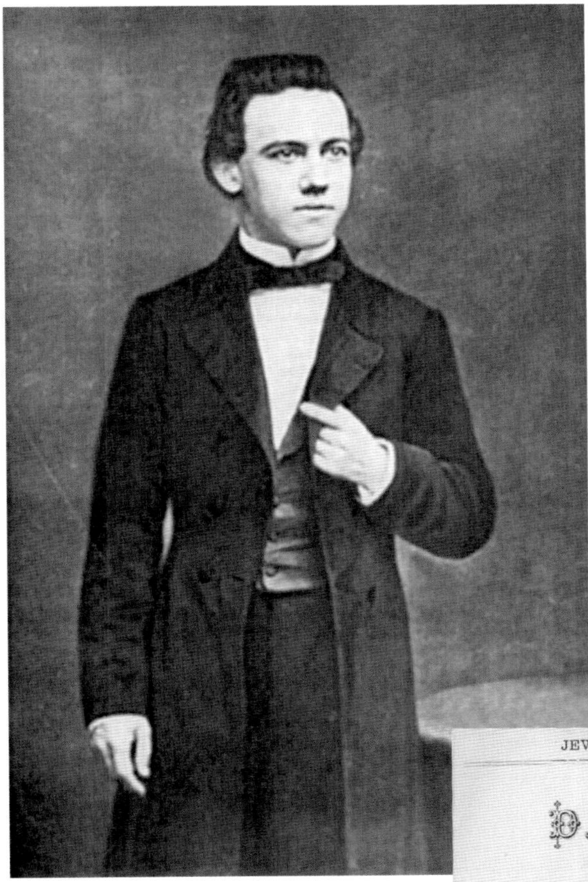

Dry Goods

Daniel Henry Holmes (1816–1898) originally came to New Orleans from Ohio to run the Lord and Taylor store opening there. In 1842, he left Lord and Taylor to open the D.H. Holmes Department Store. The store became a fixture on Canal Street for almost 150 years, with the clock hanging over the main entrance becoming a regular meeting point for locals. (Both, courtesy NOPL.)

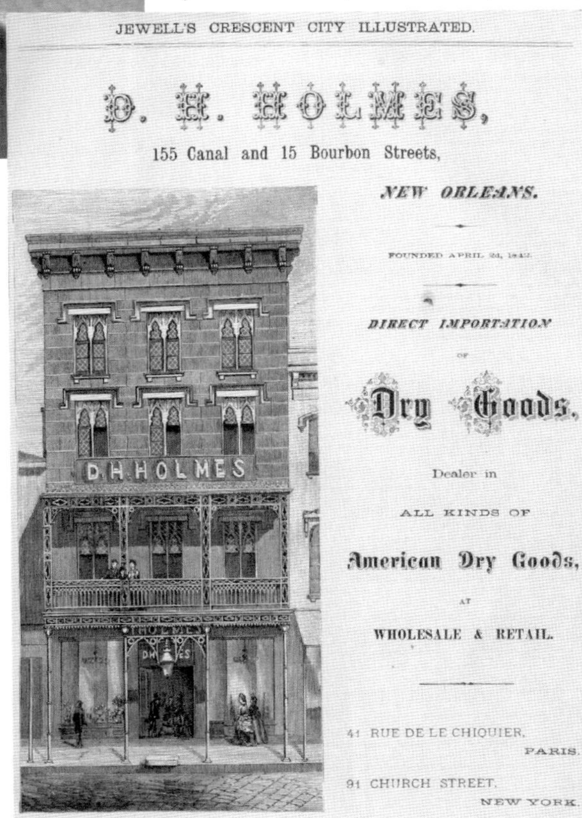

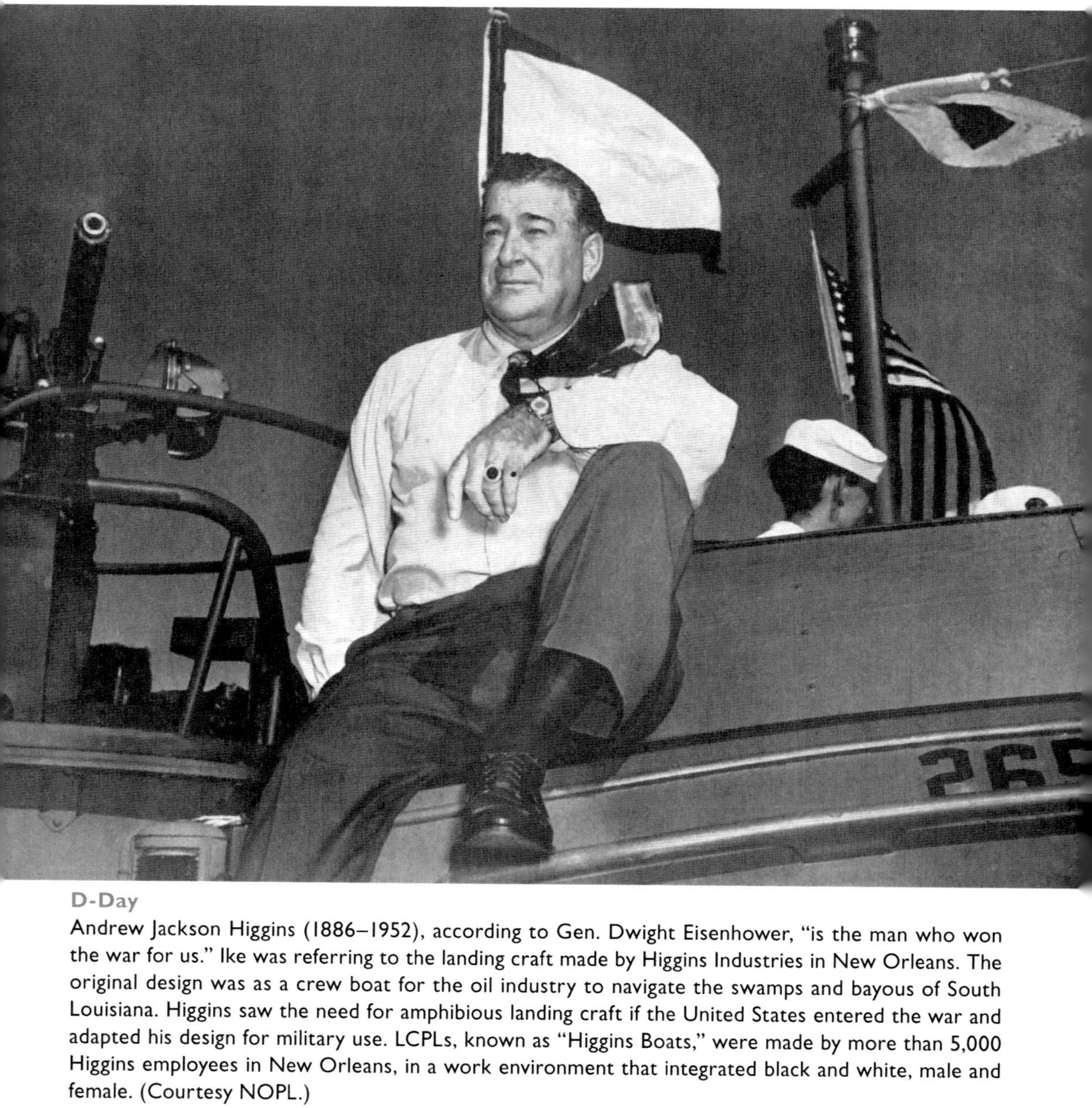

D-Day

Andrew Jackson Higgins (1886–1952), according to Gen. Dwight Eisenhower, "is the man who won the war for us." Ike was referring to the landing craft made by Higgins Industries in New Orleans. The original design was as a crew boat for the oil industry to navigate the swamps and bayous of South Louisiana. Higgins saw the need for amphibious landing craft if the United States entered the war and adapted his design for military use. LCPLs, known as "Higgins Boats," were made by more than 5,000 Higgins employees in New Orleans, in a work environment that integrated black and white, male and female. (Courtesy NOPL.)

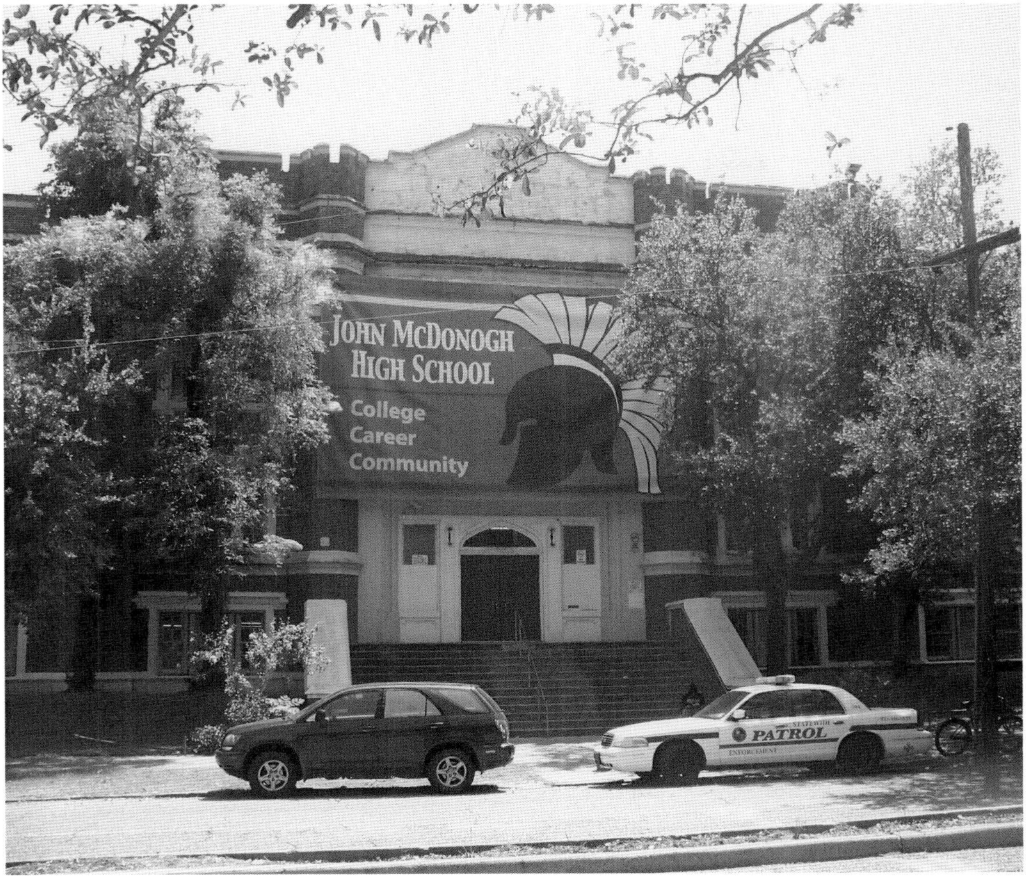

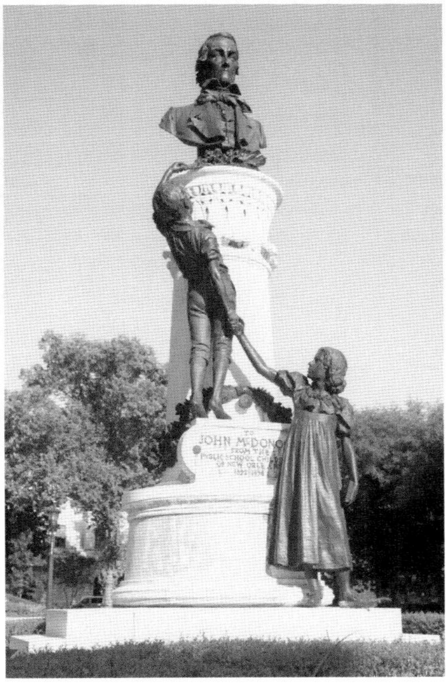

Benefactor

John McDonogh (1779–1850) started in the shipping business in Baltimore. After a trip to Liverpool, he learned the potential of bringing manufactured goods to New Orleans. He set up regular shipments and simultaneously opened a store to sell the goods. His business did quite well and made him a rich man. When he died, he left his extensive estate to the city of Baltimore and the city of New Orleans, for the construction of public schools. More than 30 schools were built in New Orleans, usually named with McDonogh's last name and a number, as well as John McDonogh High School. (Above, courtesy author; left, courtesy Tonya Armbruster.)

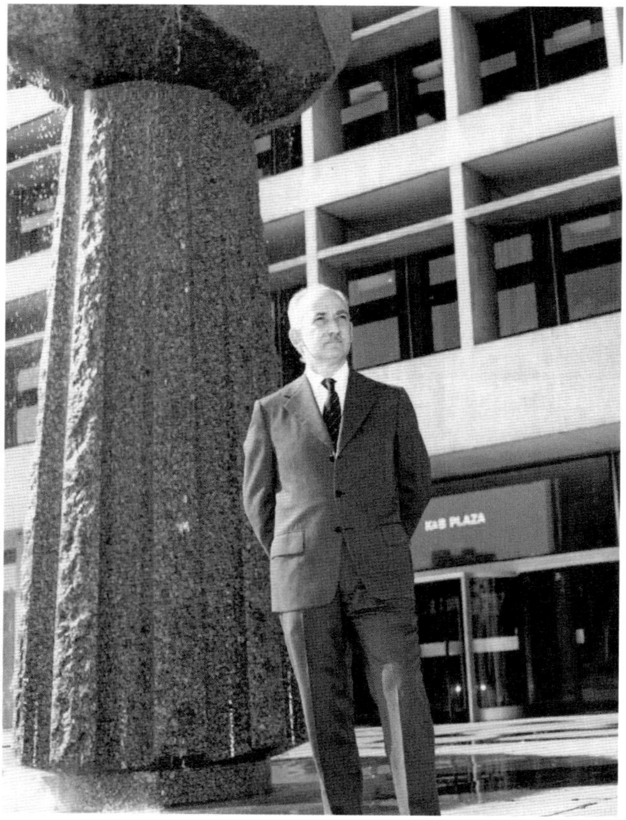

K&B Purple

Sydney J. Besthoff III was the last chief executive officer of K&B Drugstores, the chain started by his grandfather Sydney J. Besthoff, along with Gustave Katz. Katz and Besthoff opened their first drugstore together in 1905 and expanded the chain to over 180 stores in several states by the time it was sold to Rite-Aid in 1997. Now, Sydney J. Besthoff III is a philanthropist and patron of the arts. The Besthoff Sculpture Garden at the New Orleans Museum of Art (NOMA) was funded by Besthoff and his wife. The museum presents plays in the garden, ranging from Shakespeare to Lewis Carroll's *The Hunting of the Snark*, seen below. (Left, courtesy Sydney J. Besthoff III; below, courtesy Bart Everson.)

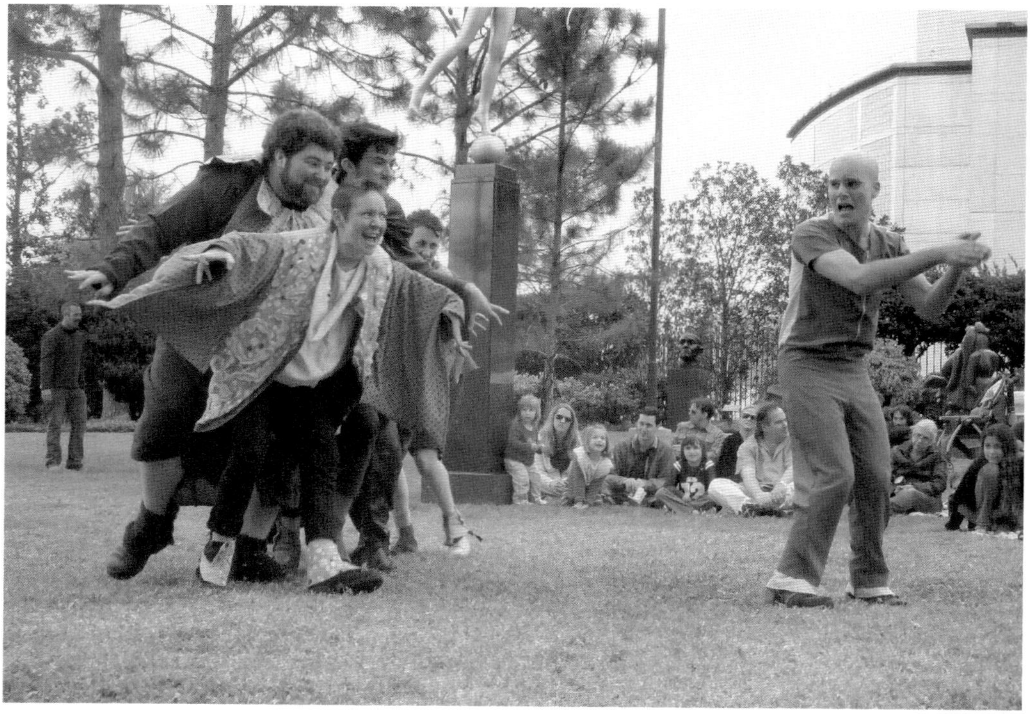

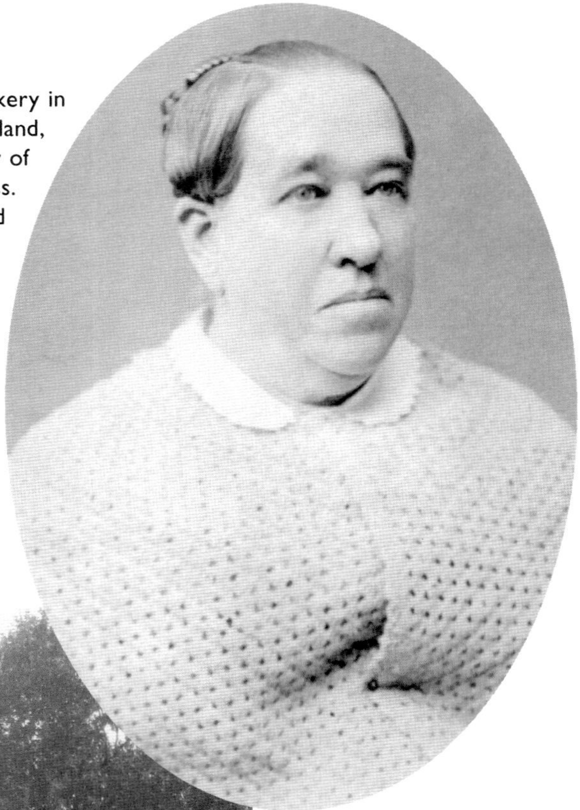

Bread Woman

Margaret Haughery (1813–1881) owned a bakery in Uptown New Orleans. Born in poverty in Ireland, she made her way to New Orleans like many of her countrymen, and built a successful business. Margaret was a washwoman when she arrived from Ireland. She saved her wages and eventually bought a dairy cart. She regularly shared her profits with the Sisters of Charity and used some of the money to acquire a bakery. The bakery fed orphans and the poor as well as sold bread and crackers to the community. When Margaret died at the age of 69, it was discovered that, in spite of the incredible amount of giving she had done in her life, she still had a sizable estate, which she left to charity. (Right, courtesy NOPL; below, courtesy Carlos "Froggy" May.)

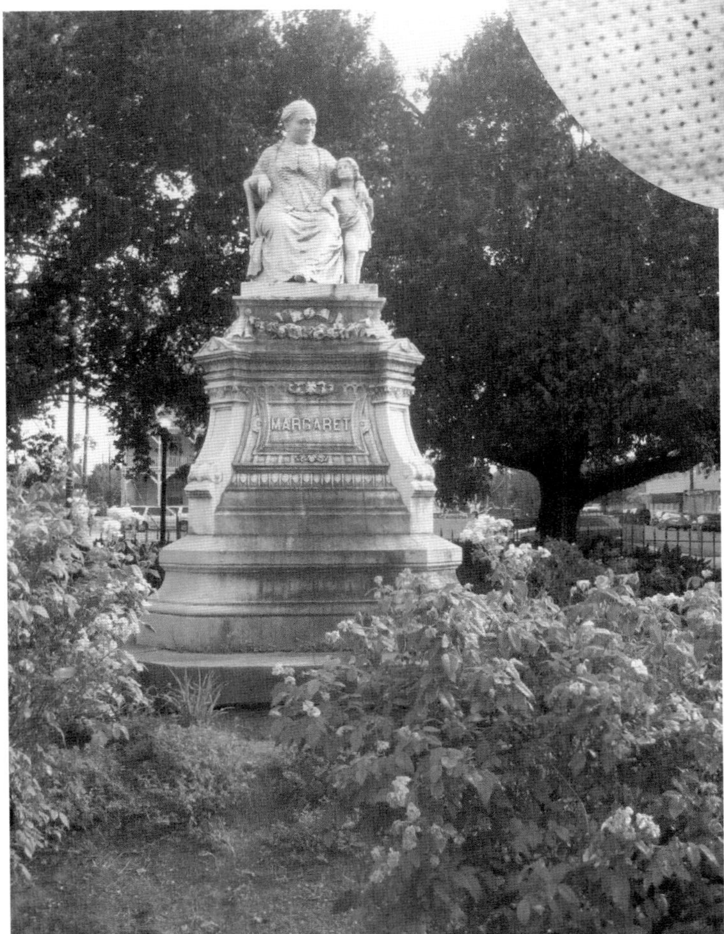

INDEX

LEGENDARY LOCALS

AN IMPRINT OF ARCADIA PUBLISHING

Find more books like this at
www.legendarylocals.com

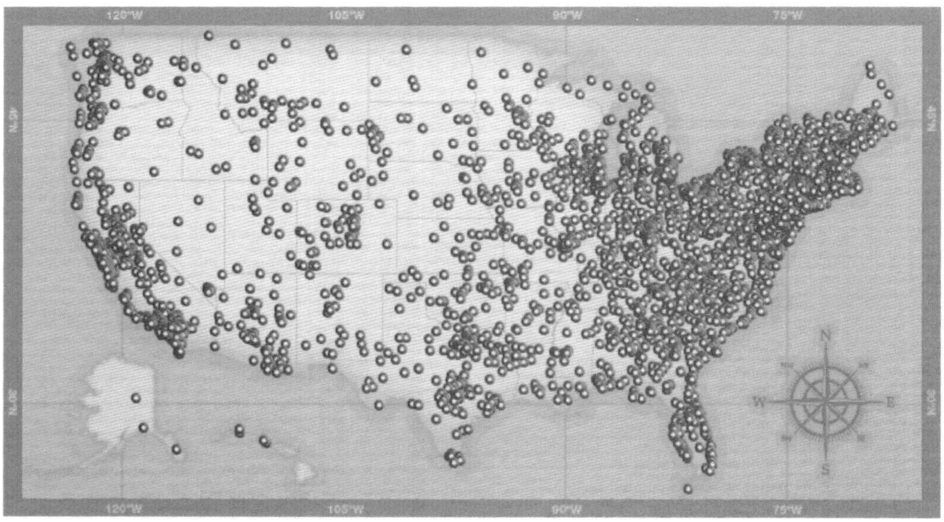

Discover more local and regional history books at
www.arcadiapublishing.com

Consistent with our mission to preserve history on a local level, this book was printed in South Carolina on American-made paper and manufactured entirely in the United States. Products carrying the accredited Forest Stewardship Council (FSC) label are printed on 100 percent FSC-certified paper.

MADE IN THE USA